I0762931

PRAISE FOR CASEY SHERMAN

THE KILLER AND FRANK LLOYD WRIGHT

"Casey Sherman maps the human trail between genius and catastrophe. The reporting is exacting, the storytelling propulsive. Along the way we get Wright unvarnished: charm, ego, scandal, and the choices that put a killer in his house. This is true history with the snap of a thriller. As an armchair architecture enthusiast, even one who has visited Taliesin, I thought I knew a lot about this story, but I turned the last page seeing Wright, and the tragedies that shadowed him, anew. Haunting."

—Laurie Gwen Shapiro, author of *The Aviator and the Showman: Amelia Earhart, George Putnam, and the Marriage That Made an American Icon*

"*The Killer and Frank Lloyd Wright* is the wildest of wild rides! In Sherman's capable hands, we see all aspects of this tragic story beautifully told: the love, the anguish, the blood, the fire, and the brilliance of one of America's most iconic and gifted architects. Fans of history and true crime will rejoice!"

—Kristin Dilley, cohost of the *Mind Over Murder* podcast

"Only Casey Sherman could have captured the scope, the intimacy, the passion, and the tragedy of Frank Lloyd Wright. This book is of literary and historical importance—full of suspense and fascinating details, it also reads like a riveting, cinematic novel. It will blow you away!"

—Laurent Bouzereau, director of HBO's *Faye* and *Jaws @ 50*

BLOOD IN THE WATER

"A riveting true crime tale."

—*Publishers Weekly*

"What I most admire about Casey Sherman is that he's more than a writer. He's also an outstanding investigative journalist, and he uses these skills to great effect in bringing this mind-boggling case to life. *Blood in the Water* is a twisty true crime narrative of greed, suspicion, and revenge, taking us from the high seas to the mansion of an enormously wealthy family. Compelling and cinematic, it keeps you guessing about the complicated family at the heart of this saga until the very last page. And it shows us that no matter how sophisticated our technology becomes, we can never have all the answers about what happens behind closed doors."

—Shawn Cohen, *New York Times* bestselling author of *College Girl, Missing*

"*Blood in the Water* is a book for every true crime fan's 'to be read' pile…though you won't want to wait to read it! The tautly woven narrative showcases Sherman's lyrical writing style and formidable research skills, guaranteeing a deep dive into family drama and depravity that's nearly impossible to turn away from. Sherman is at the top of his game!"

—Kristin Dilley, cohost of the *Mind Over Murder* podcast

"*Blood in the Water* is utterly immersive. Casey Sherman is a master true crime storyteller. Like always, he brings characters to life, which makes it hard to tear yourself away from the page!"

—Zibby Owens, host of *Totally Booked with Zibby* and bestselling author of *Blank*

"Right from the opening pages, Casey Sherman's *Blood in the Water* establishes a sense of foreboding. All signs point in one direction, but—even if you know the Nathan Carman case—you can't help but think, and perhaps even hope, that there will be surprises, something to make you believe there is more than darkness in the tale of a family mired in tragedy, accusation, and intrigue. As each thread of the story is pulled and facts are revealed, the reader is offered chances to examine their own thoughts, feelings, and beliefs about human behavior and how we decide what the truth is when there are few clear guideposts."

—Holly Frey, creator of *Criminalia* and cohost of *Stuff You Missed in History Class*

A MURDER IN HOLLYWOOD

"A wild ride beneath the glitz and glamour of 1950s Hollywood, proving once again that Casey Sherman is a master of the genre. Riveting, eye-opening, and impeccably researched, *A Murder in Hollywood* is a cinematic tour de force that pulls back the curtain on one of Tinseltown's darkest moments, reinventing our understanding of Lana Turner as an enduring icon of feminine power. Casey Sherman's research is revelatory—a game-changer that shifts the spotlight from scandal to the strength and resilience of a woman fighting for her life and her legacy."

—Ben Mezrich, *New York Times* bestselling author of *Dumb Money*, *Bringing Down the House*, and *The Accidental Billionaires*

"If you like a lively Hollywood yarn or crave a good gangster tale—or both—*A Murder in Hollywood* is the book for you. Casey Sherman turns his sharp eye to the famed Lana Turner murder case, and he delivers the liveliest, grittiest, juiciest page-turner of the year, a true story that reads like Harold Robbins on steroids. Lovely Lana, the bottle-blond heartthrob, gets top billing. Surrounding her is a fantastic cast of featured players: hoods like

Bugsy Siegel, Mickey Cohen, and Johnny Stompanato; Hollywood giants like Clark Gable, Joan Crawford, and even Sean Connery. It's the kind of book that's just plain fun to read, but when you're done, you'll wonder at the toxic effects of ambition, greed, and unfulfilled dreams of love…even in the land where dreams are supposed to come true."

—William Martin, *New York Times* bestselling author of *Back Bay* and *December '41*

"A must-read for fans of true crime and Hollywood history, *A Murder in Hollywood* never disappoints! Casey Sherman deftly serves just the right mix of glamour, glitz, and grit to keep the reader turning pages. It's a stunner from start to finish."

—Kristin Dilley, cohost of the *Mind Over Murder* podcast

"In his stunning new book, *A Murder in Hollywood*, Casey Sherman takes us behind the glitz and glamour of 1950s Technicolor to a front row seat at a real-life film noir, the story of Lana Turner and her terrifying love affair with LA gangster Johnny Stompanato. It's a violent and harrowing tale of female empowerment, a page-turner more gripping than any film in which she ever starred."

—Terence Winter, executive producer of *The Sopranos* and creator of *Boardwalk Empire*

"Casey Sherman's *A Murder in Hollywood* is a riveting page-turner. This book shines a much-needed light on sexism and overt violence against women in Hollywood during the twentieth century. Bravo to Sherman for exposing a toxic Hollywood culture against the backdrop of one of Tinseltown's most famous crimes."

—Tamara Leitner, bestselling author of *Don't Say a Thing*

"A well-researched and new take on one of Hollywood's most notorious mysteries. True crime fans and celebrity mavens will enjoy."

—*Library Journal*

HELLTOWN

"With *Helltown*, Casey Sherman delivers the kind of true crime that keeps eyes glued to the pages—smart, impeccably researched, and utterly absorbing. Destined to be on all the year-end best nonfiction lists, this is an unqualified triumph by a writer at the top of his game!"

—Gregg Olsen, #1 *New York Times* bestselling author of *If You Tell*

"Searing and important, *Helltown* is an immaculately researched and rivetingly propulsive chronicle illustrating a pivotal part of our history. Brilliantly weaving together true crime, a grotesque criminal, the political landscape, and the brilliant minds who wrote about it—Casey Sherman is a master at bringing history alive. Compelling, complex, and revealing—do not miss this!"

—Hank Phillippi Ryan, *USA Today* bestselling author of *Her Perfect Life*

"Master storyteller Casey Sherman takes us back in time to the 1960s and into the dark mind of a charismatic killer. Set against the idyllic backdrop of Cape Cod, *Helltown* is a riveting, often spine-tingling true crime story."

—Terence Winter, executive producer of *The Sopranos* and creator of *Boardwalk Empire*

"*Helltown* is an immersive and captivating journey into the mind of a serial killer."

—Associated Press

"*Helltown* will render even the calmest reader unsettled when the book has been concluded. Author Casey Sherman continues his excellent work in the true crime realm with his latest effort. The narrative relayed by Sherman is engrossing and never wavers in its intensity."

—*Seattle Book Review*

THE LAST DAYS OF JOHN LENNON

"Incredibly tense and thriller-like… I totally recommend it."

—Lee Child, #1 bestselling author of the Jack Reacher series

"A must-read for music fans, true crime aficionados, or anyone looking for a deep, insightful dive into a dark chapter of American history."

—*Town & Country*

"A first-rate book…a winner."

—*Baltimore Post Examiner*

ALSO BY CASEY SHERMAN

A Rose for Mary: The Hunt for the Real Boston Strangler

Black Irish

Black Dragon

Bad Blood: Freedom and Death in the White Mountains

The Finest Hours: The True Story of the U.S. Coast Guard's Most Daring Sea Rescue

Animal: The Bloody Rise and Fall of the Mob's Most Feared Assassin

Boston Strong: A City's Triumph Over Tragedy

Above and Beyond: John F. Kennedy and America's Most Dangerous Cold War Spy Mission

12: The Inside Story of Tom Brady's Fight for Redemption

The Ice Bucket Challenge: Pete Frates and the Fight Against ALS

Hunting Whitey: The Inside Story of the Capture and Killing of America's Most Wanted Crime Boss

The Last Days of John Lennon

Helltown: The Untold Story of a Serial Killer on Cape Cod

A Murder in Hollywood: The Untold Story of Tinseltown's Most Shocking Crime

Blood in the Water: The Untold Story of a Family Tragedy

THE KILLER AND FRANK LLOYD WRIGHT

The True Story of Mass Murder in Paradise

CASEY SHERMAN

Cover design by Pete Garceau
Cover images © Bettmann/Getty Images, Frank Lloyd Wright Preservation Trust/Getty Images, Jim Packett/Shutterstock

Published by Sourcebooks
1935 Brookdale RD, Naperville, IL 60563-2773
(630) 961-3900
sourcebooks.com

Library of Congress Cataloging-in-Publication Data

Names: Sherman, Casey, author
Title: The killer and Frank Lloyd Wright : the true story of mass murder in paradise / Casey Sherman.
Description: Naperville, IL : Sourcebooks, [2026] | Includes bibliographical references.
Identifiers: LCCN 2025053195 | hardcover | epub
Subjects: LCSH: Wright, Frank Lloyd, 1867-1959 | Wright, Frank Lloyd, 1867-1959--Friends and associates | Mass murder--Wisconsin--Spring Green
Classification: LCC NA737.W7 S54 2026 | DDC 720.92--dc23/eng/20260106
LC record available at https://lccn.loc.gov/2025053195

Printed and bound in the United States of America.
MA 10 9 8 7 6 5 4 3 2

For my dear friend Frank Capolino, who has taught me valuable life lessons about selflessness and caring for others and how best to find strength and determination in the face of the most difficult of challenges. You are an inspiration.

PROLOGUE

"Ugly things happen... The best and worst of everything came to me."

—Frank Lloyd Wright

SPRING GREEN, WISCONSIN

AUGUST 15, 1914

Uncle Jenk smelled death. The foul odor of blood and burned flesh punched through his nostrils and made him nauseous. For a brief moment, he felt like a young man again, crouched in the mud-caked trenches during the Battle of Champion Hill in Mississippi more than five decades ago, watching the bodies of his comrades from the Sixth Wisconsin Light Artillery Battery stumble and fall in ghastly heaps after getting cut down by Confederate cannon, rifle, and sword. But this was not the Civil War, and he was not a young man of nineteen any longer. The Reverend Jenkin "Jenk" Lloyd Jones was now seventy years old, and he had worked the majority of his life to put such horrors behind him and to prevent them from happening again. Yet here he was, dragging the grotesquely injured and the dead away from Taliesin, his nephew Frank Lloyd Wright's burning property just down the road from his own home on Tower Hill.

Uncle Jenk found himself leaning on his wooden cane while commanding as many as seven hundred local townspeople as they fought the flames that were still lifting high above the torched bungalow. Volunteers had formed a bucket brigade, hauling pails of fresh water from a tiny pond that was adjacent to the property and also from a nearby river. One survivor discovered a fire hose near the garden wall and began dousing the flames with his burned hands in a desperate effort to save the structure.

An eight-year-old girl living nearby had seen the dark plumes and at first thought they were coming from a chimney at Taliesin. But within seconds, it appeared that the whole hill wore a ruffled cap of smoke. Then she heard the screaming of men and the cries of children. The girl climbed on her horse, Beauty, and, together with her father, rode down the hill toward the inferno. That was when she saw the beleaguered survivors, "men in sooty, bloody clothes, their faces sweat striped masks barely recognizable."

A nearby private school run by Uncle Jenk's sisters was being used as a makeshift triage hospital for victims suffering from severe burns and deep cuts to their limbs and skulls. An urgent call was issued to a hospital thirty-eight miles away in the city of Madison for any available doctors, nurses, and medical supplies as word of the tragedy continued to spread. Shocked by the news, two nurses with suitcases filled with medicine and bandages climbed on the 7:00 p.m. train and rolled away from the state capital. The charred bodies of the dead, including three children, had been carried to a home a half mile away from the bungalow and covered with sheets until they could be positively identified.

"Who could have done such a thing?" Jenk asked himself. Only the devil was capable of such a hideous act. For the fire and the deaths were no accident but the work of a killer.

Jenk was one of the first people to notice the blaze and had used bells and whistles to summon legions of villagers from across the countryside. But once he had realized that the fire was no act of God but had been deliberately set, Jenk also called in John T. Williams, the newly elected sheriff of Iowa County, to form a posse along with lawmen from two other towns. The mad rush to answer the call for assistance nearly added to the growing calamity as Sheriff Williams and his deputies were almost killed when the brakes of the speeding automobile they were traveling in failed on their way to the scene. The vehicle hit a patch of water in the middle of a dirt road and was lifted off the ground and onto two wheels, spilling one of the lawmen out of the car.

A murderer was on the loose, possibly hiding within the vast cornfields that covered the quaint, picturesque Wisconsin valley. Limping because of a shrapnel injury to his foot during the Siege of Vicksburg, Jenk moved slowly through the yellowing cornstalks with a shotgun in his wrinkled, aged hands. A devout pacifist since witnessing the carnage of the Civil War and a renowned Unitarian minister, he felt uncomfortable carrying a loaded weapon again. But he was also determined to find the man responsible for this terrible crime before others got hurt.

The posse was aided by a pack of eager bloodhounds that pressed their wet snouts down against the dry earth. The tracking dogs inhaled five times each second while their floppy ears waved across the ground, lifting the scent to their sniffers.

For three long hours, the bloodhounds barked and yipped while straining at their leashes, but the dogs found no trace of the man they were looking for amid the towering, mature cornstalks. Those men lucky enough to have survived the attack managed to provide a description of the assailant to police. A composite sketch was quickly drawn up and wired to all points along railroad lines within a radius of fifty miles from the crime scene.

During the long and fruitless search, Jenk thought about the dead and the living. He especially thought about his nephew, an architect, made famous for his ingenious designs and also infamous for the ridicule and scorn he had brought to his family and his profession. Up to this point, Frank Lloyd Wright had led a blessed life. His extraordinary talents had provided him with great prominence and prosperity. But his most recent actions, which many deemed selfish and even cruel, had put societal mores and the sacred institution of marriage on trial. Now his critics and some of his closest friends questioned whether he was cursed.

1

Frank Lloyd Wright never had to decide his career path or his destiny. Instead, his true calling was decided for him. "My mother was a teacher and she wanted an architect for a son," he recalled. "I happened to be the son and of course, naturally an architect."

Frank Lincoln Wright was born on June 8, 1867, two years after the end of the Civil War, in the small town of Richland Center, Wisconsin. There is still much debate as to exactly which house he was born in. Many believe the precise location was a small home known as the Wertz House at the corner of Seminary and Park Streets and a short walk from the Baptist church where his father, William Carey Wright, served as minister. William Wright was married and the father of three young children when he met twenty-four-year-old Anna Lloyd Jones while she boarded at his home. His dying wife, Permelia, told Wright that Anna would make a wonderful stepmother for her children, Elizabeth, George, and Charley.

Bearded and handsome with a high forehead under a thick tousle of brown hair, William Wright had made his way to the Midwest from Hartford, Connecticut. He was a jack-of-all-trades. A graduate of Amherst College, he had studied both medicine and law and later became a professor of music, teaching students piano and at the Young Ladies Boarding School in Utica, New York, before answering the call of his preacher ancestors back to the days of the Reformation in England. As a preacher, William Wright had an unorthodox style of giving his sermons while standing outside the pulpit. It was out of necessity, as the diminutive man explained to his flock: "Children should be seen and not heard, but I would have to be heard, not seen if I stood in the pulpit."

After his wife Permelia's death, William Wright was immediately drawn to Anna Lloyd Jones, who worked at the time as a teacher at a frontier schoolhouse. Anna was just five years old when her parents emigrated from Wales to the wilds of the Wisconsin countryside where they farmed and spread the Unitarian gospel. Growing up in Spring Green, Anna rode horses, not sidesaddle but straddling the large animals just like the boys did. She was also known to wear a flamboyant blue Union soldier's cape with a hood and brass buttons while riding several miles to her schoolhouse. Anna roamed the fields alone at night and was said to have had a fearless independence and love of nature. "She knew the ferns, the flowers by name," Frank would later write in his memoir. "There were berries by the roadside too, wild cherries and plums, and grapes. She might reach out and take them on the branches to the saddle bow, eating from them as she rode."

Anna was much taller than William Wright, unlike Permelia, who had been tiny, slender, and delicate. Since single men were scarce after the Civil War, Anna leaped at the chance to marry the educated East Coast dilettante. After their wedding, Anna quit her job as a schoolteacher so that she could care for her husband and her stepchildren. With a wedding ring placed on her finger, Anna's feelings about Elizabeth, George, and Charley soon changed. "She was very sweet to us children til after they were married," Elizabeth "Lizzie" Wright later wrote.

Lizzie claimed that Anna had a terrible, uncontrollable temper and that she was jealous of the close relationship the girl had with her father. "When she told me many a time that she hated me and all my mother's people, I had no reason to doubt it."

Anna would beat Lizzie without warning with a meat tenderizer, drag her across the floor by her hair, jab a fork dangerously close to her face while threatening to poke her eyes out, and douse her with freezing cold water.

"She seemed so full of venom and hate," Lizzie remembered.

For years, Lizzie woke up screaming from nightmares that her stepmother was chasing her around with a butcher knife.

William Wright asked Anna's siblings if madness ran in the Lloyd Jones family. She stayed in bed for days at a time. But when Anna learned that she was pregnant, she forced Lizzie, then five years old, to take care of most daily chores in the household while she looked after her own health. Lizzie recalled standing to wash dishes in the basement of their home while her stepmother entertained friends in the parlor.

While pregnant, Anna took a pair of scissors to the pages of a magazine called *Old England*, cut out images of ten wood engravings by artist Timothy Cole showcasing England's grand cathedrals, and placed them in flat oak frames and hung them on the walls of the room that would become her son's nursery. As an infant, baby Frank would wake up from his naps to the image of St. Paul's Cathedral, designed by Sir Christopher Wren, in London and the Christ Church Cathedral in Oxford. Anna also bought her son a set of wooden blocks to help him unlock his creativity.

"Yours was a prophetic birth," she later told him.

Despite working several side hustles as a tax collector, political party official, and music teacher, William Wright could not earn enough money to provide for his family, so he uprooted them and moved to McGregor, Iowa, and then back East to Pawtucket, Rhode Island.

While living in Pawtucket, young Frank learned the music of Bach from his father. The lessons were often painful. William would rap the boy's knuckles with a lead pencil and force his hand into position on the keys of a

Steinway square piano in the sitting room. Young Frank was also assigned to climb into the dark chamber, lit only by a tiny oil lamp, behind the church organ and pump its wooden lever whenever William played. This was tiring work for the seven-year-old boy, whose arms and back grew sore while lifting the wooden lever. Frank cried bitterly while working feverishly to keep the air in the billows of the organ, but he refused to take his hands off the lever out of fear that his father would beat him severely for giving up before the musical piece concluded. Afterward, William would find his son in the dark chamber covered in sweat and agonized by pain. He would then lead the boy home without a word of thanks, sympathy, or understanding. "When they got there his mother, seeing the state the boy was in, looked reproachfully at the father," Frank recalled in his memoir, writing about himself in the third person. "It was always so. The differences between husband and wife all seemed to arise over that boy. Mother always on the defensive, father taking the offensive. So the lad grew afraid of his father."

Frank was terrified of his father, but he was also proud of the man. It was through William's eyes, not Anna's, that he would gain his first understanding of architecture. While listening to the works of Bach and Beethoven, he was taught by his father to see a symphony as an edifice of sound, a structure with a foundation of wood, brass, and string instruments laid down to build a sweeping, melodic score.

William moved his family once again, this time to Weymouth, Massachusetts, just a few miles south of Boston. They lived in a gray house. Frank remembered it and the town as a drab old place. Anna tried to create a protective shield around her son. She would not let him eat certain foods. Pie and cake were out of the question as Anna feared they would make him sick. Frank did not want to be coddled by his mother. "Well, let's see if it will then!" he told her. "Bringing up your children on graham bread, porridge and religion, are you?"

Young Frank was an introverted child, a far cry from the boisterous self-promoter he would later become. He played alone, learned to draw and make things with his wooden blocks. He had a wild imagination and spent much of his time daydreaming in his bedroom rather than outside climbing trees or playing soldier like the other boys in his Weymouth neighborhood. The family survived on only the bare essentials, as William's salary as a minister was "a pittance in keeping with the parsimony and poverty of the ideals of life—intolerance and infallibility it paid for." Much to the embarrassment of Anna, her husband held donation parties to solicit extra money from members of his congregation.

After the birth of his sister Maginel, whom Frank described as a "frail little thing" who for her first months was handled carefully on a pillow, his family moved back to the Midwest and settled in a modest home in Madison, Wisconsin, on the shores of Lake Mendota. It was there that Anna vowed to get Frank out of his own head and into nature. It was time for the boy to learn how to become a man. Anna sent a letter to her brother James Lloyd Jones, who rode forty miles by wagon with a cow tied to the back so that the family could have fresh milk. To prepare for her brother's visit, Anna cut young Frank's hair, which he previously wore long like a girl. Anna wept as her eleven-year-old son's golden curls fell to the floor. Uncle James took one look at the delicate young boy and ran his calloused fingers through his thick brown beard and then took him by the hand. "Ready now, Frank?" Uncle James asked. "We're going west. Going to make a farmer out of you, my boy."

Young Frank climbed into his uncle's wagon and rode back to the Lloyd Jones family farm. Life there was much different than he had been used to. Gone now were the books, the music, and his building blocks. He awoke every morning before dawn to the sound of Uncle James rapping loudly on the stovepipe. "Four o'clock, my boy, time to get up."

Frank could hardly believe that it was time to wake up as he felt that he had just laid his head down on a pillow for a restful sleep. Still, he knew better than to argue with his uncle. He reached for his denim overalls and blue cotton suspenders and got dressed quickly. Uncle James made him wear a hat, which he hated to put on his head every morning. It was then off to the barn to milk the cows until his hands ached. The remainder of the day consisted of feeding the calves, splitting oak rails while Uncle James nailed them to fence posts, and a host of other chores. Frank marveled at the manly skills that his uncle displayed on the farm. Uncle James could break colts, swing an ax with "ringing accuracy," handle a kicking cow that others were too afraid to get near, and fix any machine. By contrast, Frank was ashamed by the toll that farm life was taking on his young body. His back always ached, and his elbows, knees, and feet were in constant pain. Dinner was much the same every night: boiled beef and potatoes. But at least he was able to indulge himself in a slice of pie or cake. Frank would then climb into his bed in the attic with a low ceiling and single window and drift off to sleep each night by 7:30, too tired to move.

The next day, it was rinse and repeat.

After several months of grueling farm work, Frank had reached his breaking point. He grabbed a hammer, one that he had used each day and that made his fingers stiff and sore, and threw it in a creek. Frank fled the farm and started walking home. "So he limped along," he later recalled. "The home by the blue lake and mother seemed very dear and all he wanted, but—how far away!"

Young Frank reached an old ferry boat that would take him across the river and eventually back to his home. By this time, Uncle James had mobilized other members of the Lloyd Jones clan to search for the boy. James's brother Enos found his young nephew sitting on the barge with his skinny legs dangling over the side, waiting for the vessel to depart.

"Where are you going, Frank?"

The boy could not come up with the words. Instead, he began to cry. Uncle Enos understood his situation.

"Yes, yes. I know, my boy. Work the soreness out by keeping right on working."

Uncle Enos squeezed Frank's soft arm and then flexed his own bicep and asked his nephew to feel hardened muscle. "Your muscles will be like that, Frank, if you keep working on it. Adventures make strong men and finish weak ones."

Enos led the boy back to Uncle James's farm. Frank would run off again before being brought back by Uncle James himself. After that, he committed himself to making the best of his situation. Frank and other members of the Lloyd Jones clan met regularly at the family chapel, which he described as a "simple, shingle wooden temple," where they prayed, celebrated weddings, and mourned departed relatives. Radical Unitarians known and criticized by neighbors for their seriousness and piety, the Lloyd Jones family's motto was *Truth Against the World.*

Frank felt a kinship with his mother's side of the family that had been missing on his father's side. "These sons and daughters of Richard Lloyd-Jones [his great-grandfather], Welsh Pioneer, in his Valley had already gone far toward making the kind of life for themselves that he would have approved," he proudly wrote. "The united family had its own chapel, its [own] gristmill…and owned, cultivated or pastured pretty much all the land in sight of the Valley and its branches. Lloyd-Jones family life was growing in human welfare and consequence."

When he wasn't working, Frank built dams with sticks and stones in the river. He explored wild pastures and appreciated how the sunlight reflected on the leaves on the tree trunks. He grew an appreciation for nature and his role in it. "The spot of red made by a lily on the green always gave him an emotion," Frank wrote about that time, always in the third person. "Later, the red square as [a] spot of flame-red, became the crest with which he signed his drawings and marked his buildings."

Uncle James tolerated the boy's daydreams, occasionally snapping his fingers when Frank stared off into the pastures: "Come back, Frank, come back!"

But young Frank's mind wasn't occupied by enforced idleness. Instead, he had his eye on tomorrow. The sight of blooming chokecherries, the braided foliage of the sumac trees, the world of daylight gold, the marvel of mosses, and the warm living breath of fern beds were now embedded in his imagination for his future use as an architect.

"Study nature, love nature, stay close to nature," Frank would later tell his students. "It will never fail you."

2

Young Frank would continue to devote his summers to working on the Lloyd Jones farm while spending the remainder of his time living with his parents and siblings in their modest, brown wood home in Madison where he was enrolled in school. By this time, Anna's abuse of her eldest stepdaughter, Lizzie, had gotten even worse. She beat the girl with a heavy hardwood roller until she was black and blue and threatened to place her head over a log and chop it off with an ax. William Wright sent Lizzie to live with relatives back East out of fear that his wife would explode and harm the girl again or possibly kill her.

Frank, by now fourteen years old, did not appear preoccupied with his mother's abhorrent treatment of his half sister. Instead, he focused on ideas to spruce up the house. Outside his attic bedroom, he hung up a sign that read *Sanctum*. Inside the room, he placed small oil paintings on the walls next to the engraved images of English cathedrals that his mother had kept since his birth. He met Robert "Robie" Lamp, his first true friend, a teenage boy with disabilities, and used his newly formed, farm-fed muscles to protect him from local bullies who poked fun at the way he walked. Together they read Jules Verne's thrilling novel *Michael Strogoff: The Courier of the Czar* and John Ruskin's *The Seven Lamps of Architecture*, in which the English author spelled out the demands that good architecture must meet: sacrifice, truth, power, beauty, life, memory, and obedience. The book taught Frank many things, including to dedicate his craft to God, the honest display of construction, the organization of physical effort in the construction of buildings, ornamentation drawn from nature, that buildings should respect the culture from which they were developed, and to conform to existing values, which discouraged originality for its own sake. Frank would carry some of Ruskin's ideas with him throughout his architectural career while discarding others, such as the essayist's adherence to English Gothic design, which he described as the safest choice of style.

Frank and his friend Robie were industrious teens. They started a printing press with another neighborhood boy in the small barn in the back of Frank's house. The enterprise made little money. It was a common theme in the Wright household. William Wright never earned enough money preaching or teaching music, and yet he surrounded himself with musical instruments and books with little care about providing the bare necessities for his family. For food, Anna had to rely on provisions sent to them from the family farm. William and Anna argued over finances as well as the overwhelming attention she paid to their son. "The lad was his mother's adoration," Frank later wrote. "She lived much in him. Probably that didn't help either."

William took out his frustrations on his son. He thrashed Frank until the point that he fought back. Bigger than his diminutive father, Frank grabbed him and threw him to the ground on the stable floor and held him there until the man promised to leave him alone. Frank was shamed and shaken by the experience. William could no longer manhandle his growing son. "Father ought to realize it," Frank told his mother. While he had sympathy and even admiration for his talented father, he never saw himself as William's son. After their wrestling match, their relationship was forever broken and would remain a source of great pain for Frank. "Perhaps the father never loved the son at any time," he wrote in his memoir. "Memories would haunt the youth as they haunt the man."

William retreated from his son, his tortured wife, and their children. He was like a ghost in their home, rarely interacting with any of them. Anna kicked her husband out of bed and sent him to sleep on the couch. This was no temporary measure; she told him that she would never share his bed again. In 1884, he filed for divorce.

"Well, Mr. Wright. Leave us. I will manage with the children," Anna said to him. "Go your way. We will never ask you for anything except this home… We will never ask for your help. If you can send us anything, send it. If you cannot, we will do the best we can."

Frank defended his mother and stood by her side. He struck back at his father, not with his fists but with something that would inflict permanent damage to the man. Frank changed his middle name from Lincoln, which his father had chosen at his birth to honor the slain president, to Lloyd in honor of his mother's family.

Although outwardly angry at his father, Frank tried his best to understand the man and what he was going through.

"All real crises in Life, are they not finally so simple?" he later wrote. "And who may judge the silent changes gradually taking place in the human heart like organic changes taking place in trees or plants, and like them, when manifest as complete, to be accepted?"

His mother did not see it that way. Despite her own toxic and violent behavior, she blamed her husband for the divorce and was deeply ashamed. According to Frank, Anna Wright never thought of another man in her life and never ceased to believe that William would come back to her. Anna wore the scarlet letter of "divorced woman" on her sleeve, and that invisible label had a visible impact on her son. Her shame was his shame. Frank retreated within himself, and his sensitivity and overwhelming shyness returned. In his subconscious, he felt that people were judging him for his parents' so-called *social crime*.

Anna recognized that her son was headed down a dark path and took steps to secure her prophecy for him. She brokered a meeting for Frank with Allen D. Conover, the dean of engineering at the University of Wisconsin. Despite a poor academic record in high school, Frank was allowed to enroll in the college to study civil engineering on a trial basis in 1886 as he was declared a special student. Conover also had a private architectural practice in Madison and hired Frank to work for him in the morning and afternoon between classes, earning him thirty-five dollars per month. He walked to classes each morning carrying a lunch that he would eat later at Conover's office.

Frank thrived at the drafting board while working for Conover, but he quickly grew tired of his classes. He later described his university years as nothing more than a "dull pain." Frank did not see the point of most of his classes. He liked mathematics because it worked. Unlike the theoretical debates in his university lectures, there was a finite answer to every math question. Frank studied stereotomy, graphic statistics, and analytical and descriptive geometry. He was drawn to a particular math professor named Charles Van Velzer, who had "opened for his pupil the stupendous fact that two plus two equals four." Yet as if he were studying the classics, Frank felt that math had unlocked the key to his creativity. He discovered there was poetry in mathematics and soon dreamed that a civil engineer like himself could be a composer of symphonies.

A flamboyant but shy student, Frank wore a top hat and carried a cane as he peacocked around campus. Yet he had zero success courting any of the young women living at Ladies' Hall, a dormitory strictly for women.

He managed to land a date with a young student named May, whom he took to a dance on campus. Once they got there, she immediately left him to dance a waltz with another man. "Standing out from the crowd, he felt like the bull's-eye of a big target," Frank recalled in his memoir. "Some boy took pity on him and showed him where to stow his coat and hat. Then when he came back to look for his unfortunate lady, he couldn't find her." Frank eventually caught up with May, hoping for a last dance and a kiss good night, but he was too awkward to accomplish either.

His only moment of sheer adrenaline and excitement came when in November 1883, he stumbled upon a building collapse at the south wing of the nearby state capitol building. Frank saw a cloud of white lime dust rising high in the air and heard the agonized cries of workers trapped in the wreckage under fallen masonry and heavy iron beams. "Some fell dead on the grass under the clear sky," he later wrote. "Others fell insensible." The image of one laborer who was pinned by an iron beam outside a fifth floor window was seared into his brain as a red stream of blood poured from the man's crushed foot and down the stone wall of the building. Several workers were killed in the collapse, which was caused by columns that were built too thin and too small to distribute the weight of the roof properly. Survivors later described seeing floor-to-ceiling cracks in the walls. The architect for the project, David Jones (no relation), was blamed for the disaster, although he had called for thicker, sturdier columns in his design. Jones was later found guilty of manslaughter.

Frank would describe the event in his memoir as "a vivid tragedy [that] had its life-long effect upon the incipient architect." Although Frank called Jones "good and conscientious," he understood that a chief architect on any project would achieve full credit when things went right while also bearing full responsibility when things went wrong. The tragedy had taught him a valuable lesson that would stay with him for the rest of his life.

Outside of his math classes, college meant nothing to Frank. He felt intellectually threatened by the rules and regulations that came with college life. He yearned to be free to pursue his life's dream, one that had been nurtured by his mother while he was still in the cradle. At the University of Wisconsin, he felt that he was surrounded by students who were future "might-have-beens" or "never-weres," as his uncle James would have described them. Adding to his trouble was the bitterness he felt as a product of a broken home as well as the "unsatisfied longings, humiliations and frustration" of poverty and struggle. It was time to break out on his own. When he turned eighteen, Frank quit school and pawned his father's Swiss watch, some of his old books, and his mother's mink collar. He took the money and purchased a one-way train ticket and headed to Chicago.

3

Frank Lloyd Wright was ready for his real education. The city of Chicago was booming and in the midst of a massive rebuild after the Great Fire of 1871. The inferno had swept across twenty-one hundred acres of the city, killing up to three hundred people while leaving another one hundred thousand without homes. Eighteen thousand structures, most of them made of wood, were destroyed in the blaze, forcing Chicago city planners to start again from scratch. Many of the world's greatest architects descended on the city in droves.

Frank Lloyd Wright as a young, aspiring architect. "Yours was a prophetic birth," his domineering mother, Anna Lloyd Jones, had told him. (Frank Lloyd Wright Foundation)

The move to Chicago was not an easy one for Frank, who fought with his mother about leaving college with only two terms left before his graduation.

"There are great architects in Chicago, Mother, so there must be great buildings too," he told Anna. "I am going to be an architect. You want me to be one. I am nowhere near it here."

Frank reminded his mother that she had sent him off to the family farm to gain experience and learn how to become a man. He felt that a move to Chicago would be the only way for him to achieve the next level of personal and professional growth. He also believed that college had placed a major financial burden on his poor mother. "Here at the university, I am doing nothing but draw and draw and see professional generalities glitter, spending money we haven't got or you have to slave to get," he told her.

Frank's uncle, Jenkin Lloyd Jones, was building a new Unitarian church in Chicago, and the aspiring architect hoped that he could land a job with the firm that had designed it. Anna reached out to Uncle Jenk for advice. "On no account let the young man come to Chicago," Jenk warned her. "He should stay in Madison and finish his education. That will do more for him than anything else. If he came here, he would only waste himself on fine clothes and girls."

Frank did not tell his mother that he had pawned some of their belongings to raise the seven dollars needed for the train ticket to Chicago. He did not tell her that he was leaving either. He knew that when he failed to return home from classes in the evening, his mother would sound the alarm bells. Frank promised himself that he would write to her as soon as he found a job.

He stepped out of the Chicago and North Western train carriage and onto the platform at Wells Street Station under a light drizzle on an early evening in late spring 1887. The first thing that Frank noticed was a sputtering light in the train station and out in the street. He had never seen electric lights before, and his first impression was that they were dazzling but ugly. He followed his fellow train passengers to the Wells Street Bridge and over the Chicago River. Frank paused on the bridge and peered down to the black waters below. He appreciated the somber beauty of the moment, gazing down at a tugboat puffing clouds of steam while pulling a large boat filled with grain. Frank was shivering and hungry and had no place to go. He had stubbornly resigned himself to the fact that he would not go anywhere near Uncle Jenk, nor seek his help or use his name.

The light drizzle had developed into a hard rain by the time he neared the Chicago Opera House. He fished in his pocket for a dollar and purchased a ticket to a production of *Sieba*, which was being performed by the Grand Corps de Ballet. The opera house was dry and warm. The music was unlike anything he had ever heard his father play. Frank thought the music was not good and that the overture was "too sentimental." Still, he was thankful for a place to dry off from the torrential rain.

When the show ended, he stepped back out into the Chicago night and continued to walk through the city. The skies had cleared, and Frank was energized. He marveled at the sight of his first cable car and the seemingly never-ending rows of saloons, tailors, dry goods stores, and candy shops, all with signs on their storefronts written in Polish, German, Italian, and Chinese. He eventually got himself lodging at the Briggs House, a hotel on Randolph Street. Before climbing into bed, Frank wrapped a sheet around himself and caught his reflection in a mirror. "A human item," he thought of himself. "Insignificant but big with interior faith and a great hope. In what? I could not have told you."

Any uncertainty that Frank may have had as he drifted off to sleep was erased when he awoke the next morning. He had a plan. He leafed through the city directory and wrote down the names of all the architects listed, paying close attention to the firms he had heard about while working in Allen D. Conover's office back in Madison, Wisconsin. He also recognized the name J. L. Silsbee, the firm that had designed Uncle Jenk's new church. Given his pious uncle's total disavowal of his career plans, Frank refused to call on the architectural firm. Instead, he beat down the doors of several rival firms.

He had checked a bag at the train station, one filled with his architectural sketches, and had no drawings with him as he visited the offices.

Since Frank had nothing to show, he was not taken seriously by anyone, even though he was a "university man." He continued to wander the streets of Chicago, feeling completely underwhelmed by the city's new architecture. All the buildings looked very much alike to him, "industriously varied without variety."

"Were all American cities like this one?" he asked himself. "So casual, so monotonous in their savage, outrageous attempts at variety?" Frank believed that the city's architects were all drawing off the same ideas, or lack of them.

After four days of diminished returns and surviving on only a few bananas each day, Frank swallowed his pride and paid a visit to J. L. Silsbee's office. As he entered through the door, the budding architect was immediately impressed by the collegial atmosphere of the office and a collection of Silsbee's sketches lining its walls. He had learned from his previous mistake and this time had brought with him the satchel containing his drawings. A man at the firm, Cecil Corwin, later described by Frank as a "fine-looking, cultured fellow with a pompadour and beard," approached him with rolled-up sleeves. "Let me see your drawings."

Frank pulled the sketches out of his bag, and Corwin studied them carefully.

"You made these just to please yourself?"

"Yes," Frank replied.

"You've got a good touch," Corwin told him.

Corwin then brought the drawings into J. L. Silsbee's office and shut the door. A few minutes later, the door opened, and Silsbee revealed himself in the doorframe. Tall, dark-faced, and aristocratic-looking and wearing gold eyeglasses attached to a long gold chain, the boss studied Frank for a moment. "All right, take him on," Silsbee announced. "Tracer's wages—$8.00 [per week]."

Silsbee then turned, stepped back into his office, and slammed the door.

At first, Frank was outraged. Given his experience working with Conover as well as his college education, he felt that he should have earned three times that amount. But his disappointment soon gave way to gratitude as Cecil Corwin took him under his wing and invited him to vacate the hotel and stay with him.

One night after dinner, Corwin took Frank down to the corner of Oakwood Boulevard and Langley Avenue to see Uncle Jenk's new parish, All Souls Church, which was near completion. Frank studied the building, which didn't look at all like a church to him but instead resembled something built in the Queen Anne style, asymmetrical, complete with a wraparound porch. He then felt a firm hand on his collar.

"Well, young man. So here you are," Uncle Jenk said to him in a booming voice.

Frank grew nervous, just like the days as a young boy when he ran off from the family farm, only to get caught and brought back again by one of his strappingly built uncles.

"I've been expecting you, young fellow," Jenk continued. "Your mother wrote—distracted. I'll telegraph [her] you're found."

Frank begged his uncle not to inform his mother. He told Jenk that he had already written to Anna and had sent her some money because he now had a job with J. L. Silsbee. Instead of being angry, Jenk was impressed to learn that Frank had not used his family influence to find work with Silsbee.

As Frank began building a career for himself in Chicago, his mother was left to clean up his debts in Madison. Unbeknownst to her, he had taken out a loan from a local bank and appeared to have no intention of paying it back. Frank also purchased a pair of dancing gaiters to protect the gap between his shoes and his pants on credit from a clothing store in Madison. When Anna visited the store to buy something for her daughter, she was handed a bill for seven dollars.

While Frank had inherited some valuable qualities from his father, he had also taken after the man in his frivolous, devil-may-care spending. He had no concept about how to build up savings. As money trickled in, he spent it on nice clothes, theater tickets, and tables at "cozy restaurants" and the elegant Tip Top Inn in the Pullman Building where the menu offered stuffed lobster and imperial steak for two.

Unsatisfied with his pay scale, Frank quit working for Silsbee and offered his talents to another architectural firm, Beers, Clay, and Dutton. The stint did not last long. Frank immediately felt pressure to design great buildings while he was still in the process of learning what type of architect he wanted to be. He was thrown into the deep end of the pool without first learning how to swim. He had no mentor at the firm and was learning very little, so he decided to go back to Silsbee and ask for his old job back.

"You've quit already, have you?" Silsbee asked him.

"Yes, sir."

"What for?"

"Well, I didn't want to look as though you were taking me away from Mr. Clay [of Beers, Clay, and Dutton], if you let me come back."

Silsbee appreciated the young architect's candor as well as his need not to embarrass the rival firm. Chicago was a big city but a small town as far as architectural firms went. Word spread quickly among the city's draftsmen, and Frank did not want to burn any bridges so early in his career. He was rehired by Silsbee and given a bump in pay.

Frank finally addressed the debts he had left behind in Madison. Anna wrote to her son, telling him that she was so poor, she was now contemplating suicide as the only way to relieve her financial burden. "I have been very sad of late," Anna wrote in a letter. "I am afraid that I cannot pay my debts by fall… What can I do about your debt here?"

Frank began sending his mother money to cover both his debts and her own. He brought his mother and his younger sister Maginel to live with him in Chicago. Maginel was an aspiring illustrator and graphic artist who would go on to attend the Chicago Art Institute and later illustrated books written by L. Frank Baum, creator of *The Wonderful Wizard of Oz*. Frank, his mother, and younger sister settled temporarily into a redbrick house on Forest Avenue in Oak Park. Frank had originally wanted to find them all a home somewhere on Chicago's North Shore, but Anna could not take the chill and raw winds rolling off Lake Michigan.

Although Frank was now earning eighteen dollars per week working for Silsbee, he felt stymied by what he believed was a lack of creativity in the office. Frank felt that he could match and even eclipse Silsbee's talent for freehand drawing. He also believed that Silsbee was a mere copier of styles, from Gothic Revival to the more modern shingle style, which focused on a limited material palette of cedar shingles. To inspire himself, Frank devoured books that he borrowed from a local library, including *The Grammar of Ornament* by Owen Jones and *Dictionnaire raisonné de l'architecture française du XIème au XVIème siècle* by French architect Eugène Viollet-le-Duc. "I believed the *Raisonné* was the only really sensible book on architecture in the world," he wrote in his memoir. "That book was enough to keep, in spite of architects, one's faith alive in architecture."

In order for him to break through this creative inertia, Frank was desperate to make a move. He had read in the newspaper about a radical firm that was in the process of building the world's grandest theater and office tower, the Auditorium Building, at the corner of South Michigan Avenue and Ida B. Wells Drive.

"Adler and Sullivan, architects, room 56, Borden Block, of course gave the attention to the rising Auditorium Building, in which the next President of the United States is to be nominated, and its great hall will be all ready for that event," one reporter wrote in 1888. "If Chicago is great, the Auditorium will be—already is, even in its partial development—the greatest architectural exponent of that fact. It will rest by the waterside as the cathedral of Chicago."

For the first time, architects were being described in print not as draftsmen or builders but as artists of brick, mortar, and steel. Frank wanted desperately to be a part of this new radical form of architecture, which was pioneering the idea of the skyscraper. Leading the charge was the firm's general partner, Louis Sullivan, who had joined Dankmar Adler's company a few years before. Frank was approached by a friend who had been turned down for a job by Sullivan.

"He's looking for someone to make the finish drawings for the interior of the Auditorium," Frank was told. "I can't make them, but you can. I told him about you and he asked me to send you over to see him."

Frank gathered his drawings and rushed over to the Borden Block to meet with Sullivan, whom he later described as "a small man immaculately dressed in brown. His outstanding feature his amazing big brown eyes. Took me in at a glance."

Frank felt that Sullivan could read his innermost thoughts. He nervously unrolled his drawings for the man's inspection. Sullivan was not impressed by what he saw. He told Frank to create some drawings with ornamental details and return. Frank immediately obliged and went to work. He locked himself in his bedroom in Oak Park with a drawing board, a T square, and a triangle. He promised himself that he would only use the tools for guidelines. Instead, he used his free hand to draw Gothic ornaments that he had seen on other Adler and Sullivan buildings.

When he returned to Sullivan's office, Frank showed his freehand imitations of Silsbee's work, imitations of Sullivan's ornamental drawings, improvised Gothic drawings in the style of Owen Jones, and finally his own original designs.

"You've got the right kind of touch, you'll do," Sullivan said as he scratched his scalp with the sharp point of a lead pencil, triggering a small avalanche of dandruff to fall onto the drawings. "How much money have you been getting?"

"Not enough," Frank replied.

"Well, how much is enough?"

"Twenty-five dollars."

A deal was struck, and Frank returned to Silsbee's office to let his boss know that he was quitting again.

Anna fretted over her son's decision, thinking it was too rash. "Oh, my boy, stop where you are now. I thought you were doing well. You are in too much of a hurry," she pleaded with him. "I told you not to leave Silsbee until you get more experience. Of course, my boy, you have not yet [had] the experience. You are not yet twenty."

Frank did not heed his mother's advice. He now had the job of his dreams. It was time for him to find someone to share his good fortune with. Serendipity would soon reveal itself with a painful bump on the head.

4

Her name was Catherine Tobin, but her father called her Kitty. She moved effortlessly across the dance floor during a *Les Misérables*-themed costume party at All Souls Church in a flowing pink dress under a head of blond curls. She was turned away from Frank while still walking in his direction. Before he could step out of the way to avoid her, she crashed right into him, their foreheads knocking together. Kitty, a tall and pretty girl, tumbled to the ground upon the collision, while Frank grew dizzy and saw stars. He managed to pick her up, and they both laughed awkwardly over the crash encounter. Frank led Kitty to her parents to apologize, but she took full responsibility for the mishap. Instead of being angry over the bump on their sixteen-year-old daughter's forehead, Kitty's parents invited Frank over for Sunday dinner.

He showed up late to dinner at the Tobin family home on Drexel Boulevard. Kitty's father, Samuel Clark Tobin, had an easy way about him and did not make Frank feel guilty for arriving a few minutes later than the scheduled suppertime. Kitty's mother, Flora, acted differently. Although she was fine-looking with auburn hair and adored by Kitty and her two brothers, Flora had a dominant personality and clearly ruled the home. But Frank learned right away that Kitty was treated differently from her brothers and "pretty much had her own way in that household," including the use of her own particular plate and silverware for dinner.

After dinner, Kitty put on a pair of boots, gloves, and a short plaid walking jacket and took Frank by the hand on a tour of homes in her Kenwood neighborhood on Chicago's prosperous South Side. While Kitty appeared confident and sure of herself, Frank was nervous. "I was grown up pretty well in architecture, the sphere in which I lived in earnest," he later recalled. "But where people were concerned, I had nearly everything yet to learn."

Although Kitty was a great talker and fun to be around, she did not drink or smoke and was devoted to her church. She taught Frank how to act more naturally in polite society, and their relationship grew quickly from hand-holding affection to a steady romance. Watching their relationship unfold from the sideline was Anna Wright, and she was not happy at the notion of sharing her son with another woman.

"Why all this fuss over a perfectly natural thing?" Frank asked his mother.

"Frank, have you thought of the consequences to this young girl, of your singling her out at the exclusion of all others?"

"No, of course I haven't," he replied. "But isn't she the best judge of what that means to her? I don't see how I can judge for her. And if she can't, how about her father and mother?"

"Her mother's in trouble with her already," Anna informed him. "It seems beyond her mother's control."

Frank grew furious over the notion that Anna had paid a visit to Flora Tobin's home without first consulting him. His mother added that Kitty was accustomed to having her own way and had been giving her mother heaps of trouble. Their conversation quickly devolved into a shouting match, with Frank swearing at his mother over her anxiety, anguish, prying, and gossip. Anna got up from her chair and stormed out of the room.

Frank told Kitty about his mother's meddling, and she confided that her own mother had forbidden their relationship because of her young age. "I've had pretty nearly everything myself but an out-and-out spanking. If I can stand it, don't you think you can?"

Their courtship lasted a year. During this time, Kitty fell behind in her classes at Hyde Park High School and was teased mercilessly by her classmates, who sent her a drawing of a large kitty cat with the words "Perfectly Frank" underneath.

Frank turned twenty-one, and Kitty was seventeen. He proposed marriage, and their wedding took place on a rainy day in 1889. In his memoir, Frank likened his wedding day to a funeral filled with a great deal of sorrow and devoid of joy: "The heavens weeping out of doors—all weeping indoors. Mother of the groom fainting. Father of the bride in tears."

Catherine "Kitty" Wright fell in love with Frank when she was seventeen years old, and together they had six children. (Frank Lloyd Wright Foundation)

Both Frank and Kitty recovered from the hysterics of the day and looked for a place to settle down. Frank asked Louis Sullivan for a five-year loan to build his own home as long as he continued to work for the firm. He purchased a vacant lot, which was inspected and preapproved by Sullivan, at the corner of Forest and Chicago Avenues in Oak Park. Sullivan warned his young draftsman about cost overruns on the project. "Now look out, Wright," Sullivan lectured. "I know your tastes... no 'extras.'"

Frank did not keep his promise. One of the first things he added to the

The home in Oak Park, Illinois, that Frank Lloyd Wright designed and built for his growing family. (Getty Images)

new home was an elegant carving in an oak slab above the fireplace in the living room that read *Truth Is Life. Good Friend, Around These Hearth-Stones Speak No Evil Word of Any Creature.* It was a play on words from the Lloyd Jones family motto: *Truth Against the World.* He had also planned to carve mottoes into the panels of the doors in all the rooms in the house, but Kitty protested. She simply did not like mottoes. Frank was surprised and angry that his young wife had disputed what he called his "superior taste in matters pertaining to [his] own work." He did not want to lose face when discussing building plans with Kitty, and a small divide began to grow between the newlyweds.

Meanwhile, Frank relished his work under Louis Sullivan, often referring to his boss as "the Master." They shared office space at the top of the Auditorium Building, along with thirty other draftsmen. Sullivan was an abrasive and sometimes abusive boss, but Frank knew that he could learn much from the forward-thinking architect. Long after the other draftsmen clocked out for the day, Frank and Sullivan would discuss architectural philosophies in the office after dark. The conversations were normally one-sided, with Sullivan doing the talking and Frank doing the listening. Frank believed that Chicago was at the "center of the united fundamentalist ugliness of the United States" and that it was their responsibility to break through and offer the world something that was boldly different.

For the Chicago Auditorium Building, Sullivan and Adler had designed a colossal Romanesque-style structure with elliptical arches and massive load-bearing outer walls. The building, completed in 1890, served as the economic and cultural base of Chicago. Frank's contribution to the Herculean effort was to add ornamental flourishes throughout the building. Everything Frank drew had been first conceived by Sullivan. The boss would relay his ideas to his talented apprentice and then divert his attention to other aspects of the project. "I became a good pencil in the Master's hand," Frank recalled. "And because I could be this to him, he had more freedom now than he had ever enjoyed before."

Some Wright scholars suggest that Sullivan's interest in his younger apprentice was more than just professional and that Sullivan was sexually attracted to Frank. Sullivan was a member of the Lotus Club, a private all men's club that glorified the male figure. The club's notebook contained several drawings, some by Sullivan, of naked men wrestling and swimming. If there was a sexual undertone to their relationship, Frank himself never discussed it in any of his writings.

Chicagoans marveled at each phase of the construction cycle. "The Auditorium progresses steadily toward completion and the architects continue to bend their energies to the end that has been nobly conceived and splendidly developed shall be finally consummated in correspondent dignity and majesty," a local reporter glowingly wrote in January 1889, nearly a year before the building's completion. "As Chicago's grandest structure approaches its perfect form, it more and more commands the wonder and delight of all beholders."

When the Auditorium finally opened its doors in December that same year, adoring critics called it "a magnificent example of modern building" and compared the ten-story, 240-foot office tower and opera house favorably to other architectural achievements such as the Capitol Building in Washington, DC, and the State House in Albany, New York. At that time, the Auditorium was the largest building in the United States and carried a hefty price tag at $3,200,000. The building housed 130 offices, a four-hundred-room hotel, a bar, restaurants, and a theater filled with forty-two hundred seats.

Frank was invited to the grand opening celebration, where he watched Spanish opera star Adelina Patti, who composer Giuseppe Verdi believed was the finest singer who ever lived, perform. He later called the occasion "a gorgeous civic and social event to be remembered."

While he was building a reputation as an up-and-coming architect, Frank was saddled with his growing responsibilities as both a husband and father. Kitty gave birth to their first child, Frank Lloyd Wright Jr., known as Lloyd, within the first year of their marriage. Five more children came after, and the Wright household filled up quickly, perhaps too quickly for Frank. "The young husband found that he had his work cut out for him," he remembered sourly. "The young wife found hers cut out for her. Architecture was my profession. Motherhood became hers. Fair enough. But it was [a] division."

Sullivan's confidence in Frank grew, and the boss soon put him in charge of the firm's thirty draftsmen. Contracts to design hotels, factories, and opera houses flowed into the office in a steady stream, and Frank often found himself working all hours and taking the late train home on an empty stomach. Despite being the highest paid draftsman in Chicago, Frank always felt strapped for cash. He began moonlighting and taking on commissions to build homes by himself. While Sullivan was sketching plans for the Wainwright Building, a tall, steel office building considered the country's first skyscraper, in downtown St. Louis, Frank met secretly with wealthy prospective homebuyers in Oak Park who had asked the architect to design them a home similar to his own.

Despite taking these jobs on his own without consultation with Sullivan and oftentimes using a pseudonym in an effort not to get caught, Frank convinced himself that he was doing nothing wrong because the firm seldom designed and built private homes. He performed his freelance work at night and on weekends from the upstairs drafting room of his Oak Park home. When Sullivan discovered that Frank had been moonlighting, he confronted his apprentice. "Your sole interest is here, while your contract lasts," Sullivan informed him. "I will not tolerate division under any circumstances."

Frank felt conflicted. He believed that he was being unjustly persecuted by Sullivan, but he also knew that it was wrong to sneak around behind his boss's back. Sullivan went as far as withholding the deed to Frank's house over his alleged breach of contract. Frank appealed to Dankmar Adler, who was even more offended by the young architect's behavior than Sullivan was. Instead of pleading for the mercy of his employers, Frank threw his pencil down and walked out of the office, never to return.

He now had a growing family, a demanding wife, and no real means to support them. Frank had to come up with a plan. He decided to go out on his own. Frank would have to gamble heavily on his own talents as well as his mission to radically alter the landscape of the American neighborhood.

5

As an architect, Frank demanded the honesty of structural expression. He constantly rearranged the furniture in his Oak Park home to fit whatever aesthetic pleasure had inspired him at that moment. While moving sofas and high-backed chairs that he had designed himself, Frank worked through a series of architectural problems in his head. The home he had designed for himself was different from the other houses on his block. On the exterior of the home, Frank used shingles to cover the rectangular foundation below its large triangular gable roof. He referred to the style as "Seaside Colonial." The base of the home also featured large polygonal window bays. The two-story structure stood in stark contrast to the more traditional turnip dome and corkscrew spire homes that lined Forest Avenue. The interior was open concept, as Frank wanted to liberate space and move away from Victorian design with smaller rooms that functioned as designated spaces: a parlor, a formal living room, a dining area, etc. Instead, Frank wanted to create a unified environment for his family and friends.

He now had to convince others to open their minds and break away from the traditional Queen Anne style of the era. He quickly found a prospective home buyer who was willing to take risks.

In 1893, Frank was commissioned by a prominent Chicago businessman named William Winslow to design a grand home for his family in the suburb of River Forest. The interior resembled Frank's house in Oak Park, centered by an inglenook fireplace and surrounded by a living room, library, dining room, and entrance hall. Frank added a semicircular room with stained glass windows. The overall design of the home resembled a symmetrical monolithic block built close to the ground with a low and gently sloping roof and wide eaves. In his sketches, Frank wanted to celebrate the horizontal instead of the vertical. He was maniacal in his pursuit of a radical new style to call his own. He incorporated elements that he would later call his "Prairie School" design.

Once completed, the home drew admirers and critics too. "The Winslow House had burst on the view of that provincial suburb like the Prima Vera in full bloom," he wrote in his memoir. "Incessantly it was courted and admired. Ridiculed too, of course. Ridicule is always modeled on the opposite side of that shield. The first house soon began to sift the sheep from the goats."

The goats, those freethinkers who were comfortable enough in their own skin to give Frank free rein in his designs, were still few and far between while the sheep were plentiful and willing to pay good money for Frank's work. One client, an attorney named Nathan Moore, demanded the opposite of what Frank had conceived and delivered to William Winslow. "I don't want to go down back streets to my morning train to avoid being laughed at," Moore told him.

Frank took the job, convincing himself that he would not "sell out" against his own radical ideas as long as he designed a worthy home in the name of Tudor style half-timber. Moore was delighted by the end result, which featured large, steeply pitched roofs, but Frank resented the praise that was bestowed on it.

The money he had earned on the project did not go very far either. As his father had done before him, Frank routinely spent lavishly on things that he could not afford. He bought each of his children a musical instrument.

For instance, his son Lloyd got a cello, while his siblings were given a violin, a piano, and a flute. He also built a large playroom for his growing brood on the upper floor of their Oak Park house. Despite the gifts, Frank kept his children at arm's length. "The children were their mother's children," he would later write.

Frank hated the sound of the word *Papa*. "The architect absorbed the father in me," he said. "Is it a quality? Fatherhood? If so, I seemed born without it."

Frank refused to discipline his children and admittingly would sometimes forget their names.

He also grew frustrated each time they entered his office without permission and interrupted his work. But Frank's children adored their father and received his affection in nontraditional ways.

"He bought my clothes, my shoes, my toys," his second son, John Wright, recalled. "He performed all the functions of fatherhood, only he performed them differently. He took no personal interest in my religious or academic training. But when it came to luxuries and play, he tenderly took my hand and led the way."

The Oak Park home was not a depressing place. It was quite the opposite. As later described in John Wright's own memoir, "Papa's parties were the best of all. He had clambakes, tea parties in his studio, cotillions in the larger drafting room; gay affairs about the blazing logs that snapped and crackled in the big fireplace... From week to week, month to month, our home was a round of parties. There were parties somewhere all of the time and everywhere some of the time."

Frank had borrowed money to build out the children's playroom and was slow to pay it back. This triggered a visit from the local sheriff, who demanded that Frank come up with eighty-five dollars to settle his debt. Somehow, he came up with the money but had another major bill looming. Frank had purchased $850 worth of groceries on credit. The grocer, named

Gotsch, went to Frank's home and pleaded with him to pay what he owed. The grocery store owner explained to Frank that it would be cheaper for him to pay his bills regularly instead of in one lump sum months later. The young architect felt remorseful and once again cobbled together the money to pay the bill. He blamed himself for getting the family into one financial mess after the other. But amazingly, Frank also put some of the responsibility on others. "It was my misfortune too, that everybody was willing to trust me," he recalled. "I don't know why they were willing, either, because I don't imagine my appearance or my way of life would appeal to a businessman any more than my buildings appealed to local bankers later on."

Frank was also trusting of others. He never carried keys, and his home was always unlocked. One morning, Frank heard stirring in the downstairs living room. It was a burglar rifling through the family's belongings. Instead of grabbing something he could use as a weapon, Frank turned on the lights so that the burglar could see better. "Papa told him he could hurt himself working in the dark and asked him why such a handsome young fellow didn't go out and work in the light where he could be seen and appreciated," his son John remembered. "When they parted, the burglar liked Papa and Papa liked the burglar."

Frank even had trouble keeping up with the rent on his new office space located on the tower floor of the Schiller Building, where his old bosses Adler and Sullivan were also headquartered. He found himself falling seven or eight months behind on payments. But like he had with other debt collectors, Frank found ways to charm the building manager. He apologized profusely for the oversight and promised to pay the hefty sum back.

"Never mind, Mr. Wright, you are an artist," the building manager told him. "I have never lost any rent owed me by an artist. You will pay me."

That was exactly how Frank thought of himself, as an artist and not a businessman. He had secured five commissions during his first year on his own. During this time, he was also offered the opportunity of a lifetime, a six-year, all-expenses-paid sabbatical to study architecture in Paris and Rome with the promise that he would master the Beaux Arts style that was popular at the time in Europe and bring it back to Chicago. Frank would have to abandon his emerging Prairie School designs and adopt French neoclassicism instead. He told his would-be benefactor that it was too great a risk for him, despite almost guaranteed prosperity for his family.

"I can't run away," Frank said. "Run away from what I see as mine… I can't go, even if I wanted to go because I would never care for myself, after that." He did not see any freedom in such a journey. "I'd rather be free and a failure and 'foolish' than be tied up to any routine success," he thought to himself. He found personal freedom in his Prairie School designs, which focused on organic simplicity that was harmonious with nature—trees, flowers, and the sky itself.

After incorporating natural elements in his designs, Frank managed to pull them all together while building his first official Prairie School–style residential home in Kankakee, Illinois, in 1900 for a prominent businessman named Warren Hickox. Frank's design blurred the boundaries of architecture and the natural world by incorporating two large half-octagonal bays with thin bands of leaded glass spanning the bays and extending the interior of the house into the natural landscape outside.

Frank was willing to defend his appreciation for nature with guns if he had to. Back in Oak Park, he found himself in a showdown with members of the town board over their plans to trim trees in the neighborhood. Frank argued that the trees should be allowed to grow as they pleased. He warned tree trimmers not to make any attempt to cut back the foliage around his home, and rumors spread that he had a "well equipped arsenal awaiting the first trimmer." The trimmers then notified the town council that they would not risk their lives by attempting to cut the tops off the trees in the vicinity of Frank's residence. He urged members of the council and their fellow critics to move to Chicago if they wanted more sunshine, as he had moved to Oak Park because there was shade there, and he did not intend to have the shade taken away from him.

Frank's professional reputation continued to grow, and so did the demand for his services. He hired several draftsmen, including a woman named Marion Mahony, who was known for her exquisite renderings of murals, tables, and chairs. Mahony was one of the first licensed female architects in the world. Frank adored Mahony for her creativity and her intellect. He did not pursue her romantically but instead kept his wandering eye focused on other women in Oak Park. It appeared that every woman wanted to be with him, and every man wanted to be him. One client called him "one of the most remarkable men he had ever met," while others said that Frank exemplified "a splendid type of manhood" and that he was "one of nature's noblemen."

As for women, the growing division between Frank and Kitty over her nearly singular focus on their children had taken a toll on Frank's selfish heart. He sought attention from others, and he got it. Frank showed off his architectural designs at an exhibition for the prestigious Chicago Club, where one critic marveled at his design of a chimney front, a gold chimney breast, and some copper articles. "The innovation…makes it very interesting," the critic wrote. "And awakens more discussion than anything else in the gallery."

In March 1901, Frank delivered one of his most important speeches to members of the Chicago Arts and Crafts Society at Hull House, a nonprofit organization that offered education, childcare, and legal services to Chicago's poorest residents. He titled his essay "The Art and Craft of the Machine." His intent was to explain the machine's unique relationship with art, which sometimes took away the artist's creativity, while also advancing artistic concepts with mechanical levers and tools.

The machine is intellect mastering the drudgery of earth that plastic art may live; that the margin of leisure and strength by which man's life upon the earth can be made beautiful, may immeasurably widen; its function ultimately to emancipate human expression!...

Now let us learn from the machine. It teaches us that the beauty of wood lies first in its qualities as wood. No treatment that does not bring out these qualities all the time can be plastic or appropriate or beautiful. The machine teaches us that certain simple forms and handling are suitable to bring out the beauty of wood and certain forms are not; that all wood-carving is apt to be a forcing of the material, an insult to its finer possibilities as a material having in itself intrinsically artistic properties, of which its beautiful marking is one, its texture another, its color a third.

The machine, by its wonderful cutting, shaping, smoothing, and repetitive capacity, has made it possible so to use it without waste that the poor as well as the rich may enjoy to-day beautiful surface treatments of clean, strong forms...

I will venture to say, from personal observation and some experience, that not one artist in one hundred has taken pains to thus educate himself. I will go further and say what I believe to be true, that not one educational institution in America has as yet attempted to forge the connecting link between science and art by training the artist to his actual tools, or, by a process of nature-study that develops in him the power of independent thought, fitting him to use them properly....

Upon this faith in art as the organic heart quality of the scientific frame of things, I base a belief that we must look to the artist brain, of all brains, to grasp the significance to society of this thing we call the machine.

The oration made him a sought-after speaker in Chicago. He also spoke before several women's clubs, including the Daughters of the American Revolution, about his love of Japan. Frank first visited there in 1905 with Kitty and another couple. She had hoped that time together and away from their children would rekindle the flame of desire that he had once had for her. Frank had planned nearly every detail of the trip, which took them by steamship from Vancouver Harbor to the port of Yokohama. The voyage took seventeen days to complete. After landing in Japan, Frank and Kitty took a train and rode along the coastal highway from Tokyo to Kyoto. He collected several Japanese prints along the way as they visited ancient Shinto shrines and other historic sites.

Frank took with him a four-by-five camera and photographed the natural landscape of mountain paths and dense woods as well as uniquely styled buildings in cities like Osaka, Kobe, and Takamatsu.

He would later compile forty of his photographs and fifteen woodblock prints of Japanese architecture and waterfalls into a personal album that he would draw inspiration from for the rest of his career.

Frank fell in love with Japan: its people, its architecture, and its ancient customs.

"Men and women so care for their very young, and their very old," he wrote in his memoir. "It is said their country is the paradise of old age and of childhood."

Frank studied how Japanese citizens lived in what he viewed as immaculately clean homes with little or no dirt. He also marveled at the minimalist lifestyles of those he came into contact with.

"I saw the native home in Japan as a supreme study in elimination—not only of dirt but the elimination of the insignificant," he later wrote.

In these ancient Japanese dwellings, Frank saw modernization. The architect was influenced by Japanese designs that focused on bare-essential living and compared them favorably to his own Prairie School style. "By heaven, here was a house used by those people who made it with just that naturalness with which a turtle used his shell," he added.

Frank's first visit to Japan was life-changing. The island nation's beautiful simplicity would lure him back time and again.

But the three-month tour did not bring him any closer to Kitty. Instead, he returned home with the greater realization that both his heart and his soul now belonged to someone else.

6

Flawless. It was the only way that Frank could describe her. She was more beautiful than any woman he had ever seen, and he could hardly take his eyes off her, even while showing her husband his architectural designs for their new home.

The year was 1903, two years prior to his first visit to Japan, when Frank was thirty-six years old. He sat in the parlor of his neighbor Edwin Cheney's house in Oak Park, discussing plans for another of his Prairie School–style homes, but one vastly different from the home that he had just completed for his client B. Harley Bradley and his wife, Anna, in nearby Kankakee, Illinois.

Cheney, a brilliant and prosperous electrical engineer, admired Frank's design for the Bradley House, which was built with ninety art glass windows to blur the separation between the interior and exterior of the home. Cheney wanted the architect to build for him something equally bold but less ostentatious. The house would be much smaller, with all the rooms on one floor, forming a single longitudinal space under a hipped roof.

The one-story house would feature a square floor design with an entrance on the side that gave way to a reception area and a large living room. The design also included a nine-foot privacy wall, a wraparound brick terrace,

The home in Oak Park, Illinois, that Frank Lloyd Wright designed and built for Edwin Cheney and his wife, Mamah Borthwick Cheney. (Frank Lloyd Wright Trust)

and a separate apartment for the sister of Cheney's young wife Martha, or "Mamah," as she was called by her friends.

During the meeting with Cheney, Frank had a difficult time focusing on his design sketches each time Mamah entered the darkened parlor, which was illuminated by flickering candles. It was as if she carried her own light with her. She radiated in both her appearance and her speech. Mamah was sleek and moved with grace and charm. She was blessed with silky black hair and smoldering, deep-set eyes, and neighbors said she looked like a Greek goddess. She also had an infectious laugh and a delicate yet commanding voice, which had served her well when she delivered the commencement speech at her graduation from the University of Michigan just a few years before.

Unlike Kitty Wright, who had led a bit of a sheltered life, moving only once from her parents' house and into the home she now shared with her husband, Mamah had already lived a life of high adventure. Her father, Marcus, was a railroad car builder, and her mother, Almira Bowcock

Borthwick, was a highly educated graduate from the Lyons Female College in Iowa.

Similar to what Frank's own father had done, Marcus moved his family around, first from the city of Boone, Iowa, then to Chicago, and eventually to Oak Park, Illinois, for a better opportunity to educate his children. Mamah attended public school in Oak Park and, at sixteen years old, was offered the opportunity to travel with her older sister Jessie on a riding, hunting, and fishing expedition in the Dakota Territory, where settlers and Indigenous Americans were still recovering from the Great Sioux War just eight years before and tensions remained high. Mamah and her sister rode by train over eight hundred miles from Chicago to Pipestone, Minnesota, at the edge of the Dakota Territory.

The sisters took advantage of the trip by hunting and riding as much as they could on the open frontier while also fishing with pitchforks for northern pike on Devils Lake in North Dakota.

A reporter from a local Oak Park newspaper called *The Cicero Vindicator* was there at the station when Mamah and her twenty-two-year-old sister Jessie returned from their northwest trip, writing that the two "Misses Borthwick" got off the train "loaded with beautiful specimens, ruddy complexions and wonderful stories."

Mamah returned to school in Oak Park, where she focused on her studies and the arts. The sixteen-year-old starred as Lady Macbeth in the school play and earned positive notice from a local theater editor. "Miss Mamah Borthwick's rendition of the instigation scene…where that worthy's wife incites him to strike the blow that would give him kingly honors, was exceedingly well-rendered and therefore deserves special mention," William Halley wrote in the *Vindicator*.

Mamah headed off to the University of Michigan the same year that Frank settled in Oak Park with Kitty and their growing family.

Mamah arrived for college at Ann Arbor alone. Her father had planned to accompany her but had to rush back home after getting word that his son was critically injured after getting crushed against a freight train car while trying to unhitch a broken-down locomotive. When she departed the train in Ann Arbor, Mamah set about getting herself a room, as there were no dormitories available to women at the time. She dropped her bags at a local boardinghouse a few blocks from campus and then introduced herself to fellow students of the class of 1892.

Mamah majored in arts and literature and quickly won high praise from the chairman of the literature department. "[Martha] was uniformly counted among the best members of her class," Professor Edward L. Walter wrote in a letter of recommendation. "With an active mind, [she is] unusually quick in the mastery of languages [and] clear in expressing herself."

When she returned for her sophomore year, Mamah met a young classmate from Detroit named Edwin Cheney, who had enrolled at the school as a freshman. Mamah spent most of her time with her Kappa Alpha Theta sorority sisters and was oblivious at first about Cheney's romantic pursuit of her. Edwin was the fair-haired son of a Civil War veteran and successful tool manufacturer named James Wilson Cheney. Edwin was a member of the glee club and pursued Mamah by serenading her over a new invention called the telephone. As college students, they appeared in one photograph together, a group picture for the school yearbook. Edwin is seen staring off camera somewhat vacant-eyed, while Mamah is looking directly into the camera lens, wearing her graduation cap.

Cheney earned enough credits to graduate the same year as Mamah. On graduation day in June 1892, Mamah delivered the class prophecy, a satirical prediction of the future endeavors of Michigan graduates, to what the *Chicago Tribune* declared "the largest class in America this year." The University of Michigan handed out degrees to 689 graduates that day, and all of them got to hear Mamah's humorous two-thousand-word free-verse poem. Addressing William Warner Bishop, who would one day organize the

Vatican Library, she told the large audience, "The favorite scriptural verse of Warner Bishop. In later years, has truly been fulfilled, that all the land whereon his feet have trod," Mamah stated. "Is his, and his alone forever more." Her speech was considered to be outrageous at the time, as women rarely skewered their male counterparts in public. But she saved her most scathing tongue-in-cheek prediction for her future husband, Edwin Cheney.

"Ed Cheney sings in Allen's microphone. To advertise its merits far and near, And even when at College in Course I, in Physics where he earned his credits-lip."

It was her way of teasing him for his almost single-minded electrical engineering pursuits. Mamah also acknowledged that she and her fellow female graduates would be looking for teaching positions as business and other professional opportunities were not open to them.

At the close of her speech, Mamah beckoned, "And now my sovereign master, Dear Apollo. Receive me back into thy sweet oblivion… For thee alone I have awakened. For thee again, I seek pathetic dust."

Mamah's last name was misspelled *Berthwick* in the newspaper article that chronicled the exercise. She graduated with a bachelor of arts degree and would remain in Ann Arbor for one more year to earn her master's degree. She then returned to her family in Oak Park while Cheney was building his engineering career with the Chicago Edison Company. She focused her attention on organizing a national convention for her sorority, Kappa Alpha Theta, which coincided with the World's Columbian Exposition, better known as the Chicago World's Fair. Theta members from across the country were struck right away by Mamah's intelligence and outgoing personality. "She will help in sending us new members," one sorority sister wrote to another about Mamah. "And in making us known and creating a favorable impression of us abroad."

Following the convention, Mamah and a classmate named Mattie Chadbourne moved to Port Huron, Michigan, along the St. Clair River, where both predictably took jobs as schoolteachers. They shared a room at a boardinghouse, first on Military Street and then closer to school on Seventh Street. Mamah ingratiated herself in the community right away, joining the Young Women's Club where she was eventually elected vice president. Cheney frequently traveled by train more than six hours to see her. She also volunteered at the Port Huron Ladies Library Association. Beautiful, talented, and refined, Mamah easily made friends with her fellow teachers and other women outside school.

After about a year, Chadbourne became seriously ill and had to resign from her position and move back to Chicago. Not wanting to remain in the city alone, Mamah gave her resignation letter also and returned to Oak Park before the school year began in 1896.

By this time, Edwin Cheney was also living in Oak Park with his parents and his sister.

When Mamah returned to town, she joined a local theater group and starred in several benefit performances of a play called *Mrs. Jarley's Waxworks*, where she had the lead role. The material for the show was plucked from Charles Dickens's novel *The Old Curiosity Shop*. Outfitted in a colorful shawl, duster, and big bonnet, Mamah delighted the crowd with her comedic flair. But all was not joyful for Mamah and her family. In January 1898, her mother, Almira, passed away after a brief illness. That same year, one of Mamah's college mentors, Professor Edward L. Walter, was killed when the passenger ship he was traveling on, the SS *La Bourgogne*, collided with the Scottish sailing ship *Cromartyshire*, off Cape Sable Island, Nova Scotia. Walter was among the 562 victims that went down with the ship.

Edwin Cheney consoled Mamah in her grief and then proposed marriage. The two appeared to be polar opposites. While Mamah was carefree, vivacious, and intellectually curious, Cheney was fastidious, career-minded, and somewhat dull. Still, he had generated wealth for himself, first by working for the Chicago Edison Company and then as vice president and manager of the Illinois Maintenance Company. He was even prosperous enough to be included in the exclusive Who's Who list of Chicago's most important people. The couple got married on June 15, 1898. Mamah invited more than a dozen classmates from the University of Michigan to attend. The bride wore a wedding dress made of white silk grenadine with lace trimmings.

The wedding ceremony took place in the parlor of her father's Oak Park home. Two hundred guests attended the reception. Following the wedding, the Cheneys took a train to New York and booked passage on a ship for a two-month honeymoon trip to Europe. They returned to Oak Park in late August, and the realization that Mamah's future would be focused on caring for her husband and any children they would bring into the world began to set in.

7

By the time Frank met Mamah in 1903, she had already given birth to her first child, a son named John. She had also been saddled by more grief. Her father, Marcus Borthwick, died after a bout with pleurisy in 1900. His funeral was held at the home shared by Mamah and her husband. In his obituary, the seventy-two-year-old family patriarch was described as "one of the oldest employees of the Chicago and North Western Railway."

The following year, Mamah's sister Jessie, the person she had shared her great adventure in the Dakota Territory with, died while giving birth to a daughter. Jessie was just thirty-seven years old. Jessie's husband placed their infant child in the care of Mamah and Edwin Cheney and left Oak Park, never to return.

Mamah's other sister, Lizzie, moved into her home to help care for their sister's baby, who was named Jessie after her mother. When Mamah became pregnant with John, she urged her husband to find a new home, bigger than the one they were currently renting on North East Avenue in Oak Park.

For the couple, there was only one architect to consult: Frank Lloyd Wright.

Tongues were still wagging about the home that Frank had designed for local banker Arthur Heurtley and his wife, Grace, on Forest Avenue in Oak

Park the year before. Just a short walk from Frank's own home and studio, the Heurtley house was built with two colors of Roman brick, laid in alternating projecting bands, with a Romanesque arch over the entrance and a large open reception hall inside. Blurring the interior with the exterior space, Frank also designed the home with an open-air elevated porch with access to the living room.

The house was already considered to be one of Frank's greatest residential designs, and the competitive Edwin Cheney wanted the architect to build him a monument to his own success, one that would rival or even eclipse the Heurtley house.

Cheney purchased a lot at 520 North East Avenue, and a building permit was issued on January 14, 1904. Frank's design looked like a magician's illusion. From the street, the home appeared as if it had just one floor when in fact, it had two. He had raised the building's basement to the ground level and then camouflaged it with a tall brick wall. Frank positioned the front door out of view and around the side of the house. He had abandoned ideas for a front porch during the advent of the automobile to avoid the loud noises made as vehicles rumbled their way down unpaved roads in Oak Park. The house was also designed with fifty-two windows of iridescent glass to evoke an image of Japanese bamboo curtains.

Both Edwin and Mamah Cheney were thrilled with Frank's design to remove walls and integrate living spaces, as it would allow Mamah to entertain guests in a more relaxed environment. As secretary for her Kappa Alpha Theta sorority, Mamah frequently played hostess to her sorority sisters from as far away as Indiana and Ann Arbor, Michigan. The new home would be 2,694 square feet, a relatively small but stunning showcase for all who entered.

During the entirety of the project, Frank grew closer to Mamah. He had developed an image in his head of the most beautiful woman in the world, and Mamah fit that ideal perfectly. Like him, she wanted to break the rigid shackles of conformity in the Edwardian era.

After the house was completed, the Cheneys invited thirty people over to christen their new home on New Year's Eve. Frank and his wife, Kitty, were among the guests who danced around a glowing grate fire. Frank and Mamah stole glances at each other while a small orchestra played "America." At midnight, they kissed their respective spouses, who failed to recognize the electricity that was building between the two.

Kitty had no idea that her husband longed for Mamah, whom she considered to be a friend. They both belonged to Oak Park's Nineteenth Century Club, along with Ernest Hemingway's mother, Grace. Mamah and Kitty delivered a lecture together about Johann Goethe's plays and poetry.

At first, Frank and Mamah fought against the gravitational pull between them. When Frank left for an architectural tour of Japan with Kitty, Mamah stayed in Oak Park, pregnant with John. In 1905, she gave birth to a daughter, Martha, and occupied herself with her motherly duties while also planning local stage productions with Grace Hemingway. It appeared that their love for each other would go unrequited, a mutual adoration from afar.

Frank probably viewed his attraction to Mamah similarly as he had viewed his design for a windmill that he had been commissioned by his aunts on the Lloyd Jones' side to provide water for their school in Wisconsin. In his drawings, he designed the octagonal windmill with a balcony that was accessible through an interior stairway. The wooden structure was built in two parts, which he called *Romeo* and *Juliet*. Although weather-beaten, Frank predicted that the structure would survive any storm.

"Romeo and Juliet shall live to crash down together," he later wrote.

Frank's own version of Juliet lived close by with a husband and two children of her own. He knew that his pursuit of her would be self-destructive, but he was at a personal crossroads.

"Everything personal or otherwise, bore heavily down upon me. Domesticity most of all," he recalled. "What I wanted, I did not know. I loved my children. I loved my home. A true home is the finest ideal of man, and yet…"

He thought back to his father's decision to leave his mother when Frank was a teenager. He had resented the man then but had grown to better understand the heavy burden that William Wright believed he was under when he decided to leave his family.

Frank asked Kitty for a divorce. She said no. Such a thing was virtually unheard of, as less than 1 percent of all marriages in America ended in divorce in the early 1900s.

Kitty told her husband to wait a year, and if his feelings toward her remained the same, she would grant his request.

Frank put his pursuit of Mamah on hold briefly while facing the crushing loss of his uncle James, who was killed while trying to save two farmhands. The workers were attempting to move a heavy thresher machine over a bridge. The bridge gave way, and the engine fell down into a dry stream bed. After the loud crash, steam and hot water escaped from the thresher, scalding the men to death. James raced to the scene and climbed onto the engine in an attempt to free the workers. His foot slipped, and his leg got caught in the spokes of the wheel. After the serious injury, James fell into a coma and died six days later. The man who had taught Frank how to become a man during those long days on the farm was now gone.

Uncle James's untimely death also revealed a dark secret—he was deeply in debt. He had purchased several farms and convinced many of his relatives to cosign on his loans. After several bad harvest seasons, James found himself behind on his mortgage payments and never informed his family members that his finances were in disarray. Those who cosigned the loans were forced to sell nearly all their belongings to pay James's outstanding debt. Some even had to declare bankruptcy.

Frank had just turned forty years old, and he admitted that he was losing his grip on his work and even his interest in it. He felt like he was back on the farm working for his uncle James. "I had added tired to tired," he later recalled. "Continuously thrilled by the effort but now it seemed to leave me up against a dead wall. I could see no way out."

What Frank wanted was freedom from his stagnant marriage to Kitty. As many men do when faced with a midlife crisis, he bought a car: a four-cylinder, three-seat, bright yellow Stoddard-Dayton convertible roadster. The automobile was not a vehicle; it was a spectacle. With brown leather upholstery, brass trimmings, and a paint coating of straw yellow, everyone in Oak Park recognized it as Frank raced at speeds of sixty miles per hour, well over the speed limit. Riding in the car could be dangerous. "When the top was down there wasn't anything to hold you in except a rise of about four inches at the side of the seat," his son John Wright recalled.

Frank's neighbors called it "the Yellow Devil." He routinely drove the wives of his clients around town. Frank cut a dashing figure behind the wheel of the roadster, always wearing a linen duster and goggles wrapped around his brown, wavy hair. For local women who went to bed with their stodgy husbands each night, Frank Lloyd Wright was a hard man to resist.

One day, he offered Mamah Cheney a ride in his automobile. It was a ride that would change both of their lives forever.

8

Kitty Wright was not blind to her husband's wandering eye. As one of her closest friends observed, "Every tone in her voice rings with fearless honesty…against sham—compromise and all disloyalty." The friend, Janet Ashbee, also observed the "tragic lines" formed around Kitty's mouth that were always present and would only disappear when she laughed.

Janet Ashbee was the wife of Charles Ashbee, an English architect and student of the Arts and Crafts movement, who had forged a special bond with Frank during a visit to the United States. They were mirrors of each other. Both were the products of overbearing mothers and fathers who had abandoned them. Frank took Ashbee to visit his mentor, Louis Sullivan, and the British architect believed that his new American friend would become an even greater builder than his master.

The Wrights entertained the Ashbees in their Oak Park home. At first, Janet noted that Kitty was "endearingly tender and light on her feet, so youthful in her smiles and gestures." Kitty, with her wide gray eyes and wispy yellow hair, radiated beauty, and Janet could hardly believe that she was the mother of six children.

As the relationship between the couples grew, Janet noticed that Frank had turned cold toward his wife. It was a feeling that was all too familiar to her. Charles Ashbee was bisexual but was open with Janet about his attraction to men. She stayed in the marriage for thirteen years, bearing him four children. Janet found a kindred spirit in Kitty as both struggled to hold on to their marriages to men who found their sexual satisfaction in the arms of others.

Soon, Mamah Borthwick became a regular passenger in Frank's bright yellow convertible. While he had kept the wives of his other clients at arm's length, even in his car, his drives with Mamah were different. They were giving themselves up to the gravitational pull and were becoming cozy together. He acted differently while driving Mamah in the roadster. No longer did he need to hide his feelings for her. As the vehicle's tires traveled over each bump on the town's unpaved roads, their bodies bounced up and down before landing closer together in the front seat. "The motor car brought a disturbance of all values, subtle or obvious, and it brought disturbance to me," he later surmised.

In August 1908, Frank found himself on a road trip with Mamah, her husband, and his mother. Cheney got behind the wheel of his own touring car and drove the group in from Oak Park to Wisconsin to see a few of Frank's projects there. Frank left Kitty at home with their children. Cheney must have been completely unaware of his wife's growing affection for Frank and did not see the architect as a potential romantic rival. Cheney appeared to be comfortable in his own skin and was apparently well respected by both men and women. "He [Cheney] was a prince of a man," an Oak Park neighbor named Verna Ross Orndorff recalled. "He was middle-aged, dark eyed and bald. You could hardly call him a Don Juan, but he was so charming and gracious that he didn't have an enemy."

The trip was mentioned briefly in the *Wisconsin State Journal*, and it reportedly included a tour of Rocky Roost, which was owned by Frank's childhood friend Robie Lamp, who had hired him to join three cabins into a singular cottage with an upper level and a wraparound porch. Their journey crossed 350 miles and included two overnight stays. During the trip, Cheney catered to his mother's needs as a dutiful son, and this distraction provided the opportunity for Frank and Mamah to spend some time alone with each other and grow even closer.

When he returned home to Kitty, Frank took a few days gathering his thoughts while racing over the prairies north of Oak Park atop Kano, a jet-black, five-gaited, three-year-old saddle horse whom he had named after the founder of judo. In his mind, he narrowed down the necessities that he felt he needed in order to live a full life and developed a case for himself in an attempt to win his freedom from Kitty. To Frank, marriage should not be considered a lifelong commitment, especially if one spouse wanted out. "Marriage not mutual is not better, but is worse than any form of slavery," he later wrote in his memoir. "Only to the degree that marriage is mutual is it decent. Love is not property. To take it so is barbarous. To protect it as such is barbarism."

In September 1909, one month after their road trip to Wisconsin, Frank and Mamah decided to tell Kitty and Edwin Cheney that they had fallen in love with each other. The meeting took place in Frank and Kitty's living room. Once again, Frank asked Kitty for a divorce. A year had gone by, and there was no rekindling of his affection for her. Despite the promise she had made to him, Kitty remained steadfast in her refusal to divorce Frank and break up their family. Both Kitty and Cheney tried convincing their respective spouses that theirs was a fleeting infatuation, one that would die over time. With eight children across both families to consider, Frank and Mamah were asked to wait a year to consider their decision. Frank had heard this from Kitty before. He knew that another year would not bring him back to his wife, but instead it would metastasize his resentment toward her. Mamah convinced Frank that they should both agree to the terms laid out by Kitty and Cheney and he reluctantly gave in to their wishes.

Over the next few weeks, Mamah worked to convince her husband to free her from their marriage.

At one point, she penned a poem to her husband with which she described her intentions. "I am going to leave you," she wrote. "But do not despair, I shall never forget. That you are here, and I am there."

Mamah did not have the courage to show the poem to Cheney. Instead, she tucked it away in a drawer for safekeeping. Still, Cheney must have recognized that no amount of time would be long enough for Mamah to reconsider her feelings for him. He filed for divorce, citing abandonment. Cheney demanded custody of their two children, John and Martha, and asked her to wait until she married Frank before running off together somewhere.

Mamah was now free to express her love for Frank, but Kitty still refused to let him go.

"I would in any case have separated from Catherine—though I might have continued under the same roof with her for the sake of the children, even that I told you I was determined not to do so," he later admitted in a letter to his mother.

He then decided that he could not wait another full year for Kitty to accept that their marriage was over and instead made plans to leave his family.

He made this decision at great risk to his reputation and career. Frank Lloyd Wright was now the most famous architect in America, due to the popularity of his Prairie School homes as well as public commissions to design massive structures such as the Larkin Company Administration Building in Buffalo, New York. That project had been virtually handed to Frank by his friend and supporter Darwin Martin, who served as secretary for the mail-order soap company. Frank's design called for a six-story building with a seventy-six-foot-tall skylit courtyard with a Roman-style atrium surrounded by balconies. The interior was designed to be open and airy since workers could rarely go outside because of all the smoke coming from a nearby rail line. Critics called it "a monster of awkwardness," while Frank insisted that his own architectural work was a monument to productivity.

The Larkin Building project, with its technical innovations including air-conditioning, radiant heat, and glass doors, had turned Frank Lloyd Wright into a household name. He was the Leonardo da Vinci of early twentieth-century North America, praised throughout the continent and across Europe.

Despite his fame, Frank hoped that he could separate from Kitty quietly and without fanfare. Instead, stories about his infidelity exploded under salacious headlines in newspapers across America.

9

The separation from his family was subtle at first. Frank moved to the Chicago Beach Hotel, located in the city's fashionable Hyde Park neighborhood. He told friends that he wanted to be closer to the construction of a spectacular new home that he later described as "one of the great masterpieces of twentieth century architecture and interior design," known as the Robie House.

In reality, he stayed at the 450-room hotel on the shores of Lake Michigan so that Mamah could join him day and night. She enrolled at the University of Chicago, where she took writing classes in the hope of becoming a popular author and essayist. There, she studied writing composition under Robert Herrick, the author of thirteen novels, including *The Web of Life* and *Together*, a highly sexualized novel about a bored housewife who commits adultery. It was as if in writing that novel, Mamah's professor had possessed the key to unlocking her innermost thoughts.

In the evening, Frank and Mamah drove through the neighborhood in the yellow roadster and enjoyed dinners at the Chicago Beach Hotel, as well as quiet, intimate moments inside Frank's hotel apartment.

In the morning, after enjoying breakfast together, Mamah would head off to class while Frank drove his automobile to 5757 South Woodlawn

Avenue in Hyde Park to oversee the construction of the Robie House, named after its owner, Frederick C. Robie, a prominent businessman and executive at a bicycle company. Robie told Frank that his new home should reflect his interest in advanced technology, as Robie was also a car enthusiast, and modernity.

Robie had purchased the land for $13,500 in 1908, although its original settlers were the Indigenous peoples of the Potawatomi, Ojibwe, and Odawa Nations. For the lot of land and the home that was to be built on top of it, Robie had set aside $35,000, which was seven times the amount spent on a typical home at that time. At first, the business executive attempted to design his own home, but friends steered him toward Frank Lloyd Wright.

Frank's goal was to build Robie a home that was completely original and American, without a shred of influence by European or Asian architectural design. The building, built of brick and limestone, would be as long as it was high. Frank sketched a three-story structure with low-sloped, cantilevered roofs sheltering the floors. It would be something of an optical illusion to passersby, as it appeared to be a low-lying two-story home. Both the walls and the windows were set back from the building's dramatic overhangs.

Frank worked nature into his design by carving pots and planters into the base walls. He wanted the home to look like it had been standing there for centuries. In his drawings, Frank penciled in ivy shrubs that crawled their way across and over the walls and through the property. For the interior, he designed two large entertaining areas on the first floor: a billiards room for adults and a playroom for Robie's children. Both rooms were connected by a large fireplace in the center of the space. Frank, considering the increased automobile traffic in the area, also designed a courtyard with a low brick wall to keep Robie's children from jetting out into the street as cars rumbled by.

The second floor featured low ceilings to signify a more intimate space. This was where Frank set both the main living room and the dining room. The living area featured a fireplace and a long row of twelve doors built with stained and clear glass, which cast the room in a splash of light and deep shadows. Private bedrooms for members of the Robie family dominated the third floor of the home. Frank did not want the bedrooms to feel clustered together or boxlike, so he designed each of them with vaulted ceilings. The main bedroom, Robie's private hideaway, featured a cozy fireplace and an en suite bathroom, which was something very rare for the time. The architect also wanted to eliminate what he believed were wasted spaces. Therefore, he built the Robie House without attic space or a cellar.

Frank oversaw every phase of the home's design, including furniture, lighting, rugs, and textiles.

The finished product would be considered the consummate expression of Frank's Prairie School–style design.

Once completed, Frederick C. Robie and his family would live in the house for just one year. Robie was forced to sell it in order to settle his recently deceased father's debts.

Frank himself did not stick around to take a bow for what at that time could be considered his crowning achievement in home design. He had decided to leave the United States and his family behind for an extended tour of Europe. So strongly did he believe that it was the right decision, the only decision he could make at that time, he was willing to give up a major design commission from auto magnate Henry Ford.

"I am leaving the office to its own devices," he wrote to his friend Darwin Martin. "Deserting my wife and the children for one year, in search of a spiritual adventure, hoping it will be no worse."

Frank's son John vividly remembered the night his father left. Frank said nothing to his younger children, who were all fast asleep at the time. John, then a teenager, confronted his father near the front entrance of their Oak Park home and punched him in the nose. "He left…quick, overnight—he didn't even say goodbye," John recalled. "I often wonder why he didn't leave sooner. Was he a saint or fool? I believe that he was directed by a force beyond his control to save his life. It has always been a mystery to me why Mother didn't leave too."

The pretext for Frank's trip abroad was an invitation from German publisher Ernst Wasmuth to visit Berlin, Germany, where they would collaborate on a folio of his architectural work. But he had no intention of making the long journey alone.

Frank conspired with Mamah to plan a secret rendezvous in New York City, where both would book passage on a cruise liner to Europe. Mamah told her husband that she was taking their young children to spend time with her friend Mattie Chadbourne in Boulder, Colorado. Chadbourne was now married and expecting a baby in September. Mamah told Cheney that she would stay with Chadbourne until the birth of her child. Before she left, she had an intimate encounter with Frank at the Chicago Beach Hotel, where she had visited under the guise of attending her sorority's national convention.

Mamah took her children, John and Martha, along with her niece, Jessie, with her to Boulder, as she knew that it would be her last opportunity to spend time with them before heading to Europe with Frank, where they had planned to spend a year traveling and working on his book. She gathered the children and boarded a train west. They had the luxury of a Pullman sleeper car and spent most of their time staring out the window as the landscape shifted dramatically from vast, flat lands to gigantic mountain ranges.

After several days, their Union Pacific train pulled into the station in Denver. Mamah had seen mountains before during her youthful adventure in the Dakotas, but her children were awestruck by the dramatic, snow-peaked mountains of the Front Range along the eastern edge of the Rockies. After watching their fellow passengers disembark in Denver, Mamah and the children continued on to Boulder. There, they gathered their suitcases, climbed into a carriage, and traveled past the city's newly opened and luxurious Hotel Boulderado. They found their way to Chadbourne's house at 404 Mapleton Avenue, where Mamah's pregnant friend was there to greet them.

At some point that summer, Mamah confided to her best friend that she planned to leave her husband. Chadbourne was not shocked by the announcement, as she knew that Mamah had been unhappy in her marriage. In August, Edwin Cheney traveled by train to Boulder to gather the children, as they did not want to miss the start of school in a few short weeks. Mamah told Cheney that she would remain in Boulder until her friend gave birth. Chadbourne was thirty-eight years old, and hers was considered to be a high-risk pregnancy. Mamah was conflicted about her decision to leave her family but took some solace in the fact that her sister Lizzie would provide proper care for her kids until she came back.

When Cheney returned to Chicago alone with his children, the proud man attempted to stave off any whiff of potential scandal. He told friends and business associates that his wife would remain in Boulder to care for her friend and the new baby until Christmastime. It was a lie, of course. Mamah had told Cheney that she was planning to leave him, and this was her chance.

Frank received a telegram from Mamah on September 23, notifying him that her friend had given birth and that both mother and baby were doing well. Frank departed Oak Park a few hours later, leaving his family and an unpaid grocery bill for $900 behind.

Frank took a train to New York City and checked into the Plaza Hotel. Mamah joined him a short time later. This was an all-or-nothing gambit for the two lovers. Frank was ready to jeopardize his career and standing as America's preeminent architect. Mamah was likely fully aware that she would never be looked at the same way by her fellow members of polite, Edwardian society again. In fact, she would be branded with a symbolic scarlet letter by many of her friends and family.

After passing off their suitcases to a porter, the two locked hands at the pier and climbed the gangway and onto the deck of the SS *Kaiser Wilhelm der Grosse*, a 1,506-passenger ship that would carry them toward an uncertain future.

10

Before he boarded the ship bound for Europe, Frank leaked news about the trip to a member of the press. Of course, he mentioned nothing about his travel companion to the newspaper reporter. The story only garnered a six-line mention in the back pages of *Oak Leaves*. "Frank Lloyd Wright left Thursday for Germany to superintend publication of a book to contain his architectural work," the reporter wrote. "He expects to be absent for a year, and the work may take even longer."

The item was also picked up by the *Chicago Sunday Tribune*, which included the line "Frank Lloyd Wright of 500 Forest Avenue, Oak Park, left Thursday for Germany, where he will spend a year in travel" in its News of the Society World column.

By alerting the reporter of his trip abroad, Frank had attempted to craft his own narrative, one that focused on his work and his genius, not his illicit affair with his married mistress.

Some found it odd that Frank had left Chicago before the official dedication of the Unity Church, a project that he had spearheaded for nearly five years. The project had been personal to Frank, as the family on his mother's side were all devout Welsh Unitarians. Frank began the project in 1905 after the original church burned to the ground. The minister of the church, a

Harvard Divinity School graduate named Rodney Johonnot, had dreamed of a chapel that was modern and would symbolize the tenets of "unity, truth, beauty, simplicity and reason."

Frank submitted designs that called for a structure built out of concrete, as the material was cheap and in line with Minister Johonnot's modest budget. Virtually no one had seen a design for any church like it before. Both Frank and Johonnot were like-minded in that each man valued the idea of unsophistication over grandiosity. As he would later write in an essay titled "In the Cause of Architecture," "Simplicity and Repose are qualities that matter the true value of any work of art… All that is meaningless has been eliminated. A wild flower is truly simple."

Frank and his team of draftsmen designed a gigantic cubic, fortress-like monolith sheltered under a sprawling flat roof. The building would be 150 feet long and 100 feet wide. Frank, always a proponent of deep, meaningful mottoes, had the words *For the Worship of God and the Service of Man* chiseled over the entrance of the church. Getting inside the chapel would not be an easy feat for worshippers, a reminder of the effort and hard work they would have to put forth for their ascension to heaven. Once parishioners walked through a series of low, dark passages, which Frank called cloisters, they were rewarded with a splash of bright light coming from twenty-five skylights of amber-tinted glass in the chapel's inner sanctuary.

Frank's motivation was simple: "to get a sense of a happy cloudless day into the room…daylight shifting through between the intersecting concrete beams, filtering through amber glass ceiling lights. Thus managed, the light would, rain or shine, have the warmth of sunlight."

Unity Church committee members were largely impressed by the architectural marvel.

"We extend to the architect, Mr Frank Lloyd Wright, our most hearty congratulations upon the wonderful achievement embodied in the new edifice and further extend to him our most sincere thanks for the great service which, through the building, he has rendered to the parish and to the community," the congregation's board of trustees wrote in a statement. "We believe the building will long endure as a monument to his artistic genius and that, so long as it endures, it will stand forth as a masterpiece of art and architecture."

Uncle Jenk, pastor of nearby All Souls Church, was slated to speak at the dedication ceremony, as was Reverend Samuel A. Elliott, son of Harvard University president Charles Elliott. The Unity Church, renamed Unity Chapel because it bore almost no resemblance to other churches in the area, was opened to much fanfare in late September 1909. Curiously missing from the event was the architect himself, who was sailing in the middle of the Atlantic Ocean and about to make his first visit to the Old World.

When Frank and Mamah arrived in Berlin, he registered them both as "Frank Lloyd Wright and wife, Chicago," at their new short-term residence, the Hotel Adlon. They were both more than four thousand miles away from their families in Chicago and felt no trepidation about posing as a married couple. While Frank and Mamah met with his publisher and toured notable buildings in the historic city such as the modern, industrially designed AEG Turbine Factory and the recently completed Baroque- and Renaissance-style Berlin Cathedral, the couple appeared not to have a care in the world. Frank finally had a companion and lover who doted on him and

Mamah Borthwick Cheney fell in love with Frank Lloyd Wright and left her family and fled to Europe with him in 1910. (National Library of Sweden)

catered to his every whim, while Mamah had a partner of brilliance who could match her intellectual curiosities.

At the Hotel Adlon, which was located directly across from the Brandenburg Gate, the couple enjoyed its luxurious amenities, which included hot and cold running water, a sparkling lobby filled with colossal marble columns, Venetian mosaics, and a Japanese fountain. Guests included members of royalty, such as Czar Nicholas II of Russia, and American business tycoons like John D. Rockefeller. Frank slipped into such opulence as easily as a delicate hand would into a perfectly fit silk glove. He enjoyed working on his folio in their spacious bedroom suite without the constant chaos that was innocently unleashed by his children back in Oak Park. For once, he did not feel the walls of responsibility closing in on him and constricting his creativity.

Frank had hoped that this honeymoon of sorts might never end. But he could not account for a nosy newspaper man who was hell-bent on shattering Frank's blissful illusion.

11

A foreign correspondent for the *Chicago Tribune*, perhaps acting on a tip from Edwin Cheney, Frank's mother, Anna, or most likely Kitty Wright, made his way to the Hotel Adlon and convinced the concierge to show him the list of recently registered guests at the hotel. Frank and Mamah had checked out of their suite four days before. The newsman ran a finger down the ledger until he spotted *Frank Lloyd Wright and wife, Chicago*, and he knew immediately that he had a big story on his hands.

The reporter telegraphed his editor at the newspaper, who then assigned journalists to flesh out the sordid tale in Oak Park. Their work resulted in a front-page story on November 7, 1909, with a sensational headline that read "Leave Families; Elope to Europe—Architect Frank Lloyd Wright and Mrs. Edwin Cheney of Oak Park Startle Friends."

Although there were other stories lining the front page about corruption inside Tammany Hall in New York, and a fire scare at Chicago's Majestic Theater, all eyes were focused on a sex scandal that was unfolding on two continents. A story such as this normally spreads boisterously through billiard rooms at exclusive gentlemen's clubs and more quietly between women whispering their secrets in the parlors of their sprawling suburban homes. The details here were smeared all over the front page and geared toward a mass audience of Chicago readers from wealthy businessmen to shoe shiners to bored housewives. The story set Kitty Wright up as a dutiful, scorned woman. The lengthy newspaper article began this way: "A wife pledging faith in a husband having gone off with another woman, and avowing affection for him in the face of knowledge of his act, two abandoned homes where children play at the hearth sides and a fly by night journey through Germany, in which a prominent Oak Park architect has as his companion the wife of a Chicago manufacturer—these are features which make an affinity tangle of character unparalleled even in the checkered history of soul mating."

The article named Frank Lloyd Wright at the beginning of the second paragraph. Readers no doubt had trouble catching their collective breath as the story continued with details about how he and Mamah (referred to only as Mrs. Cheney) had duped their spouses and orchestrated an elaborate scheme to run away together to Europe. "Investigation of the circumstances surrounding the elopement of Wright and Mrs. Cheney, which will occasion astonishment among acquaintances today and confirm a suspicion which has been strong in the minds of relatives and intimate friends reveals conditions unusual in character," the article continued. "Here is a wife [Kitty] who poses as a co-warrior and defender with her husband the struggle and allure of another woman."

Just as her wayward husband had done before he left for Germany, Kitty Wright slyly worked to create her own narrative when a reporter knocked on her front door in Oak Park and asked her for a comment. Kitty gave the reporter more than that. She invited him into the Wright home, sat him down, and sharpened her verbal knives for an all-out assault against her romantic rival.

Edwin Cheney had smartly refused to comment on the article. He was ambushed by a *Tribune* correspondent while in downtown Chicago attending the opera dressed in his evening finery.

"Will you seek a divorce or take any other court action?" the reporter asked.

"I have nothing to say," Cheney replied flatly.

Undaunted, the newsman continued to press. "Did you suspect that she was with Wright when you sent messages and letters to the Wasmuth company?"

The reporter had referred to the fact that Cheney sent letters to his wife and used the mailing address of Frank's publisher, Ernst Wasmuth.

"I don't care to talk about the matter at all," Cheney reiterated.

The reporter asked Cheney if he was aware that Mamah and Frank were together.

"If she has had anything to say about her husband, then I certainly have nothing to add."

With that, Cheney walked away.

While Mamah's husband had successfully deflected questions about the affair between his wife and Frank, Kitty eagerly told the reporter visiting her home that Cheney suspected intrigue about the relationship between Frank and Mamah and "sought by any means necessary to win her back to the love now trampled upon and spurned."

Adding gasoline to the flames, the foreign correspondent who had first unearthed the story added that when Frank visited his publisher, Ernst Wasmuth, in Berlin, he had introduced Mamah as his wife.

"This all is scarcely to be understood," Kitty continued. "People will see the bald, bare facts as they are stated now. It appears like any ordinary mundane affair with the trappings of what is low and vulgar. But there is nothing of that sort in Frank Wright. He is honest and sincere. I know him. I tell you I know him. I have fought side by side with him. My heart is with him now. I feel certain that he will come back. When, I don't know. It will be when he has reached a certain decision with himself."

Kitty attempted to dismiss Frank's infatuation for Mamah as something of a midlife crisis, not true love. She told the *Tribune* reporter that she would not divorce her husband and believed in her heart that Frank would return to her and their children.

"We have six children… They cannot think of a separation. They worship their father and love their mother. If only I could protect them now I would care for nothing else. I am living for them now."

Kitty retrieved a letter that she had planned to send to Frank in Germany. She handed it to the reporter, who later printed it in the *Tribune* article. It read, "Oak Park, Oct. 20. My Dear, we think of you often and hope you are well and enjoying life, as you have so longed to. From the children and your wife. CATHERINE L. WRIGHT."

Kitty told the reporter that she had nothing to say about Mamah. Her pledge lasted for only a few moments as she then stepped up her attack against the woman who she claimed had ruined her family. "I have striven to put her out of my thoughts in connection with the situation," she said. "It is simply a force against which we have had to contend. I have never felt that I breathed the same air as her."

Kitty believed that Mamah had placed her husband under some kind of spell. "This is simply the case of a vampire," she said, referring to Mamah. "You've heard of such things."

The story was so scandalous, the burning-hot details nearly singed the fingers of all those who picked up the newspaper that day. The next morning, another *Tribune* reporter wrote about Kitty's strength and naivete, describing her this way. "Her sex will stigmatize Mrs. Frank Lloyd Wright as a fool. Men will confess that Wright does not deserve such a wife. Few of us do. And commonly, the less deserving we are, the more prodigally does heaven shower blessings on us."

Reporters also would not leave Edwin Cheney alone. Shortly after confronting him at the opera, a newsman visited his house in Oak Park, one that had been designed by Frank. The newsman pounded on the front door until the maid responded and told him that "Mr. Cheney is not in." The reporter then staked out the home until all lights in the house were extinguished for the evening and "no amount of pounding and ringing could bring a response from the inside."

Frank and Mamah were now the talk of Chicago, the suburban hamlet of Oak Park, and soon most of the country. The couple did their best not to get swept away by the undercurrent of the growing scandal. Although he did not offer any comment for the explosive *Tribune* piece, Frank did share his thoughts in a letter to his old friend Charles Ashbee.

"I think you will believe that I would do nothing I did not believe was right," he stated in the letter. "But I have believed a terrible thing to be right… I have never loved Catherine—my wife—as she deserved… I know what a blow this will be to you—to all who believed in me; what a traitor I seem to the cause of architecture."

Frank and Mamah left Germany and traveled south to Italy, where he continued to work on his folio. Mamah was not idle during this time either. She took a train north to Sweden and met with a writer named Ellen Key, who would become her mentor. Key was one of the world's leading feminists and suffragists and had striven to educate working women across Scandinavia. Mamah was mesmerized by Key's outlook on feminism and the modern woman.

"Ellen Key greeted me at her front door. By daylight the youth in her eyes was even more apparent," Mamah later wrote. "Her body might grow old, but her spirit never would… There is so much mother love in Ellen Key… Soon we were in deep talk and I was telling her about my trip around the world, and presently, I felt Ellen's hand on mine, and tears were in her eyes and welled over as she said: 'Oh, I am glad you are a woman who understands. I was afraid you might be the other kind of American.'… Our hearts beat for the same purposes and the same end. We recognized each other as part of the great women's movement which we loved. It was a day of sheer gladness."

In Key, Mamah had found her kindred spirit. For all of her married life, Mamah had been referred to only by the dishonorable honorific *Mrs. Edwin Cheney*. Her entire name had been taken away from her due to the social mores of the day. Mamah felt that her identity had been lost. No longer was she a highly intelligent graduate of the University of Michigan and a high-ranking sorority member. While wed to Cheney, the only distinguishing part of her character was that of wife and mother, just like countless women across the United States and around the world. It was for this reason that she had decided that she needed to break free.

Although they had never met before, Mamah asked Key if she would allow her to translate her work for English-speaking audiences, and the writer agreed. Mamah brought Key's manuscripts with her back to Italy where she and Frank shared a mountainside villa in the historic town of Fiesole, just outside the city of Florence, where they enjoyed dramatic hilltop views and the ancient architecture of the fourteenth-century monastery of San Francesco. It was a self-imposed exile, but an exile nonetheless.

Waking up each morning in a small cream-white villa on the Via Verdi, Frank thought to himself, "How many souls seeking release from real or fancied domestic woes have sheltered on the slopes of below Fiesole!"

As he later wrote in his memoir, "I, too, now sought shelter there in companionship with her [Mamah], who, by force of rebellion as by way of love, was then implicated with me."

It was a village that had inspired Leonardo da Vinci during his visits there, and now Frank was hoping for a similar artistic stimulation. The town was intoxicating, and residents there allowed Frank and Mamah to show affection for each other without judgment, as they could not have known that each was married to someone else.

"Walking hand in hand together up the hill road from Firenze to the old town, all along the way in the sight and scent of roses, by day," Frank later described. "Walking arm in arm up the same old road at night, listening to the nightingale in the deep shadow of the moonlit wood—trying hard to hear the song in the deeps of life."

The couple hiked together in the fields and forests across Vallombrosa and, after a long day, slept together inside what Frank referred to as "a cloistered, little mountain inn." He called Mamah his "faithful comrade."

Meanwhile, Frank's second eldest son, seventeen-year-old John, felt rudderless without his father's strong presence. He went to work on the family farm in Wisconsin, just as his father had decades before. At night, after all his chores were completed, John would play a particular song on a hand-cranked gramophone. The title was "Lonesome," and it symbolized John's yearning for his father. John played the song over and over again until he fell asleep. "The year dad left home…I felt alone and on my own," he would write later. "It was a long, depressing [season]."

Soon, John's older brother, nineteen-year-old Lloyd Wright, would be sent on an intercontinental quest to bring their father home.

12

While in Italy, Mamah received devastating news. Her best friend, Mattie Chadbourne Brown, was dead. According to an account in Boulder's main newspaper, the *Daily Camera*, Brown's death was caused by "heart disease with involvement of the lungs… Her death has caused a shock to the entire community, her apparent excellent health giving no warning."

Brown's health must have rapidly declined after Mamah traveled to Europe. Otherwise, there was little chance that she would have left her best friend alone in her final days.

While Mamah grieved the loss of Brown, Frank sent letters to his son Lloyd, urging him to join him in Italy. Frank needed the teenager, who was studying engineering at the University of Wisconsin, to work as a draftsman for him while he compiled more than a hundred sketches for his long-awaited book. Mamah wanted to avoid what would surely be a tense family reunion, so she briefly took a job teaching at the University of Leipzig in Germany.

Reporters clamoring for any new developments in the affair saga seized upon the story about Lloyd Wright's journey to Italy. The January 18, 1910, edition of the *Chicago Tribune* ran with the headline "Frank Lloyd Wright's Son May Repair Family Break: Boy Sails for Italy Today at Request of Father, Who Eloped with Mrs. Edwin Cheney."

Once again, the primary source of information for the newspaper article appeared to have been Kitty Wright, and she used the opportunity to reinforce her belief that she was her husband's one true love despite his dalliance with his client's wife. "Reconciliation between Frank Lloyd Wright, the Oak Park architect and his wife, whom he deserted several months ago to elope to Europe with Mrs. Edwin Cheney is expected following a meeting between Wright and his son in Florence, Italy," the *Tribune* stated.

Although Lloyd may have believed that the trip focused on him working side by side with his father on architectural designs, Kitty had an ulterior motive behind her decision to allow him to go to Italy. She had received almost no word from Frank since he had left. Kitty did share with the reporter details of one letter she had just received from her husband in which he reportedly asked for forgiveness and declared his repentance.

There is no evidence that Frank had sent such a letter. Once Kitty became aware that her husband had been corresponding with their son Lloyd at school, she called a meeting at her home in Oak Park with an unidentified friend and Frank's mother, Anna. The trio debated whether they would allow Lloyd to accede to his father's wishes. Kitty agreed to let Lloyd sail to Italy if he would serve as her emissary in an effort to convince Frank to leave his mistress and all the madness behind and return home to Oak Park. Kitty was placing a great amount of pressure on their son to help her rebuild their family. She told the *Tribune* reporter that Lloyd was strong enough to stand up to his father and explained how the nineteen-year-old had "attacked and severely beaten him, the father making no resistance."

When Lloyd arrived in Florence, he worked diligently at his father's side to complete the work that was eventually submitted to Frank's publisher. The *Wasmuth Portfolio: Ausgeführte Bauten und Entwürfe von Frank Lloyd Wright* was Frank's largest collection of architectural drawings to date and would soon be published in Germany, extending his global influence.

There is no record of conversations between father and son at this time, but Lloyd likely brought up the topic of Frank's eventual return home. The other Wright children needed their father, and their mother deserved some answers. Frank's eldest son eventually sailed back to America alone, much to Kitty's dismay. Frank had planned to spend one full year living in Europe with Mamah, and he was not going to alter his plans for anyone, including his children. He had not given much thought to his future after that. He had been under enormous pressure from friends back home to reconcile with Kitty. "You have a wife and children," friend and client Norman Guthrie reminded Frank in a letter. "The ties that bind your soul to them will grow stronger as they should."

Frank had taken a giant leap of faith in following through with his decision to leave his comfortable but insufferable life behind in Chicago for a bold adventure with the one woman that he truly loved and who loved him with equal passion and commitment. Was he ready to give up the freedom he had to share his romantic feelings about Mamah openly and return to his life as it was, financially prosperous but at the same time emotionally bankrupt?

He decided to write Kitty a letter in which he outlined the conditions for his return. He was angry that she had used the media as a weapon against him and was equally outraged that she had vilified Mamah, calling her a vampire in the press. Frank did not love Kitty—he never had. But he did feel a small amount of guilt for leaving their children for a year. But Frank believed that his own mental health had demanded it, as he was in the midst of a breakdown. Had he gone to a sanatorium he would have received empathy from friends, family, and clients. But the fact that he had chosen his own therapeutic escape, albeit with the wife of another man, meant his character was attacked on all fronts. The rumors and innuendos would have to stop if he were to return to Oak Park.

On July 4, 1910, as Americans celebrated their independence back home, Frank sat down at a table inside his quaint Fiesole villa and wrote a long letter to his mother, Anna, perhaps the one person in the world whom he did not want to disappoint, given her lifetime of devotion to him. The letter began with Frank expressing great woe about his current financial situation as he recognized that he would have to earn $5,000 (an estimated $167,000 today) to keep his sons Lloyd and John in college and handle all household expenses. He also expressed frustration about bills that had gone unpaid for his children's music lessons and suggested they would benefit more by performing backbreaking work on the Lloyd family farm, as he had done in his youth. The criticism of his children was unfair given the circumstances, and he blamed himself for their pampering. "It is a constant increasing load [child-rearing]—which is a matter of course—for the privilege of being a father—they owe me nothing. They have been so taught. In fact, they feel that but for their father's extravagance, they could all have had much more. This doesn't look like much of a farm for me. The personalities of the children are dear to me—just the same. I must make the struggle."

For Frank, the struggle meant that he would have to find some way to get several of his clients to pay their bills for services that he had already rendered. It appeared that once he fled to Europe under the cloak of scandal, his clients all found creative excuses about how not to pay their bills as they worked to distance themselves from the disgraced architect. He felt that the entire world had turned against him.

"I had one time thought that I could keep what was good in life that was—and go forward to a new life," he wrote his mother. "The world is not yet arranged on that basis I find—but someday it will be—the present moral code is as inadequate for certain souls as the old science is inadequate for new achievements. Life is not a thing to be lumped or legislated for in the lump—when we progress beyond the mob stage—Eternal verities are not alone those within the grasp of present majorities—Some lie around. Let us hope."

In the letter to his mother, Frank also expressed great trepidation over his eventual return to America. "I dread the aspect my return must wear," he confessed. "I am the prodigal—whose return is a triumph for the institutions I have outraged—a weak son who infatuated sexually has had his passion drained and therewith his courage, and so abandoning the source of his infatuation to whatever fate may hold her—probably a hard lonely struggle in the face of a world that writes her down as an outcast to be shunned,—or a craven return to another man, his prostitute for a roof and a bed and a chance to lose her life in her children, that something—more shred of self respect (that) may clothe her nakedness—While I return to my dear wife and children who all along 'knew I would' and welcomed by my friends with open rejoicing and secret contempt. Why must this be so?"

Then, once again, Frank pointed the guilty finger, not at himself but at his peers in so-called polite society for choking out of him the ability to make his own moral choices.

"It is the character given by my own people, those who should know me best, and therefore it is authentic. Why could it not have worn the semblance of its truer aspect that scorn might not be added to the natural effects of ideals, lost, life sacrificed and hopes dead? Anyone who lets by his acts, the outer world touch in any way his affections must submit to having them vulgarized, brutalized and spit upon by the mob. But when one's own people give him over—ticketed and labeled libertine and weakling, in a frantic and unseemly effort to save him… Love is blind, but when love lies parallel to self interest—of what is incapable. This burns out of my heart something that grew once and still grows there but to wither and burn at the thought—always."

Frank's pencil was then sharpened and pointed directly at his mother and his wife, Kitty, who had told reporters how shocked she was when he had "abandoned" her.

> "You knew and Catherine knew that I was going to take her [Mamah] away with me as soon as I could, as I had declared openly to you both

and to her husband a year before I did take her. There was no deception that makes the 'runaway' match of the Yellow journal anywhere. She went with me knowing that you knew and Catherine knew, that I would in any case have separated from Catherine—though I might have continued under the same roof with her for the sake of the children—but even that I told you I was determined not to do—She told her husband one year before she went away with me that she would go with me married or not whenever I could take her. Marriage was never a condition with her any more than it was with me—except in order to work I felt this must take place when it might, if it might. I may be the infatuated weakling, she may be the child-woman inviting harm to herself and others—but nevertheless the basis of this whole struggle was the desire for a fuller measure of life and truth at any cost—and as such an act wholly sincere—and respectable—within—whatever aspect it may have worn without. This by my return I discredit because I seemingly endorse the character made for it publicly by those, whom by my returning to them I seem to endorse. This bitter drought seems to me—almost more than I can bear—The last weight of a degradation otherwise not hopeless. I turn from it in disgust and hard as it was to throw down what I had worked hard for twenty years to build up it is doubly hard to go to work again among the ruins—poorer in heart, in mind, in pocket—robbed even of the sustaining sense of the truth when dealing such a foul blow to the woman who trusted her all to me in the struggle as I do when I endorse the character made publicly for her by those for whom I leave her. It may be too late to do anything worthwhile now—but I am a house divided against itself by circumstances I cannot control—I can face them and down them or go down with them trying to get whole again within—but again is not the word—I have always as you know lived a divided life, but always with a hope—undefined—but a hope. Now it will be without

> the hope and so, perhaps more useful to others… I suppose I may look forward to seeing you all again before long—As Always, Frank."

While the architect had poured out many of his frustrations and, to a degree, accusations to his mother, Mamah sought advice from a confidante of her own, Ellen Key, the only woman that Mamah believed had truly understood her. She wrote Key a letter describing the onslaught of hateful attacks against her character for her pursuit of her own independence instead of living under the yoke of strict Edwardian era constructs about the woman and mother that society wanted her to be. "Trying to live, at a frightful cost, what I believed to be the only truth and light, groping in perplexity and darkness, with my poor, little dim light 'close to my breast,'" Mamah wrote. "Suddenly in my darkest hour, I found you… Still however my perplexity and doubt is great that perhaps it is not mine—Your torch however will also light me to the truth path—the true path for me."

But unlike Key, there were many that could not see or understand Mamah's path toward self-realization. Her sister, Lizzie Borthwick, who had been caring for her children, visited her in Europe and urged her that it was time to come home.

Both Mamah and Frank felt they had been beaten into submission by their families and by tabloid journalists who had been provided with enough salacious excitement to trigger one of the earliest celebrity sex scandals in American history. In a correspondence with his friend Charles Ashbee, Frank sounded utterly defeated.

"The fight has been fought—I am going back to Oak Park to pick up the thread of my work and in some degree [the thread] of my life where I snapped it. I am going to work among the ruins—not as any woman's husband, but as the father of the children—to do what I can for them… But I have been cruel. I have destroyed many beautiful things."

Among those "beautiful things" that Frank felt he had ruined was

Mamah's reputation back home. She had been a willing travel partner, and she had her own reasons for leaving her family as she did. But the intense scrutiny that Mamah had been subjected to was the direct result of Frank's fame. Had she eloped with an Oak Park dentist or grocery clerk instead, Mamah's name, or her title as "Mrs. Edwin Cheney," would have been absent from the front pages of newspapers across America, as dozens of daily periodicals had eagerly reprinted stories about the scandal plaguing the nation's most prominent builder.

It had been nearly one year since Frank and Mamah had boarded the SS *Kaiser Wilhelm der Grosse* bound for Europe, and thus far, they had survived the turbulent waters surrounding their relationship, emotionally injured but still intact. The question now—would their bond remain strong after they returned to face their families and legions of critics both known and unknown?

13

Still together of heart, Frank and Mamah had decided to return separately to America. While Frank was making the final preparations for his journey across the Atlantic, Mamah remained behind and settled briefly again in Berlin, where she planned to stay until she fulfilled the two-year separation obligation needed for a divorce from her legal husband, Edwin Cheney.

When Mamah was ordered to fill out a certificate of temporary residence with the American consul general in Berlin, she crossed out the masculine word *He* in the application and replaced it with *She*. It appeared that only men could apply for temporary residence in Berlin.

When the application called for "the name of wife," Mamah wrote down the word *Widow*.

While Frank had grave concerns about leaving her behind, Mamah was eager to show her newfound independence, which would not be tied to the architect or any man. She moved into a hostel for single women, which was supported by the Lutheran Church and located in Berlin's Schöneberg district. Mamah took a job teaching at an exclusive Berlin school for boys called the Joachimsthal Gymnasium and tried her best to keep herself active and occupied while her true love returned home to an uncertain fate.

Frank was not eager to face the music back in Oak Park, so he visited his friend Charles Ashbee and his wife, Janet, in England at their home in the Cotswolds. Their visit fell under the guise of a business trip, as Ashbee had been asked to write an introduction to Frank's forthcoming book.

Frank's time spent with the Ashbees in England represented the calm before the storm, a brief period of peace before his return to dreaded domesticity and the moral outrage and second-guessing over his decision to embark on a sensual sabbatical with his lover.

He had hoped to avoid any fanfare regarding his homecoming, but Kitty Wright had other plans. She worked with reporters to create a narrative to underscore her desire to show that Frank's return as a defeated man was her triumph. In August, well before Frank's voyage back to the United States, Kitty had convinced a *Chicago Tribune* reporter to falsely write that her husband and Mamah had agreed to end their relationship and that Mamah had returned to Chicago and was now in seclusion somewhere outside the city with her husband and two children. Kitty also told the reporter that she was planning to bring her children with her to Europe for what would surely be an emotional reunion with her husband. Under the agreement for printing the exclusive story, the *Tribune* reporter had to attribute most of his information to "friends of Kitty Wright" and the Cheneys when the likely source was Kitty herself.

"I feel that I cannot discuss my plans," Kitty told the reporter on the record. "Whether I go or stay can surely be of no interest to the public. At least it is my own business. I must decline to say what I intend to do."

Yet despite Kitty's near refusal of comment for the article, the reporter somehow managed to include details that Kitty had planned to educate her children in Berlin while her husband pursued his work to complete his folio in the German capital city. Confiding to the reporter as background information not to be attributed to her, Kitty lied and said that Frank's "affinity" for Mamah had now passed and that the infatuation between the two "soul mates" had ended. When pressed by the reporter to share her feelings about the fact that her husband had falsely declared that Mamah was his wife when the two registered at the Hotel Adlon several months before, Kitty said, "It is a tribute to his sincerity and honesty. If he were an ordinary rake, if there could be anything low or common about him, do you think he would do that? He would have used another name. He is honest in everything he does."

The reporter then gave Kitty all the credit for keeping Frank's architectural firm afloat for the past year. "Mrs. Wright, with the same zeal that she has shown in championing her husband since his departure, has carried on the work at his office in his absence."

Most readers of the *Tribune* article, which was completely inaccurate, came away with a renewed sense of admiration for Kitty Wright, who was standing by her cheating husband and even reportedly running his business, all due to her undying love for him and her commitment to repairing their family.

There is no evidence that the story reached Frank overseas, who would no doubt have been outraged by its falsehoods. At the same time, reporters hunted for new information about Mamah's family. A story ran in the suburban newspaper *The Crystal Lake Herald* on August 11, 1910, detailing Edwin Cheney's alleged whereabouts that summer. Under the headline "Found at Fox River Camp—Husband and Children Deserted in Oak Park Scandal Live at Cary [Illinois]," the newspaper announced that Cheney had built a summer camp for himself and his children to shield them "from the gaze of the curious and gossiping public who are still talking of the sensational elopement [of Frank and Mamah]."

The reporter claimed to have broken the story by getting his hands on a receipt for groceries paid for by Cheney in Chicago and shipped forty-four miles west to the town of Cary and delivered to a picturesque summer camp "secluded by a group of trees on Fox River…about which is woven a web of complicated marital tangles involving two of the most prominent families of Oak Park." Cheney kept his automobile inside a barn owned by a local farmer named George Lowe, who told the newspaper reporter that he had "become suspicious" of Cheney after reading about the Cheney-Wright troubles. "Cheney, when discovered, refused to discuss his troubles," the newsman wrote. "His wife is said to be in Berlin at present."

When Cheney returned to Oak Park, another reporter, this one writing for the newspaper the *Inter Ocean*, confronted him at his home and asked him to confirm the *Tribune*'s reporting (with erroneous information likely supplied by Kitty) that Mamah was back home. "This is the question that is agitating residents of the fashionable suburb and which rapidly is assuming the importance of a deep mystery," the newsman wrote. "Cheney denied last night that his wife had returned to him, affinity-weary, but not before the Inquirer had caught a glimpse of a woman in the hallway of the residence… and had noticed a marked resemblance between her and Mrs. Cheney's photos." The woman described in the newspaper article was not Mamah but her sister, Lizzie Borthwick.

The train carrying Frank from New York after his yearlong overseas odyssey reached Chicago's Union Station around dusk on October 8, 1910. Like everything about the architect's life at the time, news of his return had already reached the press prior to his arrival. In yet another story leaked to the *Tribune*, someone described as an "intimate friend" of the Wrights, either Anna Lloyd acting on behalf of Frank's wife or even Kitty herself, told a reporter that Frank "is coming home to square himself with the public, his creditors and his family. Mrs. Cheney is not with him." Of course, Kitty attempted to stay at arm's length with the reporter, at least on the record. "I must beg not to be pressed for any sort of a statement," she told him.

The *Tribune* article, published in late September 1910, served as a brief precursor for the fireworks that would follow Frank when he finally did make it home. On October 9, 1910, one day after Frank stepped foot inside his home for the first time in a year, the *Tribune* ran a front-page story detailing the event under the headline "Wright Returns to Oak Park Wife—Family Welcomes Architect Who Went to Europe with Neighbor's Spouse—She Is Still Absent."

Frank glared outside at the news reporters who had gathered around his house. There was no way that he would speak to them after what they had written about him during the past year. Kitty convinced her husband to at least answer their questions, as it was her who no doubt tipped the reporters off to her husband's arrival. Frank reluctantly acquiesced to the request under one condition: that he would not speak to any of them face-to-face. He retreated to a back room of the house while Kitty met with the newsmen at the front door, wrote down their questions, and relayed them to her husband. She handed Frank a piece of paper with a reporter's question scribbled on it. He examined the note and then carefully wrote his reply. Kitty stared at the sheet of paper and then nervously walked back through the house to the front door and handed the note to the reporter.

"Mr. Wright says that it is none of the public's business and that he has nothing to say," Kitty told him.

The reporter was undeterred. There was no way that he would go back to the *Tribune* newsroom and tell his editor that he received a "no comment" on the biggest celebrity sex scandal in America. Instead, he pressed Kitty to get him the information that the newspaper was depending on for its front-page story. "Doesn't Mr. Wright think that a frank statement of his view of the situation right now as he returns will relieve him of a lot of importunity at the hands of acquaintances and the public in general?" he asked her. "Any sort of an explanation and an announcement that he expects to resume his work here probably will hasten the time when curiosity over the affair dies."

Kitty must have understood where the reporter was coming from after having spoon-fed information to newsmen, including the embarrassing tidbit that Lloyd had beaten up his father, for the past year. She retreated into the house and scampered toward the back room. Frank must have relished the moment, as he was now in control of what Kitty said to the press. They discussed the situation for several minutes until Kitty was forced to return to the newsmen, who had been showering her with praise for several months, to offer his terse reply.

"No, he says he has nothing to say, no explanation to offer," she said with her head bowed. "That it is nobody's business; that his coming home is his own affair in which no one has the right to meddle."

If, given his sullen mood, Frank would not entertain the reporters, Kitty was more than willing once again to play the heroine in the story. The last thing she wanted newsmen to believe was that her husband had returned to her against his own free will. She invited them into the parlor for a few minutes and gathered her children to greet them. Kitty had put on many shows before. The theme for this one was that the Wrights were a big happy family once again. "At night, the house was lighted from top to bottom," the *Tribune* reporter wrote in the article. "The faces of the young Wright children were wreathed in smiles and Mrs. Wright's countenance reflected the pleasure experienced by them. She was in buoyant spirits and conveyed the impression that the burden of care had suddenly dropped from her shoulders. Her younger son [Llewellyn] threw his arms around her and laughed during the reporter's brief visit."

It did not take long for Frank to regret his decision to come home. It is one thing to be considered an outcast when one is thousands of miles away; it is another thing entirely when one is shunned directly to their face. It was a feeling that he had never experienced before. As he wrote to his friend Darwin Martin just two weeks after his return, "I am accustomed to being an alien but not to see women drawing their skirts aside as they pass and my old friends crossing the road to avoid me."

Frank was not the only person who had misgivings about his return. Kitty, who had campaigned so publicly for their reconciliation, expressed her own regrets in a letter to Janet Ashbee. "Each morning I wake up hoping it to be the last. Womankind seems to be so moveable a 'feast.'" Still, she had no intention of granting her husband the divorce he had been yearning several years for. Frank's relationship with Mamah had taken on much water, and there was now little hope for their future together.

14

Frank remained separated from Mamah for several months from the fall and winter of 1910 to the early spring of 1911. During that time, he worked diligently to rebuild his business by receiving and paying off old debts and to reestablish a connection with his children. His attitude toward Kitty remained cold and distant. There were no more parties at their Oak Park home, and any family fun or frivolity was rare. Frank and his wife were merely occupying the same space, not the same heart and mind. He was hounded by reporters on a nearly daily basis. He was no longer famous. He was now infamous, an adulterer who had spat on society's moral code. Frank believed that he, not Kitty, was the true victim in their relationship and that he had suffered so that others might one day endure such freedom from marital oppression, especially when seeking legal divorce. Kitty's refusal to grant his request had placed Frank in an emotional prison.

"The passions have all contributed to the progress of life," he wrote in his memoir. "Sacrifice began as selfishness and even love began as lust… Legislation can be no friend to moral growth except by the 'Hands off!' or the 'Stand back please,' that allows the individual in the purely private and deeply personal concerns of his own life, to do or die *on his own.* I, too, believe that for any man to have found no lasting relationship in love in this brief life is to suffer great waste. Flogging, ridicule nor censure are needed to make such waste socially exemplar and effective."

There were no letters written or sent between Frank and Mamah, and it is unclear whether they had any contact during this time. Each was alone, an ocean apart. The architect spent his days remodeling his home and studio. He split the house into a duplex of sorts where one half of the structure would be transformed into his expanded home office and an apartment for himself, while Kitty and the children lived on the other side. Working at all hours there, he could cut himself off from being subjected to his wife's presence. He also convinced his mother, Anna, to sell the house he had purchased for her next door and use the money to buy land in Spring Green, Wisconsin. The wheels in his head were already spinning as to what he would eventually do with the property.

For her part, Mamah continued to teach, as she was fluent in German. Her Swedish language skills were not as polished, but she made her best effort to translate Ellen Key's latest book, *Love and Marriage*, in which she called for the transformation of the fixed laws of marriage. Mamah felt that the Swedish author had written the book for her. "All thoughtful persons perceive that the ideas of the morality of sexual relations upheld by the religions and laws of the Western nations are in our time undergoing a radical transformation," Key wrote early on in her book. "Those who regard monogamy as the only standard of sexual morality and the only legitimate form of personal love, do not mean the ostensible monogamy now established by law but circumvented by custom. They mean real monogamy: one man for one woman during that man's lifetime; one woman for one man during that woman's lifetime, and beyond that complete abstinence. In the way of development, they acknowledge only one gradual realization of this ideal; in the tendency of the present day to adopt several lines of development they see nothing but decadence."

Mamah and Frank were in a committed, monogamous relationship that just happened to occur outside their marriages to people they were bound to by law, not love. Mamah knew that Key's work was to be released in America by a prominent New York publisher, and she hoped that the book would educate both men and women, the pious and the heathen, about the unnecessary shackles placed on couples in the form of legal marriage contracts. "Wasn't love enough?" Mamah may have asked herself. She was in a dark place without Frank and without her children. Mamah still considered herself to be a good mother and believed that her decisions and sacrifice might help them in their future relationships when they grew to adulthood.

Mamah corresponded with Key regularly about her book and about her own feelings of despair. Having great difficulty finding her own words to describe her current state of mind, Mamah quoted a Robert Browning poem instead.

If I sink
Into a dark tremendous sea of cloud
It is but for a time. I press God's lamp
Close to my breast—its splendor soon, or late
Will pierce the gloom. I shall emerge one day.

The last line of Browning's poem captured both the anguish and fortitude of Mamah Borthwick.

She was down but not defeated, and she looked forward to her eventual return to America as a free woman.

Frank was anything but free at the moment. He shared a house with a woman he despised, and his finances were in shambles as clients were slow to return, many afraid that the stench of scandal surrounding the architect might spread to them. Out of desperation, he asked an old client for a $20,000 loan to help cover his expenses and pay off his debts. The client denied the request, but Frank's friend Darwin Martin eventually stepped up and provided him with a loan for $25,000. The loan paid for the remodeling of Frank's house in Oak Park and the installment owed for the German publication of Frank's folio. Martin had little faith that Frank would ever pay the loan back. "What you term 'a fine nature and a good heart' is commonly termed 'sucker,'" he later wrote.

Frank used some of the money from the loan to travel back to Berlin in March 1911. He told Kitty and his friends that he had to settle some issues with his German publisher over the continued delays of his book. This departure must have resulted in a contentious conversation with his wife. Kitty had previously told a reporter that she would accompany her husband when he returned to Europe to put the finishing touches on his folio, but Frank had no interest in traveling with his wife. Knowing that Mamah was still living in exile in Berlin, Kitty may have made Frank promise her that he would not see his mistress while in Germany, and he may have reluctantly obliged. Both must have known that Frank's vow would just be smoke. He had all intentions of spending as much time as possible with the woman he loved, regardless of the wedding band that held his finger like a vise.

Back in Berlin, the couple reunited with the same fiery intimacy that they had experienced together lying side by side in their villa in Fiesole the year before. Frank and Mamah toured Paul Cassirer's gallery, where Frank, now flush with cash, purchased several prints from well-known Secessionist artists. They also visited a bookstore in Berlin where he bought a rare copy of *A Hymn to Nature* by Goethe. It was a book that Frank would cherish for years to come.

Frank left Mamah in Berlin and sailed back to America in mid-March, their reunion much too brief for the both of them. Mamah remained in Germany until the end of the school year in June and began preparations for her return to Oak Park and the end of her two-year legally mandated separation from Edwin Cheney. Before traveling back to the United States, she visited Ellen Key in Sweden at her newly built home, called Strand, in

Hästholmen overlooking Lake Vättern. The home would become a cultural hub for artists and intellectuals from across Scandinavia and Europe. During the visit, Key urged Mamah to pay a visit to their publisher in New York immediately upon her return. They undoubtedly also would have discussed all that may have awaited Mamah when she got back to America. Would she continue to be villainized by the media? Or had gossipmongers taken their sizable pound of flesh from her and were now willing to leave her alone?

Reporters did not write about Frank's return to Germany back in March. In their collective eyes, the story was over. Frank had seemingly returned amicably to Kitty, and the institution of marriage had won out over true love.

Mamah said her goodbyes to Ellen Key at the front entrance of her home, which had the inscription *Remember to Live* carved into the wood. Mamah then traveled to Copenhagen before eventually boarding a passenger ship bound for America, where she would be forced to confront her recent past and blaze a path toward her future.

15

Mamah arrived in New York aboard the SS *United States* on June 27, 1911. She had planned to meet with the publisher to discuss the pending release of Ellen Key's work in the United States, but the publisher was away on his honeymoon at the time. Mamah had the option of partnering with another publishing company for her translations of Key's books, *Love and Ethics*, *The Morality of Woman*, and *The Torpedo under the Ark*. Frank brought her manuscripts with him back to Chicago, where he got a publisher there to agree to release Mamah's English translations if Frank would cover the production costs. He did so with money that had been loaned to him by his friend Darwin Martin.

That year, Frank had eight commissions to design houses and buildings, which was almost a 50 percent decline from 1905, when he had secured thirteen commissions for his work. Money was tight and margins were thin. Yet this did not stop him from dreaming about leaving Kitty for good and building a monument to his love for Mamah on the land that had been purchased by his mother, Anna, in Spring Green, Wisconsin.

Frank had first been struck by the idea while living with Mamah in Italy. During his time in Florence, Frank was enamored by the Sina Villa Medici, a nineteenth-century palazzo surrounded by gardens and built on a slope overlooking a golden valley filled with cypress and olive trees. Frank had committed the images to memory and later embedded them into the architectural drawings for his home in Wisconsin. Like the Villa Medici, Frank would place his own home in the same position on the side of a hill with high walls and plush gardens.

But Frank did want to simply build a house on a hill; he wanted his home to belong to it naturally, not like caves as they often organically appeared but native in spirit. "I scanned the hills of the region where the rock came cropping out of the strata to suggest buildings," he wrote in his memoir. "How quiet and strong the rock-ledge masses looked with the dark red cedars and white birches, there, above the green slopes… There must be some kind of house to belong to that hill, as trees and the ledges of rock did."

Frank wanted a house and hill that would marry each other and live happily ever after.

He did not want to ruin the home by overbuilding and overdesign. "Was there no natural house? I felt I had proved there was. Now, I wanted a natural house to live in myself…having itself all that architecture had meant whenever it was alive in times past."

Once he decided on an exact location for construction, he began to imagine the world of natural beauty that he would create around it. "I saw the hill-crown back of the house as one mass of apple trees in bloom, perfume drifting down the Valley… I saw plum trees, fragrant drifts of snow-white in the spring, loaded in August with blue and red and yellow plums… I saw rows and rows of berry bushes… Black cherries? White cherries? Those too."

He envisioned white hives where bees would store their honey next to a chicken yard and "spirited well-schooled horses, black horses and chestnut mares with glossy coats and splendid strides… I saw sturdy teams ploughing the fields."

His home would rise unbroken above the hill to, in his own words, "crown the exuberance of life in all these rural riches."

Frank would take stone from a quarry a mile away and employ local farmers and laborers to pile them on top of the hill for use in building a foundation that would have the appearance of a native slope. More stone would be placed in the walls outside the home, "bespeaking strength and comfort within."

Mamah knew about Frank's plan to build them a Midwestern oasis and may have even encouraged it. She returned to the Chicago area in July 1910 to settle her divorce with Edwin Cheney. Unlike what Kitty had done with Frank, Cheney did not alert reporters to his wife's arrival. She did not visit the home she had shared with her husband but instead took refuge in Spring Green, which was 184 miles northwest of Oak Park. Frank's sister Jane Porter and her husband took her in. Plans were quietly made for Mamah to reunite with her children, Martha and John, in Canada, away from the prying eyes of reporters.

A month later, Cheney appeared in court in Chicago and asked a judge to grant his divorce from Mamah. The exasperated husband was accompanied by his mother, Armilla Cheney.

"About June 28, 1909, Mrs. Cheney left me stating she was not going to return," Cheney testified. "She also stated three days prior to that time that she was going away and would not come back. Since then she has not returned, neither has she offered to return."

This was the first public acknowledgment that Cheney had been separated from his wife for more than three years. This new information contradicted Kitty's assertion that both she and Cheney were shocked when their spouses left them for Europe in the fall of 1910.

"While we lived together, I conducted myself kindly toward her and showed her every kind of attention possible and supported her to the best of my ability," Cheney continued.

"Did you ever give her any reason to leave you?" asked his attorney, Eugene G. Fassett.

"No, no occasion at all."

"And have you at all times had the care, custody and control of your children?"

"Yes sir," Cheney replied. "There is an agreement between us that the children are to remain in my custody."

Armilla Cheney also testified on her son's behalf that her daughter-in-law "had left him without cause and has since then not returned."

There was no doubt that Cheney was a dutiful father toward their children and had never laid a hand on his wife. He did not speak ill of Frank or Mamah. She had simply fallen out of love with him, if she had ever loved him in the first place. Most women of the time would have stayed in a loveless marriage because divorce was frowned upon, but Mamah Borthwick was not like most women.

The Cheney divorce proceedings were covered by a reporter from the *Chicago Tribune*. The front-page headline read "Cheney Divorces Wife Who Eloped—Affinity Tired of Her." The article was accompanied by an enchanting portrait of Mamah along with a photo of her husband, looking beleaguered. The story treated Mamah as a cold, uncaring wife while portraying her romantic rival, Kitty Wright, as "a Griselda waiting patiently with her children for her husband's disillusionment and return."

While Kitty remained both admired and adored by the media and friends and family alike, Mamah's public ostracization had already begun. Upon her return, she found out that she had been expelled by the First Congregational Church of Oak Park. This rejection likely contributed to her decision to leave the suburb for good. She quickly petitioned for the right and was granted the request to change her name back to Mamah Borthwick. When asked by a reporter why she made the name change, Mamah reportedly told him that the name Cheney was "distasteful" to her because of the "unpleasant memories" that were attached to it.

Kitty offered another story to a hungry member of the press in November of that year. She informed the reporter that the partition Frank had built to separate their house into two halves had been taken down. She then invited the newsman into their home to see that she and Frank were sitting in front of a cozy fire with their children.

"Whether it was for the love of their children that resulted in tearing down the barrier between them they would not say," the reporter wrote. "But it was plain that the barrier of wood and plaster was not the only one that had been obliterated."

When asked how she felt, Kitty beamed and told the newsman, "All I can say is that we're perfectly happy. I don't care to discuss the removal of the partition," she said while waving her arm across the room. "You can see for yourself."

Frank likely had no idea that a reporter had been invited to the house and may have felt set up by his wife so that she could continue with her now-tiresome charade to project themselves as a happily married couple to the media while using their own children as props for the effort. The article appeared in newspapers nationwide as readers clamored for any morsel of news about their volatile relationship and Frank's affair with Mamah.

Meanwhile, Frank quietly went ahead with his plans to build Mamah a home in the Wisconsin countryside.

Kitty and the children had not given up hope that he would return. Frank's young son Llewellyn wrote to him, likely at the urging of his mother, in early November 1911.

Dear Papa

This is my birthday I miss you very much. Will you please eat Thanksgiving with us. We are lone-some without you. We are afraid you are sick. We have snow now and sliding. I hope you are warm as we are in the house. I am eight years old. Good bye from your loving son.

Llewellyn Wright
Birthday kisses oooooooo

It is a heart-wrenching letter from the young boy, who was desperately seeking love and attention from his wayward father. There is no evidence as to whether Frank responded to the letter or whether he attended the holiday meal. Meanwhile, Mamah was working on correspondence of her own to her mentor, Ellen Key, about her decision to leave her two children, Martha and John, in the care of her ex-husband while she lived permanently with Frank in Spring Green, Wisconsin.

I have as you hope "made a choice in harmony with my own soul"—the choice as far as my own life was concerned was made long since—that is absolute separation from Mr. Cheney. A divorce was obtained last summer and my maiden name is now legally mine. Also, I have since made a choice in harmony with my own soul and what I believed to be Frank Wright's happiness and I am now keeping his house with him. In this very beautiful Hillside, as beautiful in its way as the country about Strand… We are hoping to have some photographs to send you soon. I believe it is a house founded upon Ellen Key's ideal of love.

Frank had hoped to keep the Spring Green house's construction a secret, but members of the news media were not going to let that happen. On Christmas Eve, 1910, the *Chicago Tribune* ran its most explosive headline yet about the affair: "Architect Wright in New Romance with 'Mrs. Cheney.'" Despite the fact that she was divorced and no longer married to

Edwin Cheney, the newspaper still refused to call her by her legal name. When reached for comment for the article, Frank valiantly replied in a telegram, "Mrs. Cheney never existed for me. I am taking care of Mamah Borthwick."

The *Tribune* reporter then took credit for breaking this sensational story. "The spot [in Spring Green, Wisconsin] is ideal for such a romantic liaison as Wright and Mrs. Cheney apparently have planned," he wrote. "Up to a time that a newspaper reporter called on them yesterday they were 'far away from the madding crowd,' free from prying eyes and inquisitive ears."

The newsman referred to "Mrs. Cheney's" divorce as the result of a "spiritual hegira" in which she and Frank were "the pilgrims." He then reported that a witness had sighted the couple walking to and fro along the side of a stream, looking for a shallow place to make their crossing. "When they found it, [he] lifted the woman tenderly in his arms and stepped boldly into the ice cold water. The current was strong and the water rose to his shoulders. He never hesitated however. His sole solitude seemed to be lest the woman's feet get wet."

The reporter went on to describe "a score of curious villagers" who watched them cross the stream. "They saw a good deal of lingerie of the quality not seen in that part of Wisconsin."

The story also suggested that Mamah shied away from her Spring Green neighbors and spent most of her time inside a large bungalow that Frank had built on the property to oversee their grand estate. The reporter then approached the bungalow and saw a man inside and a woman in the kitchen preparing breakfast. He asked if Frank Lloyd Wright and Mrs. Edwin Cheney lived there.

"I'm Wright," Frank replied gruffly. "But I won't say a word."

"Is the woman living with you Mrs. Cheney?"

"None of your business," Frank reiterated. "I won't say a word."

The *Tribune* reporter left, but his work was not done. He still had to confirm that Frank was at the bungalow with his so-called mistress. He telephoned the home a short time later. Mamah picked up the phone.

"I want to speak with Mrs. Cheney," he said.

Startled and panicked to hear herself addressed by her formerly married name, she replied, "I am Mrs. Cheney."

The reporter now had his story.

Meanwhile, another *Tribune* staffer found Kitty Wright visiting her lawyer in Chicago that same day and asked her for a comment. Normally one to speak at length about the matter at hand, Kitty said little and attempted to pour cold water on the story.

"Mr. Wright went north on business," she said. "He built that bungalow as a home for his mother. If there is any woman there, it is his mother."

"His mother would not dwell there in the company of Mrs. Cheney?"

Kitty's attorney stepped in and answered for her.

"I will say that I accompanied Mr. Wright to the union depot last Thursday night when he departed for Wisconsin," the lawyer stated. "He was alone. There was no woman there, of that I am positive."

When a reporter returned to the bungalow in Spring Green, he did not find Mamah Borthwick there. Instead, Frank's seventeen-year-old daughter Catherine opened the front door.

"We have nothing to say," she offered with a nervous giggle before saying much more than she had intended. "We have become hardened to the sensational features of this case. We don't really pay attention one way or the other. As far as the story goes, I suppose that it is substantially true in the main facts, but I don't know anything about this present affair… I know Mrs. Cheney, or did know her four years ago, but I haven't seen her for some time, and I don't know whether she is still in Oak Park or not. I rather think Mother [Kitty] will be amused over this occurrence. It really seems funny that this skeleton in the closet should be dragged forth at every opportunity.

Just say for Mr. Wright and Mrs. Wright and all the little Wrights that we don't know anything about this awful story, and that it must be untrue."

"Does that statement include your father, as you have said?" asked the reporter.

"It includes all of us."

News that Frank and Mamah were cohabitating in Spring Green had nearly gutted Kitty, and she now had to act quickly in her own defense. She had spent the past two years carefully crafting a narrative that her husband had been bewitched by a ruthless and seductive vampire and that she, through her faith and love for her husband, had finally broken the evil spell. This latest story, the biggest of all thus far, had been broken the old-fashioned way, by dogged and nosy reporters who had gathered details from multiple sources and were not just spoon-fed information by Kitty alone.

When readers of the *Chicago Tribune* put away their stockings and picked up their newspapers on Christmas morning, they learned that Kitty would soon tell all about Frank's affair with his mistress. She allowed a reporter into her home to watch their son David entertain some friends from his fraternity while making merry around a "beautifully ornamented Christmas tree." Daughter Catherine was also there, just home from Spring Green.

"I have no reply to make to Mr. Wright's alleged statement of Sunday," Kitty said, referring to Frank's telegram in which he told a reporter that he was now taking care of Mamah Borthwick. "Nor have I any statement of my own to make at present. I probably shall have something to say in a short time."

Kitty's statement to the press and to the public was not verbal. It was visual. She allowed the newsman to describe a beautiful holiday setting at her Oak Park home where she was surrounded by her children and their friends. The one person absent from the Christmas festivities was the children's father, who was about to break his long-held silence over the scandal of his creation, once and for all.

16

A reporter arrived by horse carriage and knocked on the door of the bungalow, which Frank had just finished building on a great limestone crag with a commanding view of the Wisconsin River, on Christmas Day. He likely anticipated that Frank would shoo him off as he had done previously. A news editor told the reporter to be persistent as that was one of the tenets of the job. He braced himself for an angry retort from Frank and a slamming of the front door. But the reporter was surprised when Frank invited him inside. The architect told the reporter that he had hoped to stand behind the one statement he had given in a telegram when he had informed the media that he was now caring for Mamah Borthwick. But now he wanted to take a bolder approach to the situation.

"I see this as an opportunity to tell the world which thinks I have something to be ashamed of that I am not ashamed," Frank said as he paced the floor.

The reporter dug a notepad and pencil out of the pocket of his winter coat and sat with eager anticipation for him to continue.

After clearing his throat, Frank began. "In the first place, I haven't abandoned my children or deserted any woman, nor have I eloped with any man's wife. There has been nothing clandestine about this affair in any of its aspects. I have been trying to live honestly. I have been living honestly."

He reminded the reporter once again that the term *Mrs. E. E. Cheney* had never existed for him. Frank did not view Mamah as an appendage of another man or an appendage of himself.

"She was always Mamah Borthwick to me, an individual separate and distinct, who was not any man's possession."

Frank then turned the topic to his kids. "The children, my children are as well provided for as they ever were," he told the reporter. "I love them as much as any father could. But I suppose I haven't been a good father to them. Certainly I regard it as a tragedy that things should have come about as they have, but I could not act differently if I had to do it all over again."

He then praised his estranged wife for her child-rearing skills, which was something he had lacked. "Mrs. Wright wanted children, loved children, and understood children. She had her life in them. She played with the children and enjoyed them. But I found my life in my work."

Frank spoke philosophically about what he felt was his purpose in life. He did not see himself as perhaps other men saw themselves, rooted by family and gauging their own success by how well they raised their kids.

"I started out to give expression to certain ideas of architecture. I wanted to create something organic: something sound and wholesome. American in spirit and beautiful if might be. I think I've succeeded in that. In a way, my buildings are my children."

The reporter then weighed in. "Why couldn't your work and Mrs. Wright's work go on side by side?"

The question was at the heart of Frank's decision to leave, whether he had found Mamah or not.

"Mrs. Wright had little time to be interested in my work," he answered. "She was wrapped up in her children. I lived more and more in my work.

And so we grew apart. She did not understand my going away. She does not understand it now. She thinks I am infatuated with another woman. That isn't the whole of it. I went away because I found my life confused and my situation discordant."

Frank told the reporter that he could no longer remain in the home in Oak Park because he would have been living a lie and felt that he had to remain true to himself, especially when he had designs to radically change the world of architecture. "I believe we can be no more useful to the progress of society without a stubborn selfhood that we can lift ourselves by our bootstraps, and I wanted to be what I had come to feel for some years I was; I would honestly be myself first and take care of everything else afterward."

He recognized that he was self-centered and, some would say, narcissistic in his pursuit of professional excellence. Frank was undoubtedly a genius, but his superior intellect came at a steep price. However, he believed that the only way he could do right by his family was to do right by himself.

"I felt that I would find the strength and the way to help my family when I was strong myself, and no man is strong until he is himself," he added. "I can do better by my children now than I could have done had I sacrificed that which was life itself to me and remained with them a sacrifice to duty, bound a slave and not a man with coldness and falsehood in the atmosphere they breathed."

The reporter had knocked on Frank's door in search of a quote for his story. What he got instead was a long, philosophical lecture from the famous, now disgraced architect about all that truly mattered to him in life. The newsman could hardly scribble down Frank's words fast enough, knowing that they would be reprinted for the world to read.

Carrying on about his children, Frank said, "I believe in them, but no parent can live his children's lives for them… I do not want to be a pattern for them. I want them to have room in which to grow up and be themselves… When they get a little older, I hope they will see me in another light."

"You mean that the material wants of Mrs. Wright and her children are provided for?" the reporter asked.

"Everything I have done up to this time is at their disposal," Frank replied. "I have taken nothing and shall take nothing from them. Mrs. Wright has a soul of her own and much greater matters than this to occupy her heart and mind. It is not for me to say what she will do."

Frank also expressed great concern for his financial future. He told the reporter that if he was a writer, musician, or actor, there was a greater likelihood that his livelihood would not suffer because of scandal. But architectural design was a client-facing business, and he regularly came into intimate contact with those he worked for. "There will be people who will be unwilling to have me in that intimate relation," he said. "I shall have buildings to design of course. But I shall not have as many as I would have if this thing had not happened. I shall not have as many as I would have had if I had been content to live dishonestly. It will be a waste of something totally precious if this robs me of my work."

Noticing that he held the reporter in rapt attention, Frank grew even more boastful in his attempt to explain himself, but his words would alienate most readers and likely made Mamah Borthwick cringe with discomfort.

"I want to say this: laws and rules are made for the average," he stated. "The ordinary man cannot live without rules to guide his conduct. It is infinitely more difficult to live without rules, but that is what the really honest, sincere, thinking man is compelled to do. And I think when a man has displayed some spiritual power, has given concrete evidence of his ability to see and to feel the higher and better things of life, we ought to go slow in deciding he is acting badly."

Frank clearly saw himself as an Americanized version of recently deceased Friedrich Nietzsche's idea of an *Übermensch* or *superman*, a self-mastering individual who transcends conventional morality and creates their own values.

The lengthy interview now concluded, Frank ordered a worker to fetch the reporter's carriage as the two men walked outside in the courtyard. "My home stretches 300 feet along the rock," Frank said proudly. "Most of it is built in limestone laid in close imitation of the cliff."

He shared his plans for a fountain in the center of the courtyard surrounded by flowers. Along a sunbathed slope to the south, he planned to build a vineyard where his children would fill baskets with purple, green, and yellow grapes to "set about the rooms like flowers." At the foot of the slope, Frank was in the process of constructing a dam that would back up several acres of water for a pond to be inhabited by fish and waterfowl. He recalled how his mother, Anna, had refused to allow him to eat desserts as a child and spoke about the herd of prized cows that he planned to raise there to produce milk and cream: "All the cream the boy had been denied. Thick—so lifting it in the spoon it would float like an egg on the fragrant cup of coffee or ride on the scarlet of strawberries."

Frank designed the bungalow to be self-sustaining, "a complete living unit genuine in point of comfort and beauty." The property provided him everything that he had yearned for as a child and dreamed about as an adult. The home "was to be an abstract combination of stone and wood as they naturally met in the aspect of the hills... The lines of the hills were the lines of the roofs, the slopes of the hills their slopes." He allowed the shingles of the roofs to weather naturally like tree branches, camouflaging the home and blending it in with its natural surroundings. Inside, great stone fireplaces offered large gathering spots for his and Mamah's family on cold nights. Frank even had a name for his estate. He would call it Taliesin.

17

Reaction to Frank's long-awaited and long-winded interview with the *Chicago Tribune* reporter was swift and full of vitriol. Upon reading the article, Kitty Wright vowed once again that she had no intention of divorcing her husband, despite the fact that he was living with another woman. When reporters called on her at her Oak Park home, they were greeted by seventeen-year-old Catherine Wright, who told them that her mother was in her bedroom resting, no doubt embarrassed that the truth about their marriage had finally come out. After fielding a few questions, Catherine walked upstairs to consult Kitty on a response. She returned a short time later and said, "There will be no action of any kind in this case, now or in the future."

Inaction was not on the collective minds of townsfolk in Spring Green. They were angry, and many wanted to run Frank and Mamah out of their village. A group of neighbors met with a local sheriff to discuss their options.

"I was asked to open an investigation," Iowa County Sheriff W. R. Pengally told a reporter. "Wright's neighbors have decided that he is going ahead with his plans regardless of their disapproval. They don't like what he's doing and they want to put a stop to it if they can."

But what could they do short of setting siege on the bungalow with an angry mob? The sheriff admitted that he had no answers, as he did not know what charges could be brought against the couple. "The citizens who consulted me do not want to take the law into their own hands," Sheriff Pengally added. "I told them I would do my best to thwart any attempt at tarring and feathering."

The lawman stressed that he did not believe that Frank's neighbors were planning to cause him physical harm. "They want him to leave and think that he can be compelled to go by legal means or else send away this woman he is reported to be living with."

The sheriff promised to consult with the area district attorney on what legal avenues were available to them to remove Frank and Mamah from the property.

"I don't know yet, what charge will be brought against them," Sheriff Pengally said. "[But] I am ready to act the moment a citizen of Iowa County swears out a warrant for Wright's arrest." With that, the sheriff instructed each of his deputies to begin gathering evidence against the couple. No doubt this meant staking out the bungalow as if they were hunting down two bandits who were on the run from the law.

Townspeople had known Frank for several years and seemed willing to put up with his many eccentricities. But living openly with a woman who was not his wife appeared to be a bridge too far. "This love affair of his is beyond me," one neighbor said. "I've only had a common school education and when he [Frank] explains why he left his wife and children in Chicago, he gets beyond my depth."

Frank's Spring Green neighbors were not the only people to express outrage over the affair; prominent Chicago clergy members were also quick to denounce the couple.

"A man in any other walk of life who stole valuables from another could not take refuge in such an excuse," Reverend M. P. Boynton told members of his congregation at Chicago's Lexington Avenue Baptist Church. "Mr. Wright can make no valid excuse for invasion of another man's home. Monogamy is society's domestic ideal."

Other religious leaders piled on. "People of wealth and prominence are getting away with this soulmate business," said Father Edward A. Kelly, the pastor at St. Anne's Roman Catholic Church. "In a matter that is a disgrace to state and church. If a poor man were to try this affinity arrangement regardless of all marriage laws, he would quickly be thrown in jail charged with bigamy or adultery… Soul mates nothing! They are crazy, and as the state has institutions caring for such demented people, there is where they belong."

Some vocal critics of the couple demanded that Bible instruction be taught in public school to help prevent such acts of free love.

Unsatisfied with a lack of response from local members of law enforcement due to the fact that no one quite knew which, if any, laws had been broken by Frank and Mamah, a few Spring Green residents discussed taking up arms against the couple. There was also talk among townspeople that the couple had stockpiled weapons and barricaded themselves inside the bungalow in an attempt to resist any arrest and fight off any attack.

Uncle Jenk also denounced his nephew, calling Frank a "blinded egoist" and referring to Taliesin as a "haven for pleasure."

The scandal was getting more sensational with every retelling. Frank's son John, now working as a draftsman in San Diego, woke up to front-page stories about his father each day in the city's newspaper. The articles were filled with "scandal, distortions of truth about my father. This time his bold unmarried status with a woman of his choice…provided the theme," he recounted later. "A sudden pain caught my breath. These outbursts were always a trial for me, but this time it seemed tragic."

Frank had seen enough, and he had heard enough. After calling some newsmen who were attempting to peek into the windows of his snow-covered bungalow "a fine bunch of dubs," he promised that he would release what he hoped would be the final word on the matter.

The architect said that he would issue a joint statement before New Year's Day that would be signed off by himself, Mamah Borthwick, Kitty Wright, and Edwin Cheney. After coming to an agreement with the other signatories on the language he used in the statement, Frank sent it by telegram to newsrooms across Chicago and Wisconsin and urged news editors to print the statement in full. It read as follows:

> I am tired. The woman [Mamah] is tired. We are living the life that truth dictates. Our hope is that we may benefit humanity. Our determination is to be true to our ideals at any cost.
>
> Here we are, four people—a wife and a man, and a husband and a woman, who each assumed earlier in life the responsibility of marriage and children. Then *the thing* happened that has happened since time began. There was the usual struggle with conscience, the usual concession to duty, but not the usual clandestine relation furtively continued to save the face of the situation.
>
> As soon as the situation developed its inevitable character, a frank avowal was made to those whose lives were to be affected a readjustment. Time was asked and a man and a woman agreed to make certain that love was love. The wife characterized the matter as mere infatuation that would pass. For a year, the wife continued in her household separate from the man. All was wretched and false. At the end of the year, the man was called abroad on business. He made no secret of the fact that he would take the woman with him, but he neglected to inform the newspapers, and it was said he had eloped.

Frank made no mention or implication that Kitty had most likely informed the media herself instead. He continued with the statement:

> It is hard to say who suffered the most. There was a breaking of established ties—but against them was the passion of a man for a woman and of a woman for a man. The man returned—not as a husband but as a father, to ensure his family's comfort… The man knew that only with the woman that he could carry out life's purpose. A place was found for the woman. It is this place [Taliesin]. There are no obligations, no family deserted, no duties undone. But the hue and cry of the yellow press was raised, and from one end of the country to the other, "the abandoned children," "wife deserter," "affinity" and the "hegira" were proclaimed.

As for Edwin Cheney's reluctant role in this evolving drama, Frank wrote, "The husband had freed the woman, but not because he had lost faith in her womanliness."

He ended the joint statement this way. "The struggle is to live and let live. To remain true to all humanly dischargeable and still be serviceable."

Frank hoped that the joint statement would end all speculation on the matter.

After all the tough talk by law enforcement about handcuffing the couple, there would be no police raid on the bungalow, as Frank and Mamah had committed no crime. The townspeople of Spring Green returned to their lives, and members of Chicago's café society would eventually find other gossipy topics to discuss. Kitty Wright remained somewhat quiet about the situation, although she could not help herself when she told a reporter in early January 1912, "I still love my husband and hold no hard feelings against him on account of anything that has happened. I feel no resentment against Mrs. Cheney, but I believe she has queer ideas about the moral code." It was Kitty's last opportunity to portray herself as the emotional martyr of the scandalous affair.

Silent for far too long, Mamah decided that it was time to share her own feelings about her relationship with Frank. She invited a reporter from the *Chicago Examiner*, not the rival *Chicago Tribune*, which she felt had treated her cruelly, to the bungalow, where she was seen reclining on a small couch next to the architect. Frank was sketching plans for additions to their new home, while Mamah was engrossed in her work of translating Ellen Key's Swedish prose into English. Her current project involved Key's book *The Morality of Woman*. The reporter was immediately awestruck by her beauty and described her this way: "Of the dark, somewhat voluptuous type, Mamah Borthwick possesses large, dark brown eyes, that meet one unflinchingly. Her hair, which she wears parted in the middle and combed close to her head on both sides, is of an uncertain shade. When the light strikes it, one is certain that it is jet black, but closer inspection shows that it has a touch of brown."

She greeted the reporter wearing a loose-fitting peasant dress and identified herself. "Yes, I am Mamah Borthwick," she told him. "I am proud to admit it, for I certainly have no reason to feel ashamed of my name or identity. But I still do not wish to be interviewed. I have left all that to Mr. Wright and anything that he may consent to has my unqualified endorsement." Instead, she had prepared a statement for the reporter, which she demanded be printed in full to avoid any possibility that her words could be taken out of context. It would serve as an addendum to the joint statement.

"But for the life of me, I cannot find that there is anything more to be said," she stated with a sigh. "Don't you think that everything has been explained?"

Mamah was being coy. She had plenty to say for herself but also wanted to project an image of deference toward Frank. She was also careful not to take a combative tone with the *Examiner* reporter and tried her best to woo him to her side.

She gazed at the reporter, who had flakes of white snow on the shoulders of his dark top coat. "Do you know I feel sorry for you fellows," she told him. "Spring Green must be an awful place for you to be in, away from your friends and everybody you know at this holiday season. And none of you are used to the cold Wisconsin winds. I should think you all would be glad to get back to Chicago."

"Don't you suffer too?" the reporter asked her.

"No, it is different for me," Mamah replied. "I have lived out in the open all my life. I never feel that it is winter unless it is really cold."

She handed the reporter her written statement. He reviewed it quickly and promised her that he would reprint it in its entirety on the front page of the *Examiner*.

"Mrs. Borthwick, now that everything has been explained, what are your plans for the future?"

She paused before offering her response. "Why, I have no plans. That is an extraordinary question. I have never thought of living differently with Mr. Wright and my studies. What the future holds for us, neither can tell. I am busy every day, and with my work and Mr. Wright, I find happiness."

Mamah then responded to the news reports that the couple's Spring Green neighbors wanted to drive them out of town. "We do not want to be censored by the community. That is what hurts us most. We want to use the world socially as well as materially, and how are we to do this without the respect and cooperation of our neighbors? Do you suppose that Mr. Wright could have built this bungalow in the midst of the homes of his relatives with the intention of occupying it with me when not related to him in a legal way? That is foolish!"

She also discussed her translation of *The Morality of Woman* and how it mirrored her own situation. "The book itself I consider one of the most absorbing ever written," she said. "But I am given too much credit by the newspapers. Possibly, [the book] was printed at a time when it was regarded as [a] sort of defense of my position, to which the public has not taken kindly. But the text of the work did not originate in my mind. That book is from the brain of a genius—Ellen Key. I merely translated it from the Swedish in which it was written… While Mr. Wright is occupied by his art, I work on my translating."

Frank then offered the *Examiner* reporter a tour of their bungalow and showed him his leather-bound folio, which contained reproductions of plans and photographs of buildings he had designed over the past twenty-five years. "I just wanted to show you that my life has not been useless," the architect declared. "In my art, I find solace for the harsh things the newspapers have said about my life. My art is my life."

The reporter returned to the *Examiner* newsroom with Mamah's statement and his own story about his encounter with the couple. As promised, the newspaper printed Mamah's complete statement, which read, "We both live in monogamy. Our trip to Europe was requested by Mrs. Wright and Mr. Cheney to rid us of a temporary infatuation. Neither of us intended that the present condition should exist after our return from abroad, but 'there is many a slip 'twixt the cup and the lip.' Neither Mr. Wright or myself believes that every man should have two women. But we do believe that husband and wife should be compatible in every respect. When this condition ceases to exist, why live the lie? I had no home when I returned to this country. Had we waited for legal happiness, I would be homeless today. I am not ashamed of my name or identity. I have no plans. What the future holds for us, neither can tell."

Satisfied for the first time with a reporter's recounting of their relationship, Mamah retreated back to her translation work while Frank created designs for their future. He hoped to follow through on his plans to build out Taliesin, his Shangri-la and his most personal love letter to Mamah. He was aware of the ill will expressed toward him by his neighbors, but they would not scare him off his land.

"I was born and reared in this community," Frank said. "Most of my relatives and real friends live nearby. I'm sure that the majority, if not all of them, respect my sincerity, and although I do not agree with them nor they with me in many things, yet I think I have their sympathy and respect. I only ask to be left alone and I will take care of myself and protect Mamah Borthwick. Everything will come out right in the end."

Frank envisioned the couple growing old together in the Wisconsin hills. The couple had sacrificed, suffered, and made others suffer over their pledge to stay together. The dark clouds over their relationship had finally begun to clear. But neither could foresee the violent storm that was slowly beginning to form on the horizon.

18

Julian Carlton and Frank Lloyd Wright existed on different planets from each other economically, socially, and spiritually. Carlton, an African American man, was born in 1888. The Thirteenth Amendment to the U.S. Constitution to abolish slavery had been in effect for only twenty-five years. Carlton came from Cusseta, Alabama, a place that boasted about its native son, Pat Garrett, who had shot and killed William Bonny, better known by his notorious nickname, Billy the Kid. Carlton was one of thirteen children raised in a tiny, dilapidated shack by parents who had survived slavery only to scratch by day to day, wearing the invisible shackles of oppression.

His mother's name was Mariah, and his father's name was Galon. Mariah Carlton was just fifteen years old when she got married and gave birth to their first child in 1869. Mariah would be pregnant on and off for the next twelve years. She and Galon eventually moved their large brood to the city of Birmingham around 1900. At the time, hangings and lynchings of African Americans were common in Alabama and across the South. In 1900, at the start of summer, a Black boy was put to death in nearby Huntsville after he had allegedly confessed to the rape of a white woman. It is likely that the young suspect had been beaten and tortured before he may wrongfully have given answers to the questions that authorities wanted to hear. From there, so-called justice came swiftly. The boy was convicted of the crime and sentenced to death. The judge, under intense pressure from town residents, sent the boy off to the gallows, offering him no opportunity to appeal.

"The law we repeat is often slow and the Huntsville mob knew it," one reporter wrote. "And so told Judge Speake, when he promised them that the Huntsville rapist would be tried and punished at once."

Both Mariah and Galon Carlton did their best to keep their children out of potentially dangerous situations, especially with white people. An innocent glance at a white woman could result in a rope around a Black man's neck.

Julian Carlton found work at the age of twelve, sweeping the floors of a local grocery store along with his brother. The brothers did their best to keep their eyes on their mops and buckets of brownish water while white shoppers picked out their daily meats, fruits, and vegetables. Their father, Galon, worked as a day laborer and railroad porter. At the age of fourteen, Julian followed in his father's footsteps and began working himself as a porter at W. B. Leedy & Company in the business district of Birmingham. He then jumped to a better-paying job as a bellhop at the Hotel Hillman. While both parents were illiterate, their children, including Julian, had learned how to read and write.

It was 1907, and in April of that year, an Alabama newspaper, *The Elba Clipper*, ran the solemn headline "Prayer Was Spoken for Doomed Man." The story was about a lynching in Louisiana, the second in a week. According to the story, five hundred men and boys had participated in the killing of a Black man named Fred Kilbourne. He had been arrested for the attempted assault of a white woman on the plantation where he worked. That "assault" could have been a mere look, a tip of the cap, a friendly hello, or it could have been nothing at all. While behind bars in the town of Clinton, Louisiana, a large group of white men, all wearing hoods and likely members of the Ku Klux Klan, entered the jail and demanded that two deputy sheriffs turn over custody of the suspect to them. When the jailers refused, the horde of men pushed their way past the deputies, retrieved the key, and yanked Kilbourne out of the cell. Terrified, Kilbourne swore that his arrest was a mistake and begged the mob to allow him to present his side of the story to a jury and prove that he was innocent of the charge. "His captors gave him plenty of time to make his statements but remained unmoved in their determination to hang him," the reporter wrote. "When he saw that death was certain, the negro kneeled on the ground and asked that he be led in prayer. His request was granted, the prayer was mumbled by one of the leaders. Every head was uncovered. He was then hanged to the limb of a Cypress tree."

There were sixty-one men lynched in the United States in 1907, and only three of them were white. The rest of the victims looked like Carlton, who fled the South later that year.

He eventually turned up in Chicago.

Carlton probably did not yet know the name Frank Lloyd Wright, but he soon would. Frank was scrambling at this time to get his life back in order after being nearly ruined by tabloid journalists who believed that his relationship with Mamah Borthwick was as important, if not more important, than many other news stories of the day. But the April 15, 1912, sinking of the *Titanic* caused when the British luxury ocean liner collided with an iceberg in the area of the Grand Banks of Newfoundland, killing approximately fifteen hundred passengers, some of them among the richest people in the world, dominated global headlines and managed to put much less relevant news stories into their proper perspective. Frank and Mamah were no longer deemed front-page news items, and they were allowed to live together in relative peace in Spring Green.

Frank was busy bringing Taliesin to life. He had named his homestead after a Welsh poet, "a druid-bard who sang to Wales the glories of fine art… Since all my relatives had Welsh names for their places, why not mine?" he asked himself rhetorically in his memoir. "Literally the Welsh word means 'shining brow.'"

The hill where he was building had reminded him of a brow, and it was one of his favorite places to go as a boy while working on his family's farm. "I turned to this hill in the Valley as my Grandfather before me had turned to America—as a hope and a haven."

Frank designed his Spring Green home and compound to stand the test of time. He wanted Taliesin to become both a summer and winter retreat for his children, his grandchildren, and generations of the Wright family to come.

But clergy members and some townsfolk believed the property was nothing more than a monument to sin and therefore was cursed. Frank ignored his many critics and their superstitions and kept working on his safe haven in the Wisconsin hills.

19

Taliesin was not only a home. Frank had set it up to be a training center and master class for bright young architects to come and learn from the greatest designer and builder that America had yet to produce. Masons were brought onto the property to lay down the foundations for the walls in long, thin, flat edges, with those edges jutting out to resemble a rock quarry. The masons laid stone as if they were sculpting a statue out of marble, stepping back to review their work and adjusting and fidgeting with the design until it looked just right.

Frank wanted to transform these simple village masons into master sculptors. "Many of them were artistic for the first time, and liked it," he later recalled.

When winter rolled in, Frank and his team assembled the roof, finished the plastering, and put the windows in so that carpenters could work inside. The floors inside Taliesin were stone, like the floors outside. Like any construction site, there was loud noise from dawn to dusk: the hammering of nails, the moving of stone, and the sawing of wood. Amid this architectural circus and symphony, Mamah did her best to concentrate on her own pursuit, her continuous translation of Ellen Key's writings. She was happy to learn that her ex-husband had wasted little time living the life of a single man. He had taken a new bride, Elsie E. Mellor of Chicago, a former schoolteacher who was a close friend of Mamah's sister Lizzie. After their wedding, Cheney and his young wife boarded the White Star steamship *Teutonic* and sailed off to Liverpool and then to Paris for their honeymoon.

During that time, Lizzie Borthwick brought Martha and John to Taliesin to spend the rest of the summer with their mother.

A reporter summed up Edwin Cheney's nuptials this way: "By the remarriage of Mr. Cheney, one of the two great social wounds inflicted by the Wright-Cheney 'hegira' has been healed—or at least cauterized."

Meanwhile, Mamah was thrust into another controversy, but this one had nothing to do with her relationship with Frank. Some friends of Ellen Key went to the newspapers to denounce Mamah's translations of Key's books. They claimed that she had twisted Key's words about love, marriage, and child-rearing "into her own soul mate doctrines...with new and dangerous revisions." The only mistake, besides misspelling Mamah's name as *Namah* on the cover, was a slight change to the title. Key's original title, *The Morality of Woman*, was renamed *The Morality of Women*, which some critics thought was Mamah's own battle cry to isolated and underappreciated wives and mothers across America to join her in her fight for spiritual independence. The reporter failed to list any other discrepancies between Key's original work and Mamah's translations in the article and refused to identify his sources, but he did point out that in Key's other book, *Love and Marriage*, "[Key] boldly cries that ignorance in woman is not innocence, and that the woman who bears children to a man she does not love and respect is [as] unchaste as the woman who earns her bread in the streets by a life of shame."

The reporter had used Mamah as a vessel for an attack on Ellen Key and her views about the status of women in Edwardian society. He had also given Mamah a new nickname, referring to her as "Mamah of the Hills."

Key herself, however, had never expressed any concern to Mamah over the translation of her work. Mamah wrote Key another letter to update her about Taliesin and her optimism that the storm had finally passed regarding her relationship with Frank.

"You will be interested I think to know how our attempt to do what we believe right has succeeded. I can now say that we have, I believe, the entire respect of the community in which we live. I have never encountered a glance otherwise and many kind and thoughtful things have been done for us by the people around about here. I do not go to Chicago, but Frank goes and sees his children every week. My sister brought my children here for the summer during Mr. Cheney's absence in Europe for his wedding trip. He married a very lovely woman…and the children are fond of her and she of them."

The relationship between Mamah and her mentor turned rocky when Key endorsed another writer to translate her book *Love and Ethics* despite a contract that gave Mamah the exclusive rights to translate the Swedish writer's work into English for American readers. Mamah wrote another letter to Key, but this note had a much sharper tone. She reminded her mentor of their written agreement and even used Key's own words, "I would be delighted to make you the only authorized translator in your language if you learn mine," against her. Mamah continued writing the letter with a few cold strokes of her pen. "Now dear lady, no words of yours has [*sic*] been published through me that you did not give me express permission to use."

The dustup between Mamah and Ellen Key was eventually settled to their mutual satisfaction.

On a more positive note, neither Mamah nor Frank had to contend with much outside noise regarding their relationship. Although they were no longer taking direct hits from gossip-hungry reporters, the couple was blamed by one member of the tabloid press for inspiring another affair between a man from Evanston, Illinois, and a married woman. A news account under the banner headline "True Love Put above Man Law" detailed the relationship between Emerson H. Nicholoy, a graduate of Cornell University, and a woman referred to only by her married name, Mrs. John G. Coon. Apparently, Nicholoy had been living with the woman and telling others that she was his wife. The account bore some resemblance to Frank's habit of introducing Mamah as his wife during their yearlong sojourn to Europe. Friends of Mrs. Coon told the reporter that she had left her husband because of "cruelty and non-support," not to mention a domineering and overly chatty mother-in-law. The reporter suggested that the couple may have gone on a "spiritual hegira" similar to that of Frank and Mamah.

As winter fell on Spring Green, Frank became even more awed by the way that Taliesin had blended itself into the natural landscape. "I wanted a home where icicles by invitation might beautify the eaves… Taliesin in winter was a frosted palace roofed and walled in snow, hung in iridescent fringes, the plate-glass of the windows shone bright and warm through it all as the light of the huge fireplaces lit them from the firesides within, and streams of wood smoke from a dozen such places went straight up toward the stars."

Frank was slowly turning his dreams into reality and had hired another architect to work on Taliesin. Frank's son John returned home from San Diego and also joined the firm. Frank visited his younger children regularly, but Kitty still held strict against allowing Mamah to join their weekly reunions.

She was determined never to allow her husband to marry again, and despite the situation they now found themselves in, Kitty vowed that she would always be Mrs. Frank Lloyd Wright. But by January 1913, the long estranged couple had settled on a détente, a relaxation of their strained relationship.

Kitty kept her feelings to herself and away from the press. When Frank announced that he was traveling to Japan that same month, his first visit to the Far East without her, Kitty remained silent instead of lashing out against him in the media. But journalists had long memories, and one reporter worked to add a scent of scandal to Frank and Mamah's trip to Japan, calling it the couple's "second hegira," leaving in their wake "the deserted wife of the architect who still resides at the Wright home in Oak Park." The reporter was also quick to point out that Frank was also leaving behind several irate tradesmen in Spring Green, who were demanding payment of overdue bills.

Frank was nearly broke once again. Construction overruns at Taliesin had put him in a difficult financial position. But as he had done so many times in the past, he ignored his piling debts and set off on a new adventure.

20

Frank and Mamah took a train to Seattle, Washington, and then boarded a steamship to Yokohama, Japan. The architect hired a Japanese servant named Satsu, who would act as his translator during the trip. Following a short train ride from Yokohama to Tokyo, the trio checked into the Imperial Hotel. The general manager of the hotel, a representative of Japan's royal family, was considering Frank for a lucrative project to design and build a new, modern hotel that would cater to foreign guests and dignitaries.

The architect had imagined that he would be returning to a land of tranquility and beauty, but instead he had taken Mamah into a war zone. Political riots had broken out across the island nation. Citizens who were angry over the corrupt regime of Prince Katsura, Japan's premier, took to the streets with weapons and demanded his removal from office. As many as seventy people were killed or injured in the violent uprising. Frank, Mamah, and Satsu were ordered to remain in their hotel until police and soldiers managed to crush the mob. To prevent more bloodshed, Japan's Emperor Yoshihito ordered Katsura and his cabinet to step down from power.

Despite the chaos, Frank was determined to stay in Japan until he had a signed contract in his hands. The new hotel had an estimated budget of

$7 million, and Frank's commission alone would net him up to $50,000 in architectural design fees.

The money generated by the project would allow Frank to finish work on Taliesin while keeping his creditors at bay.

Frank, Mamah, and Satsu remained in Japan for five months. While in Tokyo, Frank also collected rare Japanese prints on behalf of wealthy buyers in Boston. When they returned to the United States in June 1913, the architect told friends that he had won the project to design and build what he promised would be "the largest [hotel] in the island empire." But the wheels of progress moved slowly in Japan, and plans for the new hotel would remain on hold for several years. Knowing that a promissory note from officials in Japan was not going to pay the bills, Frank set out to land another big project. While Mamah spent time with her children at Taliesin, Frank traveled to Chicago in search of his next commission.

While there, he visited his children in Oak Park and was likely pleasantly surprised that Kitty was now thinking more independently, like Mamah, and had joined the women's suffrage movement. She held a meeting at her home, where a local suffragist and the group's leader, Mary Redfield Plummer, promised to offer their members a clear understanding of the political questions of the day, which included the top priority of voting rights for women. "We will take up the most important issues of the day and have able speakers present the different sides of politics," Plummer told a reporter about the gathering at Kitty's home.

Frank hoped that Kitty's newly acquired passion for women's rights might one day allow for their divorce, but he could not focus his attention on that possibility now as he had a major project looming, perhaps the biggest of his career up to that point. Frank had won the job to design and build a vast entertainment venue in the city to be called Midway Gardens.

The project was announced to the public in January 1914 in an article in the *Chicago Tribune* accompanied by one of Frank's renderings.

He had been approached a few months before by a Chicago real estate developer named Edward Waller with a grand idea. "Frank, in all this black old town there's no place to go but out, nor any place to come but back, that isn't bare and ugly unless it's cheap and nasty," Waller explained. "I want to put a garden in the wilderness of smoky dens, car-tracks and saloons… I believe Chicago would appreciate a beautiful garden resort. Our people would go there, listen to good music, eat and drink."

Waller wanted the venue to have a large outdoor dance floor where guests would sway to the music performed by the National Symphony Orchestra. The space would be called the Summer Garden and would feature three terraces that would resemble flower boxes. To entice guests to enjoy Midway Gardens during the bitterly cold offseason, Waller also asked Frank to design an indoor space called the Winter Garden with the same structural features.

"Frank, I know you could make it unique," Waller told him.

The architect agreed, and Waller suggested they build it on the grounds of an old amusement park just off the city's Midway, which offered three acres of space. Frank asked Waller if he would send over a survey of the park for him to work with. The architect took one look at the survey, a new design came to him almost immediately, and he began to sketch. "The thing had simply shaken off my sleeve," he later recalled.

Waller was overjoyed by Frank's rendering. "I knew it," Waller said, beaming. "You could do it and *this is it*."

Waller set an aggressive schedule for construction and completion of Midway Gardens, which was scheduled to open to the public on May 1, 1914.

"It was a rush job," Frank's son John recalled. "We were to have our working drawings ready for contract in thirty days and the construction completed in ninety days thereafter… I could not start my work until Dad finished the design. When a week rolled by I became worried, thinking that probably he was neglecting his work, but Dad said he was thinking it out."

Frank soon presented John with a blank sheet of paper.

"Here it is," the architect said.

"Where is it?"

"Watch it come out of this clean white sheet."

Frank then took a pencil and moved it swiftly across the paper: up, down, right, left, and slantwise. The design was finished in an hour. John could see low masonry terraces enclosed by promenades, galleries, loggias, and an orchestra shell. Midway Gardens had just come alive in the master architect's hand.

Waller quickly signed off on Frank's design and dreamed of the financial windfall it would bring. Waller wanted to cater his massive entertainment venue to an exclusive clientele, one that was predominantly white.

The African American community of Chicago paid little attention to the hoopla over Midway Gardens. The place might offer Black residents employment eventually, but they would be discouraged from dining and dancing there. Chicago was not the Deep South, but the city was segregated socially and economically just the same.

White residents were often fearful of their Black neighbors, who carried an unfair stigma that was perpetuated by journalists. One story printed in the *Chicago Tribune* in October 1913 described the alleged attack of a young white woman by a biracial man in San Diego, California. "Mrs. Ellen Deeley, aged 20 years, was attacked by a mulatto last night in an exclusive residence section of the city," a reporter wrote. "Her screams, when the negro struck her brought [Chaffee] Grant [son of President Ulysses Grant] to the scene. As the negro fled, Grant shot at him but missed. Miss Deeley was badly bruised. The police have found no trace of her assailant." Although the incident was reported to have occurred over two thousand miles away, white women living in Chicago must have clutched their pearls and wondered if a nameless, faceless "negro" could do the same to them.

African American men like Julian Carlton had to remain vigilant when they ventured into white sections of the city. Carlton was married now to a woman named Gertrude, and together they resided in a brick row house at 4733 Evans Avenue. They made a perfect pair. Gertrude was an excellent cook, while her husband was a jack-of-all-trades. The couple found work together at the opulent home of Chicago restaurateur John Z. Vogelsang at 523 Deming Place on Chicago's north side. Vogelsang owned a German restaurant that was widely popular among the city's most successful lawyers and stock traders. Carlton worked first at the restaurant as either a dishwasher or busboy, but Vogelsang took an immediate liking to him because of his diligent work ethic and handiness and soon employed him as a butler and fix-it man at his majestic home. When Carlton mentioned that his wife was talented in the kitchen, Gertrude soon followed. "He [Carlton] was a good and honest servant who seemed rational at all times," Vogelsang's son said of him later.

Edward Waller hired John Z. Vogelsang to operate the concession and catering business at Midway Gardens. Promising "quick service and hot food," Vogelsang was soon elevated to the general manager position.

Frank and Vogelsang became fast friends. One day, the architect asked the restaurateur if he could recommend someone to fill the butler position at Taliesin. Knowing that his own servant had expressed a desire to move on to another job, Vogelsang said that he had the perfect candidate—Julian Carlton.

21

Julian and Gertrude Carlton left their small living quarters in Chicago and boarded a train bound for Spring Green, Wisconsin, in early June 1914. It appeared that no one in the boardinghouse where they lived was sad to see them go. The couple had not made many friends in the neighborhood, and some people found Carlton quite odd. While attending a party at a neighbor's apartment, one witness said that Carlton leaped around like a madman, making others feel uncomfortable. Another neighbor claimed to have seen Gertrude flee her home in terror at times. John Z. Vogelsang saw no sign of erratic behavior when Carlton worked at his home, so he gladly offered a stellar recommendation to Frank Lloyd Wright, who was looking for a new servant as well as a new cook.

Julian and Gertrude Carlton were received warmly by Mamah when they arrived at Taliesin. Mamah's children, twelve-year-old John and eight-year-old Martha, were on their summer break from school and had planned to spend June, July, and August with their mother, playing in the hills and splashing in the pond on the property on hot summer days. At least that was Mamah's plan. But the children did not like Taliesin, and once they arrived, they wanted to go home. John and Martha had just one potential playmate, a young girl named Edna Kritz. When Edna showed a desire to play with the Borthwick children, neighbors told her father that he should not allow her to visit the home because of all "the goings on" there. Edna's father responded to the warning with a simple question of his own. "Are not the children innocent?" he asked.

Edna became quite close with Martha. They played together, Edna in her simple country dress and Martha in her finest summer clothes and wearing a beautiful sapphire ring to match her eyes. One girl came from humble beginnings and was raised in the Wisconsin countryside, while the other girl was wealthy and perhaps even a future debutante. But they were children after all, and they enjoyed each other's company, along with the many desserts that Gertrude Carlton prepared for them in the kitchen at Taliesin.

Mamah was impressed by the Carltons. The husband and wife both had a strong work ethic, and they were pleasant to be around. "They're simply too good to be true," Mamah told a friend.

Mamah encouraged the children to enjoy the property while she entertained artists and the publisher of the American magazine *The Dial*.

Taliesin was a hive of activity in the summer of 1914, and adding to the bustle were several draftsmen and laborers hired by Frank to transform the property into a working farm and a studio for his apprentices. Leading the project was a local carpenter named William Weston, whose friends called him Billy. Weston brought his thirteen-year-old son Ernest to work with him every day so that he too could learn carpentry in the hope that he would eventually become a master of his craft. Young Ernest also studied under fifty-six-year-old Thomas Brunker, who served as foreman, and two draftsmen, nineteen-year-old Herbert Fritz and thirty-year-old Emil Brodelle. The young architects had been hired by Frank to work on the property and to help him prepare for a major exhibit he had planned to stage in San Francisco. Another man, David Lindbolm, was brought in to plant bushes, trees, and flower beds on the property.

Frank rarely visited Taliesin during the summer months in 1914, as he was still working on the Midway Gardens project, which was "fast growing up out of chaos."

He had struggled with its overall design. Having worked in Chicago for nearly twenty years, he believed that the city was unsophisticated and unspoiled. He decided to create something basic, something that would not resemble a papier-mâché scene painting. "Most places of the kind I had seen at home or abroad were phantasy [*sic*] developed as a cheap, erotic foolishness," he later wrote in his memoir. "In the Midway Gardens there was to be no eroticism. No damned sentimentality either. There was to be [a] permanent structure."

The work was exhausting, both mentally and physically, and Frank recalled that he would sleep on a pile of shavings at the construction site while his son John worked through the night to meet the real estate developer's overly optimistic deadline for completion. Along with lingering questions about the venue's overall design, Frank also had to deal with angry union bosses who did not want scabs working on the jobsite. One union boss pointed to a group of Frank's employees and demanded to see their union cards.

"Don't need cards," Frank told him smugly. "They're artists, sculptors. Can't you see they look that way?"

The union bosses managed to stop work on the large project at least six times during its construction. Frank also had a fight on his hands with Vogelsang, who wanted to erect a big electric sign over the venue with *Midway Gardens* blazing in colored lights. To Frank, this idea fell into the category of "cheap, erotic foolishness" and was ultimately turned down both for aesthetic and financial decisions.

"Money troubles now. Anxiety. Anger. But still hopes and active promises aplenty," he recalled in his memoir.

Although only partially completed, Midway Gardens opened to the public on June 28, 1914. To drum up excitement, Edward Waller took out a front-page advertisement in the *Chicago Tribune*, promising, "This will be a wonderful occasion; you'll surely want to be there. The Opening of Midway Gardens is the dedication of the first permanent home of high class summer music Chicago has ever had."

Opening night featured music by the National Symphony Orchestra, acclaimed concert violinist Max Bendix, and dancers Teresa and Placida Battagi, who were on loan from the Chicago Grand Opera Company. The evening gala was a success, according to the *Tribune*, as Chicago's elite came out in their tuxedos and gowns to enjoy three live musical programs and fine cuisine. "Too many persons were there for comfort, though the service was better than might have been expected for a corps of green waiters," wrote a reviewer for the *Tribune*.

Frank, his son John, and their team of "artists and sculptors" would continue their work on the winter gardens section of the venue throughout the summer.

Business at Midway Gardens soon tailed off amid great uncertainty over the June 28 assassination of Austrian Archduke Franz Ferdinand in Sarajevo, a tragedy that would eventually push America into the First World War.

At Taliesin, Mamah worked successfully to repair her relationship with Ellen Key. The Swedish writer wrote Mamah a letter of forgiveness, and she replied with a note of her own on July 14.

Dear Ellen Key,

Beloved Lady,

You cannot believe how happy you make me with your letter. It gave me great relief as well as joy in itself.

Mamah was finally coming into her own. With her translation work for Key, she earned her own money, independently of Frank. She was living her life by her own rules as a modern woman. It was a life she hoped would inspire women for generations to come. The public perception of her also started to turn in her favor. Librarians across the Midwest soon began to denounce the type of sensational, yellow journalism that had placed Mamah and Frank in the crosshairs of their neighbors, members of the clergy, and newspaper readers across the country. Librarians crusaded against what they called *affinity fiction* and refused to carry newspaper editions that published scandalous stories about the couple. Now, instead of portraying her as a manipulative adulteress and home-wrecker, newsmen wrote glowingly about her. "Ms. Borthwick is indifferent to the publicity," one reporter wrote. "She is a very remarkable woman. Her work suffices. She does it in a leisurely, concentrated fashion, working twenty minutes on a sentence of translation sometimes, and never counting the time lost… The clever woman composes and translates, while the architect wrestles with elevations and the problems of architecture. There are five men working in the drafting room… All these men are devoted to 'Mamah of the Hills.'"

Other journalists who were invited to Taliesin were also in awe of Mamah. "[She] is a beautiful woman still in the prime of her loveliness of person," another reporter gushed. "Clever in speech and fluent with pen in expressing herself, she is a woman fitted intellectually and otherwise to hold her own in a drawing room."

She had also won the approval of Frank's second eldest. "Mamah…was a cultured, respected and sensitive woman," John Wright remembered. "Her laugh had the same quality of Dad's, so did her love and her interest in his work."

Yet despite Mamah's new and improved image, some townspeople in Spring Green still refused to go anywhere near Taliesin, as they believed it to be cursed by the sinful acts of those who lived there.

22

Gertrude Carlton was startled awake by her husband as he climbed out of their bed and peered out the window of their bedroom inside the bungalow. Julian Carlton told his wife to remain silent and listen for noises.

"They're trying to get me," he whispered.

Gertrude had hoped that her husband's erratic behavior would subside once they left the choked streets of Chicago for the open fields of the Wisconsin countryside, but instead, he grew more dangerous. When Gertrude attempted to quell his paranoia by speaking rationally to him, Carlton got angry and wrapped his strong hands around her delicate throat and squeezed while she struggled to breathe.

"I'll knock your brains out," he warned her.

He began carrying a small hatchet to bed with him each night to ward off any real or imagined enemies who could bust down his door and drag him off in the darkness.

Was Julian Carlton merely reacting to the fear stirred by stories of lynchings of young, African American men that were still regularly published in newspapers? Or was he suffering from an undiagnosed mental illness?

One day, Carlton complained of a painful toothache and told his wife that he had to see a dentist in Madison. He then left Taliesin and walked to the Spring Green train station. He likely received curious looks from passersby as he kicked up gravel during his long, lonely walk to the train station, as most villagers had never seen an African American person before. Carlton did not travel to Madison that day. Instead, he bought a train ticket to Chicago. After arriving there, he sent a telegram to Gertrude informing her of his change of destination but refused to elaborate as to why he had traveled to Chicago. Carlton returned to Taliesin a few days later. He gave no explanation about his mysterious trip to his wife, and she likely did not ask out of fear that he would act on his threat to "knock her brains out."

Later, Carlton left the property again, this time to visit an apothecary shop in Spring Green. He purchased a small bottle of muriatic (hydrochloric) acid from the pharmacist.

"I need this for the farm's supplies," Carlton told him.

For the next several nights, Carlton got little sleep and instead stood as a sentry at their bedroom window with the hatchet held firmly in his powerful grip.

Gertrude did not alert Mamah or any of the workers at Taliesin about her husband's terrifying behavior. She enjoyed her time there and did not want to jeopardize their employment. "We were treated well and liked the place," she recalled later.

On August 12, 1914, draftsman Emil Brodelle barked an order at Carlton. Brodelle wanted him to saddle his horse for a ride into town. Since this task was likely not within the scope of his daily work, Carlton refused the command. The young, cocky architect did not like being told no, especially by an African American man he believed was beneath him. Brodelle launched into a verbal attack against Carlton, calling him the N-word and using other racial epithets to insult him in front of several other workmen.

Carlton stood his ground during the exchange and was determined not to handle Brodelle's saddle for him. After the altercation, he told Gertrude that he was done working at Taliesin. Carlton told his wife to notify their employer, Mamah Borthwick, that they were quitting their jobs and moving back to Chicago.

"Tell her that we're homesick," he ordered his wife.

The Carltons had been working at Taliesin for less than two full months. With several more weeks of dinner parties planned, Mamah was concerned that there would be no one to cook and clean up after her guests. She was likely unaware of Carlton's encounter with the racist draftsman when she reprimanded him over his abrupt decision to quit his job. Mamah reluctantly agreed to Carlton's request, even convincing herself that it was her decision to let him and Gertrude go. Carlton agreed to stay on for a few more days while Mamah found replacements for him and his wife.

During this time, he steered clear of Emil Brodelle, who was still outraged over the fact that a Black man had refused his demand to saddle his horse. Carlton did his best to keep to himself as Gertrude presented a happy face to Mamah and the children while she cooked for them and the Taliesin work crew.

Carlton did ask project manager Billy Weston where he kept his gasoline. It was an odd request from the butler, as he did not own an automobile.

"A rug has become soiled," Carlton explained. "I need some gas to clean it."

Weston pointed to the barn where the canisters were kept and went about his daily tasks while Carlton disappeared into the barn in search of gas.

Frank was oblivious to the goings on at Taliesin as he remained bogged down with work at Midway Gardens. Construction continued on the venue's towers, and sculptures still needed to be painted and put in place while more furnishings were added. Frank had planned to return to Taliesin on Saturday, August 15, in order to spend the weekend with Mamah and her children, but project challenges kept him hard at work at his drafting desk in Chicago.

That morning began like most others at Taliesin, with the sun rising over the nearby hills and beaming slowly into the bedrooms of Mamah and her children, John and Martha Cheney. The temperature was stifling, and Mamah had planned to take lunch that day on a screen-enclosed porch overlooking the Wisconsin River where the breeze would bring them a brief respite from the heat.

To serve lunch, Julian Carlton replaced his overalls with a white dress coat and stepped into the kitchen to see what his wife was cooking. She prepared meals for Mamah and the children along with the workers. The parties did not dine together, however; Brodelle, Weston, young Ernest Weston, Thomas Brunker, Herb Fritz, and David Lindblom all bumped elbows together at a table in a small dining room, referred to as the men's dining room in Frank's design sketches, twenty-five feet away from where Mamah and the children were sitting down for lunch in the north section of the bungalow. The time was approximately 12:30 p.m.

The kitchen was halfway between both dining areas. Carlton made two trips to the kitchen, serving the workers first before he served Mamah and the kids. When he left the racist architect Brodelle and the others in the dining room, Carlton quietly bolted the door from the outside. He then fetched three bowls of cold summer soup in the kitchen and headed for the screened-in porch. Carlton smiled politely at Mamah and the children as he set the chilled bowls in front of them. Each grabbed their napkins and tucked them under their chin. Gertrude's cooking was so delicious that they may have leaned into the soup bowls with their noses to sniff the aroma.

Carlton then unbuttoned his white tunic and reached in, wrapping his fingers around the sharp hatchet that he had hidden under this clothing. The back of Mamah's long, bare neck was exposed to him as she took the first sip of her soup.

Young John Cheney noticed something demonic in Carlton's eyes.

"Oh, Mama, look at Julian," he reportedly exclaimed.

Before Mamah could look up, Carlton swung the hatchet high above his head and brought it back down with tremendous force. The hatchet blade struck Mamah near dead center in the back of her head, splitting her skull in two. She fell forward with her head hitting the soup bowl while blood gushed from the open wound, turning the white tablecloth a dark red mess. Mamah Borthwick, the love of Frank's life, was killed instantly and without warning.

Carlton then turned his attention to the startled children. He would go for John first, as the twelve-year-old boy posed the greatest risk to him. But the child was too afraid to move. He likely stared at his dead mother for a moment while Carlton pulled the hatchet from her bloodied skull. Carlton then leaned over the table and swung it toward her son, striking him down with one fatal blow. John Cheney died in his chair. That left only Martha Cheney alive.

The savage butchering of her brother gave the girl a chance to run. With fresh blood spatter covering her summer dress, Martha sprinted out of the room and down the long corridor, screaming for help. The workmen must have heard the girl's cries, but they could not immediately investigate the noise as the door was locked from the outside.

Carlton ran down the hallway after her with the hatchet as if he were chasing a chicken around the yard. The girl made it outside the bungalow and into the courtyard. Carlton caught up with Martha near the fountain, snatched her by her hair, and struck her three times with the small hatchet. The girl collapsed onto the ground, her dress covered with more blood. Her screams subsided with each swing of the hatchet.

Carlton's white service coat was now dripping with the blood of his three innocent victims. But the killer was not done yet. In fact, the carnage was just beginning.

Carlton grabbed the can of gasoline that he had claimed he needed to fix a stain on a rug and returned to the dining room where the men had been eating and heard some rustling inside. He fished a pipe out of his back pocket and lit it with a match. Carlton took the can of gas and began pouring it onto the rug and under the door into the dining room. He took one last drag from his pipe and dropped it onto the pool of gas, the fiery embers of tobacco igniting a blaze that climbed up the door and under it into the eating area. The workers all thought it was nothing but soap suds that had spilled outside.

"The liquid ran under my chair, and I noticed the odor of gasoline," worker Herbert Fritz recalled. "Just as I was about to remark [on] the fact, a flame shot under my chair, and it looked like the whole side of the room was on fire." Flames and smoke quickly filled the dining room with Fritz and the other men trapped inside. Feeling a searing burn to his legs and arms, Fritz realized that he was on fire and stumbled toward a window that could lead to his escape from this hell.

"I plunged through [the window] and landed on the rocks outside," Fritz later said. "My arm was broken in the fall, and the flames had eaten through my clothes and were burning me."

He then rolled over and over down the hill toward a creek but stopped halfway. The fire was out. Fritz struggled back up the hill, where he saw Carlton running about the property with a hatchet in his hand. Overcome by pain, Fritz lost consciousness and collapsed in the courtyard.

The workers still stuck inside the burning bungalow had a terrible decision to make. Should they attempt to run through the flames or jump through the window where they would likely meet the sharp end of Carlton's hatchet? Either choice was a potential death sentence. One man tried to rush through the flames but was pushed back by the intensity of the fire. Young Ernest Weston ran toward the window and attempted to leap out. Carlton saw the boy coughing from the smoke and flailing his arms at the window frame. He rushed over and buried his hatchet in the teenager's back. The younger Weston, an apprentice to his father, fell out the window, got up, and stumbled to the fountain before he fell dead.

The next man to attempt an escape was Emil Brodelle, who had berated

Carlton with racial slurs just days before. Brodelle had much to live for. He had just become engaged to a woman, and they were planning their lives together. Carlton was not going to allow that to happen. He swung his bloodied hatchet at Brodelle, the blade entering the man's skull just over his left ear. Brodelle fell out the window and landed in the courtyard. The initial blow was enough to kill him.

Landscape designer David Lindblom managed to get out of the burning home. "The door was a wall of fire, so I dived out," he later told a reporter. Lindblom attempted to crawl for safety on his hands and knees, his lungs filled with smoke. Carlton watched for a moment and then swung his hatchet once more, striking Lindblom as he looked up with a blow to his forehead. It was a near-fatal wound, but somehow, Lindblom was still alive.

Billy Weston, the project manager, made his escape and was staggering toward the body of his son, Ernest, when he too was struck by Carlton's hatchet with a slanting blow. Weston was cut deeply but somehow survived the attack. He collapsed to the ground where he closed his eyes, held his breath, and played dead. "The ax struck me in the neck and knocked me down, but not unconscious," Weston later said. "I got up and ran and the negro after me. Then I fell and he hit me again and I guess he thought he had me because he ran back to the window and I got up and ran. When I looked back, the negro had disappeared."

Tom Brunker, the last man inside the dining room, also managed to survive the ordeal, suffering from severe burns and violent blows from Carlton's sharp weapon.

The flames destroyed the dining room and had now engulfed the servants' quarters. Gertrude Carlton also fled, but not before she stopped to put on her best hat. She tried to escape through the basement but found a stubborn door that would not budge. Instead, she hurled herself out a window and ran down the hill to safety. "I cannot give a single reason for his mad act," Gertrude said later. "All I know is I've been scared of him for two weeks. He's been mean to me but I never thought he'd do such a thing… The Wrights were good to us."

The fire was now rising high above Taliesin, and Julian Carlton decided it was time to make his escape. He chose a place where he figured no one would look.

23

Uncle Jenk Lloyd Jones was among the first to notice smoke coming from his nephew's bungalow. He was spending his vacation in Spring Green, hoping it would provide him a peaceful respite from the hustle and bustle of Chicago. Taliesin was burning, and Jenk rang an alarm bell, quickly saddled his horse, and rode to the property to investigate. He could not have imagined what was waiting for him there.

Severely wounded but somehow back on their feet, Herbert Fritz and David Lindblom began dragging the bodies of the dead away from the burning building. Jenk inspected the gruesome, bloody corpses of Ernest Weston and Emil Brodelle. Clearly, they had not suffered their wounds in the fire alone. The two young men had been hacked to death. Jenk summoned his sisters to open their nearby school to treat any victims who had survived the attack. Fritz and Lindblom gave him the name of the killer—Julian Carlton—and a description. Billy Weston raced down the hill to the home of a neighbor named Rieder, as he knew the man had a telephone. Weston called the sheriff and told him to bring every available deputy that he had to Taliesin.

At this point, Carlton was nowhere in sight. He had simply vanished after causing so much death and destruction.

Jenk had not brought his rifle with him on his ride to Taliesin because he believed he would not need it to lead a bucket brigade to try to save the bungalow. The Unitarian minister climbed on his horse and rode back to his property to fetch his weapon, wondering, after so many years since he had fought in the Civil War, whether he would need to kill again.

Hundreds of Spring Green villagers climbed on horses, piled into buggies, or simply ran toward Taliesin to help with whatever was going on there. Once the men learned of the deadly attack, they split themselves into two groups. While crowds of men grabbed buckets of water from the pond and nearby river to douse the flames, others, hell-bent on vengeance, spread out and disappeared into the cornfields in search of Julian Carlton.

Edna Kritz had just finished attending Saturday services at the nearby Our Lady's Assumption church and was wearing her best dress when she arrived at Taliesin with her father. While most villagers did not know their way around the property because they had been wary of visiting there, young Edna was quite familiar with the bungalow, having played inside the home several times with John and Martha Cheney. Like Uncle Jenk, Edna also believed that she and her father were responding to a fire on the property, nothing less, nothing more. The girl jumped off her horse, Beauty, and climbed the gnarled roots of the children's favorite tree, one they called Widow's Walk, where she and Martha had played house with their dolls. From her elevated vantage point in the tall tree, she noticed a blackened body lying face down in a quarry. Her hands began to tremble, and she started to cry. "Hail Mary, full of grace. The Lord is with thee, the Lord is with me," she whispered to herself over and over again.

"It is bad to be nearly nine and so afraid," Edna thought to herself. "I did not come for this—Thing, whatever it is. An unknown that is sensed all around the willows. Troubling and secret as reasons the house is strange."

Edna felt her father's arms wrap around her as he lifted her out of the tree and placed her on the ground. She stopped crying and tried to brace herself for what was to come. Father and daughter walked slowly through the rubble and climbed a set of stone stairs where they felt they would be safe. Edna took notice of a small figure lying on the ground under a large white towel. The head was partially covered. Edna could see a ball of singed hair and eyelashes on a blackened face. "That is not Martha," she told herself. Her own eyes traced the outline of the body from the face to the arms. A tiny hand poked out from underneath the towel and lay flat on the ground. Edna studied the hand and saw that the victim wore a sapphire ring on her finger. At that moment, she knew the victim was her playmate, Martha Cheney.

The killer's description was shared with local authorities, who then wired it to all stations along the railroad lines within a distance of fifty miles.

Herbert Fritz sent a brief and understated telegram to his parents' home in Chicago.

Dear Mother:

Our house burned. Am all right. Don't worry.

Herbert

But now, someone had to break the tragic news to both Frank Lloyd Wright and Edwin Cheney.

Frank was sitting down to a late lunch at the newly finished bar at Midway Gardens when his stenographer walked into the room. "Mr. Wright, you are wanted on the telephone," she told him.

There was an uneasy tone to the woman's voice. Frank looked at his son John and said nothing. He pushed his chair away from the lunch table, stood up, and followed the stenographer to the telephone.

A friend of Frank's from Madison, Wisconsin, named Frank Roth told him that Taliesin was on fire but that he had no more information to share.

Frank returned to the bar where John had his nose in his work. John did not look up at his father, but he could hear his heavy breathing. Frank then let out a loud groan as he reached for a table for support. His face was ghostly white.

"What's happened, Dad?"

Frank did not offer an answer. Instead, he gave a quiet order for his son to hail them a taxi.

"What for, Dad? What has happened to you? What's the trouble?"

"Taliesin is on fire," Frank mumbled. "Mamah, the children, the students [meaning his young draftsmen], what if they're hurt? Why did I leave them?"

At around 2:00 p.m. that day, a telegram arrived at Midway Gardens, summoning Frank back to Taliesin because "something terrible" had happened. The telegram was signed with Mamah's initials, *MMB*.

Reading the telegram, Frank breathed a sigh of relief that Mamah must still be alive.

John took his father by the arm and escorted him to the street where a taxi was waiting. The cab driver drove them both to the train station where John purchased two tickets on the next train to Spring Green. They were not alone at the station; Edwin Cheney was there too with his own ticket in hand. A crowd of reporters had gathered at the train platform. John purchased a private compartment on the train and pushed both men inside before newsmen began badgering each of them with their queries.

Once inside the compartment, Cheney reached over and clasped Frank's hand. Neither man knew exactly what was waiting for them at Taliesin, but both were praying for the best. The trio was joined on the train by Frank's lawyer, Sherman Booth.

What began as a three-hour journey of dread and hope turned more tragic at each stop for the slow-moving locomotive. Reporters descended on each train station, hoping to ask questions of the famous architect. Frank had no information to share. Instead, it was the reporters themselves who had most of the answers up to that point.

"I have often tried to erase from my mind the anguish that was in Dad's face in that feebly lighted compartment when he learned the ghastly details from the reporters and heard them shouted from the throats of newsboys along the way: 'Taliesin Burning to the Ground, Seven Slain!'"

Frank's nephew, Robert Lloyd Jones, met them when the evening train rolled into Spring Green. Frank was growing weaker by the minute and teetered on collapse. His legs were jelly when he stepped out of the train and onto the platform. Jones grabbed his uncle by the collar of his coat. "Stand up, Frank," he shouted. "It couldn't be worse. Get a hold of yourself!"

THE OGDEN STANDARD

THE TERRIBLE FATE OF MAMAH BORTHWICK IN HER BUNGALOW OF LOVE

Woman, Who With Frank Lloyd Wright, Dared Live Contrary to Accepted Rules of Conduct, Meets Disaster in a Few Short Years

Newspapers across the United States reported many of the grisly details about the tragedy at Taliesin, the so-called Bungalow of Love. (OGDEN STANDARD EXAMINER)

Frank shook his arms and his legs as if he were trying to exorcise himself from the clutches of an invisible demon.

"Thirty-six hours earlier I had left Taliesin leaving all living, friendly and happy," he later wrote in his memoir. "Now the blow had fallen like a lightning stroke."

Finally, when pressed by a reporter for comment, Frank muttered, "The Carlton's, Julian and his wife, were the best servants I have ever seen. The wife cooked and Julian was a general handyman…and Julian especially seemed to have an intelligence above the average and a good education for one of his class… Three days ago when I last saw him, he seemed perfectly normal. He must have lost his mind and yet I cannot believe that the news is true. The fact that the telegram signed M.B.B was received after the alleged murders buoys my hopes."

He would never learn who had sent him that mysterious telegram with the initials *MBB*. But Frank was still clinging to a miracle. He needed to see the dead for himself in order to make it real.

Grief like this was too much for any man, let alone two. Edwin Cheney was told that his innocent children, John and Martha, had been murdered by a madman with an axe.

But where was the killer, Julian Carlton, now?

24

The posse formed of farmhands turned vigilantes by Iowa County Sheriff John T. Williams continued scouring the Spring Green countryside after dark. The last person to report having seen Julian Carlton was the injured workman Herbert Fritz, and he had no idea where the suspect had run off to. Lawmen had found Carlton's wife, Gertrude, within an hour of the search. She was hiding in a clump of bushes by the roadside three miles from Taliesin. Sheriffs' deputies arrested her on the spot and brought her to the nearest jail for questioning. Out in the cornfields, Uncle Jenk, other members of the posse, and even bloodhounds had turned up nothing.

Some men surmised that Carlton may have escaped down the Wisconsin River in a canoe.

At dusk, a group of armed men began poking around the smoldering embers of the bungalow when they heard a noise coming from an unused furnace. Sheriff Williams was alerted and arrived at the scene moments later with his pistol drawn. Williams opened the furnace and spotted Julian Carlton, crouched on his hands and knees in the tight space. The asbestos insulation of the furnace had shielded Carlton from the flames and severe heat.

The sheriff quickly yanked the fugitive murder suspect out of the furnace and onto his feet. Carlton still had the bloody hatchet in his hand but was too ill to swing it. There was an empty bottle found in the furnace where Carlton had been hiding. When asked what it was, Carlton groaned, "Acid."

The killer had swallowed the muriatic acid that he had recently purchased at a pharmacy in town.

A crowd of men quickly surrounded the sheriff and his suspect. After the carnage they had witnessed, including the butchering of a mother and her two young children, many townspeople felt that there was no need for a trial in this case and that whatever penalty the judge ultimately handed down to Carlton was too good for him. The men cocked their weapons, and one of them brandished a rope. They planned to march the murderer at gunpoint to the nearest tall tree and hang him for his sins.

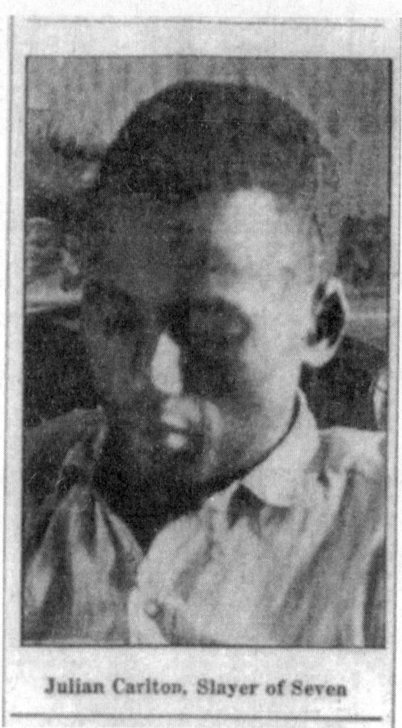

The only known photograph of accused mass murderer Julian Carlton, taken after his capture in 1914. (Chicago Tribune)

Sheriff Williams had to act quickly before the mob got out of hand. He called for a police wagon to meet them at the back of the burned-out bungalow. The vehicle swung around and formed a barrier between the angry men and the murder suspect. Carlton could not walk on his own, so the sheriff and a deputy cuffed him, lifted him up, and pushed him through the side window of the police wagon. The lawmen then climbed into the vehicle and took off down the road. They were headed to the local jail in Spring Green.

Carlton lay down in the back seat, moaning from the pain in his burned throat. The sheriff had no desire to bring the suspect to the nearest hospital to have his throat checked and his stomach pumped. The only way that Carlton could be protected from the mob was to place him safely behind bars at the jailhouse.

Sheriff Williams looked out the back of the police wagon and saw they were being followed by villagers on horseback and groups of men piled into three automobiles. The vigilantes had not given up on the idea of lynching Carlton. The sheriff ordered his deputy to gun the engine in the hope of putting themselves at a safe distance from the mob. After a few more miles, the vigilantes gave up their chase.

Later, when they arrived at the jailhouse, sheriff's deputies gave Carlton milk to soothe his throat and whiskey for the pain. Their mission was to keep the killer alive so that they could stand him before a judge to explain what he did and why he did it.

Meanwhile, six armed men were stationed back at Taliesin to protect the property from looters as Frank, John, Edwin Cheney, and lawyer Sherman Booth made their way from the train station to the crime scene.

Storm clouds had formed over Spring Green, and a strong wind whipped the solemn faces of the men as they rode by car in the direction of black smoke billowing in the distance. A crackle of summer lightning could be heard in the distance.

John felt the eyes of villagers on them during the brief journey to Taliesin. He described the scene this way: "Shadows of men taking on exaggerated proportions in the darkness, running hither and thither—rays of flashlights darted here and there—lanterns swinging in mid-air detached from the bodies that supported them."

Frank's son called the onlookers morbidly curious ghouls, "[pushing] madly to see how one looks when he suffers. Pharisees—Sadducers—sadists, standing in huddled groups whispering, and the heinous crime laid at the feet of God, who through [a killer], demanded the brutal murder of seven of His children."

Frank and Edwin demanded to see their loved ones first. They were driven to a neighbor's house where the remains of Mamah, John, and Martha had been collected and were lying under towels and blankets. First responders had managed to pull what was left of Mamah and her twelve-year-old son, John, from the smoldering bungalow, their charred bodies burned almost beyond recognition. Martha Cheney's clothes were almost burned off her body.

The children's grieving father, along with Mamah's distraught soulmate, studied the dead and offered silent prayers for their eternal rest. "She for whom Taliesin had first taken form and her two children—gone," Frank recounted solemnly in his memoir.

After an evening of much-needed rain for the village, dawn broke the following morning, and the sun shone brightly over Spring Green. A reporter for the *Tribune* awoke early to capture the mood and atmosphere on his notepad to later share with readers back in Chicago. "Dawn across the valley of Wright's landscaped Eden kingdom—a farmhand drove a herd of prized cows to the milking sheds to the tinkling accompaniment of the bell cow's music," he wrote. "A turtledove set up a melody of doleful notes from an overhanging pine. A cock sparrow as vociferous and cosmopolitan as his city bred brothers set up a row in the trampled loggia. The routine of the day had begun in the valley."

But of course this was no routine day in Spring Green. Something evil had entered the valley. That evil had wiped out a family and several men who had arrived at the bungalow on that fateful Saturday to put in an honest day's work. Now they were dead. The *Tribune* news article that day was accompanied by photos of Mamah, John, and Martha Cheney, all alive and staring innocently into the camera.

That morning, Frank and Edwin Cheney had breakfast together at the home of Frank's sister, Jane Porter, a place they called Tan-y-Deri. Neither man touched his food. The house was now a makeshift hospital as victims

Tom Brunker and David Lindblom were seriously wounded, bedridden, and cared for by nurses and other volunteers. On the night of the attack, Jane Porter's six-year-old son, Franklin, saw the victims lying on improvised beds on the porch, just below his bedroom. The young boy could hear their constant, painful moaning, which lasted well beyond sunrise.

After breakfast, Frank and Cheney split up and walked the ruins of Taliesin on their own. Frank sifted through the rubble, much of it still hot to the touch. He pulled out a broken piece of a porcelain vase and scraped away the ashes. "Satsuma. $250 in Japan," he whispered.

Scattered around him were the remnants of expensive Japanese prints that he had recently collected during his visit there with Mamah.

His long, wavy hair was uncombed, and he was still wearing the suit, now wrinkled, that he had left Chicago in the evening before. Frank lifted his eyes from the smoky pile of debris and scanned his property. "I will rebuild it all—every line of it," he pledged to himself. "As it was before when she…" His voice drifted off as he fought back tears. "This is home."

Frank and Cheney later returned to the Porter home, where they quietly discussed next steps.

"Once, years ago, she [Mamah] said that if anything ever happens to the children, I want their bodies cremated," Cheney told Frank. "I will take the bodies of the children back to Chicago to fulfill that wish."

It would be up to Frank to decide what to do with Mamah's remains. "We will bury her here," he told the ex-husband.

25

Edwin Cheney gathered the remains of his beloved children and placed them in a single casket before calling for an automobile that would take him to the train station. As he left Jane Porter's house, he nodded to Frank.

"I'm going now."

"Goodbye, Ed."

"Goodbye, Frank."

Cheney was driven to the depot, where reporters eagerly awaited any comment that he would make about the tragedy. The grieving father obliged.

"Are you not remaining for the funeral of Ms. Borthwick?" a newsman asked.

Cheney paused. "No, I am only here to take the bodies of my children home for cremation. You may say however, there will be no funeral, either here or in Chicago. Concerning Ms. Borthwick, you must talk to…to someone else."

"Will you take any part in the prosecution?"

"I don't know," Cheney replied. "I don't even know what happened. Until I do, I shall not know what I will do."

Cheney asked the reporter whether there was any news from the jailhouse regarding Julian Carlton. The reporter told Cheney that law enforcement officials believed that the man had gone insane.

"Do you believe there could be any other explanation of the crime? There have been rumors, you know?"

The reporter was referring to gossip that Carlton had not acted alone. There was no explanation given for his recent visit to Chicago. Did Carlton meet with gangsters who were angry that Frank was not using enough union laborers for the Midway Gardens project? Did Carlton meet with some rogue members of clergy who wanted Mamah Borthwick struck down for her alleged sins? Did he meet with Kitty Wright, who may have plotted murderous revenge against Mamah for stealing her husband? The conspiracy theories, while intriguing, seemed preposterous.

"I am sure that he was insane and that there was no other reason," Cheney replied, his voice firm, before he boarded the train.

Back at Taliesin, Frank could not yet afford to think about why Julian Carlton had gone on a murderous rampage as he had the overwhelming burden of burying the love of his life.

He called it a "primitive burial" with no fanfare. "I felt that a funeral service would be a mockery," Frank wrote in his memoir. "The undertaker's office too, his vulgar casket, seemed profane to me." Instead, he had his carpenters build a simple pine box.

Members of the Lloyd Jones family, including Frank's uncle Enos, brought their shovels to a quiet spot near the family chapel where Frank's grandparents had been laid to rest many years before. Frank got a pair of long pruning shears and clipped a bushel of bright zinnias and dahlias from the garden that Mamah had cultivated and lined the box with them. Frank's son John watched his father from a distance while he placed the remaining flowers over Mamah's body and her face until they were completely covered. John walked over to his father and helped him lift the box onto a small spring wagon that was also decorated with a collection of Mamah's favorite annuals and perennials. "We made the whole thing a mass of flowers," Frank remembered. "It helped a little."

With the pine box sealed shut, two of Frank's horses, whom he had affectionately named Darby and Joan, pulled the wagon slowly toward the final resting spot that he had selected for his beloved. "I watched his great but quiet suffering as he walked along the wheels," John wrote later. "The little sorrel team pulled the wagon along the road to the family chapel where no people were waiting. I watched him… I followed."

The dirt road to the chapel was bare. Neighbors did not come out to pay their respects, which was how Frank wanted it. No bell rang in the churchyard.

Frank was stoic when John and two cousins lowered the pine box into the freshly dug ground in the shadow of the family chapel. Frank did not cry; he did not pray. "His face bore the expression of one not on earth," John recalled. "It seemed to me that in that moment his soul soared up to God and Besought him to join her."

Frank then asked his family members to leave. He would fill the grave himself. Frank fought a sudden urge to climb into the dark hole with her. He tried to savor the last moments he had with Mamah, reflecting on their deep love and commitment to each other in the face of almost insurmountable odds. No one had wanted their relationship to succeed, not their families, not journalists, and not society at large. Yet they had accomplished something very rare and beautiful, but it would not last. As the African proverb went, *Somewhere, the sky touched the earth, and that place is the end.* Frank had reached his dark horizon.

"The August sun was setting I remember on the familiar range of hills," Frank wrote in his memoir. "Dimly, I felt coming in far off shadows of the ages struggling to escape from subconsciousness and utter themselves… Then slowly came darkness… I filled the grave, staying there in the dark. It was friendly."

There would be no headstone, no monument to mark Mamah's grave.

"All I had left to show for the struggle for freedom of the five years past that had swept most of my former life away, now had been swept away." Frank later explained. "Why mark the spot where desolation ended and began?"

At twilight, Frank returned to Taliesin and his work studio, which had somehow survived the fire. His son was waiting for him there. Frank asked him to return to Chicago and continue the work on Midway Gardens. But John wished to stay by his father's side in his moment of deep grief. "Memories rushed before me," he recalled. "When I had a fever, he was at my bedside. When I broke my leg, he left all his important work…[and] directed the doctor in setting the bone. He would not leave my side until I was out of danger. Time and again in my childhood he proved his devotion… And now, I did not want to go. I did not want to leave him alone."

Frank appreciated such devotion from his son. He tried to smile as he urged John once more to leave Taliesin and all its horrors behind. Only the famed architect could pick up the pieces from there.

Frank stayed at the burned-out bungalow for several more days; his only companion was a watchman who sat on the steps with a loaded shotgun across his knees. Everyone in Spring Green remained on alert for another possible attack, as rumors continued to spread that Julian Carlton may not have acted alone. Would a coconspirator come to Taliesin in the darkness, slit Frank's throat while he slept, and finish Carlton's murderous mission?

But Frank could not sleep. He stayed awake night after night, lying on a cot in the little back room of his studio. He took cold baths and roamed the property in the early morning hours, not really knowing where he was going. The sky was pitch-black, and the countryside was silent. There were no stars and no croaking sounds coming from the frogs living in Frank and Mamah's pond.

"But I would come back safely again with only a sense of the black night and the strange fear, no beauty visible any more. Grope how I might—to help from that source. And I would find my way back to bed." For the first time in his life, Frank felt utterly alone. "Something strange had happened to me. Instead of feeling that She [Mamah], whose life had joined mine there at Taliesin, was a spirit near, she was utterly gone. After the first terrible anguish, a kind of black despair seemed to paralyze my imagination in her direction and numbed my sensibilities. The blow was too severe."

For a time, try as he might, Frank could not remember the sound of Mamah's voice, and he struggled to see her face in his mind's eye. His brain had shut down, and he had blocked her from his memory. In a vain attempt to visualize the images of her that he could no longer see, Frank sat down at a small piano with broken legs, which had been thrown out the window of Taliesin in an attempt to save it from the fire, and tried to play for her. But the darkness was all-consuming. "Days strangely without light would follow the black nights. Totally—she was gone."

He was overcome by a numbness of body and soul. The famed architect lost weight, and boils broke out on his neck and back. Frank had prided himself on his vision, but now his eyesight was failing, and he was struggling to see clearly. But he refused any help or support from his family. "My mother was deeply hurt by my refusal to have her with me," he later wrote. "My children—I had welcomed them eagerly always—I did not want them now."

He felt like a stranger to all around him. Through his grief, Frank wrote a lengthy letter to be printed in Spring Green's *Weekly Home* newspaper. Titled "To My Neighbors," it served as part eulogy, part indictment of the press and critique of society, and part mission statement for his plans to rise again, phoenix-like, from the ashes.

To you who have rallied so bravely and well to our assistance—to you who have been invariably kind to us all—I would like to say something to defend a brave and lovely woman from the pestilential touch of stories made by the press for the man on the street, even now with the loyal fellows lying dead beside her, any of whom would have given his life to defend her.

I cannot bear to leave unsaid things that might brighten the memory of her in the mind of anyone. But they must be left unsaid. I believe at no time has anything been shown her as she moved in your midst but courtesy and sympathy. This she won for herself by her innate dignity and gentleness of character, but another—perhaps any other community—would have seen her through the eyes of the press that even now insists upon decorating her death with the fact, first and foremost, that she was once another man's wife, "a wife who left her children."

That must not be forgotten in this man-made world.

A wife still is "property"... The birds of prey were loosed upon her in death as well as in life to feed that Moloch of the heart that maintains itself at the cost of "the man on the street," by preaching to him in vulgar language the gospel of mediocrity... Mamah and I have had our struggles, our differences, our moments of jealous fear for our ideals of each other—they are not lacking in any close human relationships—but they served only to bind us more closely together. We were more than merely happy even when momentarily miserable. And she was true as only a woman who loves knows the meaning of the word. Her soul has entered me and it shall not be lost.

You wives with your certificates of loving—pray that you may love as much and be loved as well as was Mamah Borthwick! You mothers and fathers with daughters—be satisfied if what life you have invested in them works itself out upon as high a plane as it has done in the life of this lovely woman. She was struck down by a tragedy that hangs by the slender thread of reason over the lives of all, a thread which may snap at any time in any home with consequences as disastrous.

And I would urge you upon young and old alike that "Nature knows neither Past nor Future—the Present is her Eternity." Unless we realize that brave truth there will come a bitter time when the thought of how much more potent with love and action that precious "Present" might have been, will desolate our hearts.

She is dead. I have buried her in the little Chapel burying ground of my people—beside the little son of my sister, a beautiful boy of ten, who loved her and whom she loved very much—and while the place where she lived with me is a charred and blackened ruin, the little things of our daily life gone, I shall replace it all little by little as nearly as it may be done. I shall set it all up again for the spirit of the mortals that lived in it and loved it—will live in it still. My home will still be there.

Frank Lloyd Wright

Frank would try not to dwell on the past or the present, as there was a glimmer of light that was now pointing him toward his future. Frank vowed to rebuild his home, his only monument to Mamah, which had been destroyed by what he called "hateful forces."

26

After spending the first night locked up inside the Spring Green jailhouse, Julian Carlton was transferred to the larger county jail in nearby Dodgeville where he was guarded by nine sheriff's deputies, all armed to prevent any escape or to thwart the local lynch mob.

Given the severe injuries to his throat after swallowing the bottle of acid, the murder suspect was not saying much, but he did attempt to get lawmen to believe that he was acting in self-defense.

"They jumped on me and I had to fight," Carlton whispered to the sheriff and the district attorney.

Billy Weston and other survivors of course said that Carlton's account was untrue and that this was a premeditated, grisly sneak attack on the workmen and Mamah and her children. Weston was still recovering from his injuries and was not well enough to attend his own son's funeral.

Sheriff Williams pressed Carlton over his mysterious trip to Chicago.

"He admits he went to Chicago a week ago, but refused to tell why, or whom he saw there," Williams told a *Tribune* reporter. "I do not believe the negro is insane."

Many newspaper readers took the sheriff's words to mean that authorities believed that Carlton was no madman and no lone killer and that the mass murder was the result of a conspiracy to destroy the relationship between Frank and Mamah and ruin the architect's career. This theory was supported by a former deputy sheriff named George Peck, who had once worked as a guard protecting building materials during the construction of Taliesin. "Mr. Wright has many enemies," Peck told a reporter.

But Carlton's wife stressed to authorities that her husband was no hired assassin and that he had suffered from a severe mental breakdown. Handcuffed, sweating, and wiping away tears, she was questioned for hours at the Spring Green jailhouse. "My husband had the notion that he was being pursued," Gertrude told investigators. "He recently got to waking me up in the night at our quarters in the bungalow to listen for noises."

She told sheriff's deputies that her husband took the murder weapon to bed with him every night and had choked her and threatened to kill her on numerous occasions. Gertrude said that she had no idea why Carlton had suddenly gone to Chicago instead of visiting a dentist in Madison like he had told her. "He would not tell me why he went there," she claimed. "Saturday he served the lunch and went into the [courtyard] with a pail of gasoline. Then he struck a match and lighted his pipe. I went into the kitchen and a minute later, the whole place was afire. I saw Julian running around the barn with the hatchet in his hand… I didn't see my husband hit anybody and I did not know anything until I was arrested on the road into town."

The *Tribune* put a team of reporters on the story, which was undoubtedly the biggest and most shocking local news story of the year. The newspaper dubbed Carlton "the Spring Lake Slayer."

A *Tribune* reporter interviewed a Spring Green tavern owner who overheard two of Carlton's victims discussing him over glasses of whiskey inside the bar two weeks before the murders.

"William Weston and David Lindblom were in my place talking about the negro butler," J. M. Rouchlin claimed. "[Weston said], 'He's polite and smart, but he's the most desperate hot-headed fellow I ever saw. Don't ever contradict him. He'll fly off the handle any minute.'"

Newsmen also worked to chase down anyone who knew Carlton in the so-called Black Belt, the African American neighborhood in Chicago's South Side. A man named Harry Long had lived down the street from Carlton on Evans Avenue. "I didn't like Carlton and was afraid of him," he told a reporter from the *Tribune*. "He always did look queer to me. I thought he was off. His wife was afraid of him too."

Long said that Gertrude would come to his home often, trembling and nervous after her husband had frightened her. "She said he'd get spells when he was wild-eyed and do such strange things that she feared for her life."

Other unnamed sources told reporters that Carlton had possessed all the characteristics of an insane man. They recounted an episode where he exploded in anger after he lost a game of cards, while at other times, "he was morose and sullen, avoided other persons and gave every evidence of being a moron."

The characterization of Carlton as a troubled man contradicted John Z. Vogelsang's opinion of him and the glowing recommendation that he had given about the man to Frank when he was looking for a new butler. But the wife of one of Vogelsang's employees shared her disturbing view of her husband's former coworker who had visited their home many times. "He seemed to be nervous and quivering all the time," Mrs. Maurice Dorsey explained to the *Tribune*. "He'd fly off the handle at the slightest provocation. I remember one time when I gave a whist party [referring to an English card game] and he was playing. All of the sudden he jumped up and let out a yell that scared us all nearly to death. All the women started to run out thinking he had gone crazy. But he sat down trembling and mumbled a few words of apology. His mind always seemed to be wandering away from what he was doing and what little talking he did was about his poor circumstances and how afraid he was that he wasn't going to get along."

Other Carlton associates also claimed that he was constantly worried over his financial woes.

The question remaining on everyone's mind: Did money or madness lead Julian Carlton to commit such awful crimes? Frank's attorney, Sherman Booth, scoffed at the idea that Carlton had performed a contract killing at Taliesin but did believe that the murders were planned well in advance of that fateful Saturday in August.

Carlton was only half-conscious when he was arraigned at the jail for allegedly murdering Emil Brodelle. The day before, he had managed to sign an official statement under the handwritten transcription of his words, *The fire was accidental. I was attacked by Brodelle and I struck him in self-defense.*

Carlton's health was quickly deteriorating, and authorities wondered if he would stay alive for his trial. Sheriff's deputies carried him from his bunk and sat him down on a chair outside his grated cell. A judge read the murder warrant, and Carlton whispered a response that other spectators could not hear. A formal plea of not guilty was entered on his behalf.

He was brought to the Dodgeville courthouse again ten days later for a pretrial hearing. This time, he was carried into the courtroom on the second floor of the building by the sheriff and five deputies. He toyed with a glass of water while seated at a table and was given an orange and slices of apple and bananas, which he chewed and spit out. Carlton's squat and somewhat stout frame looked emaciated, as he had lost several pounds since his arrest. Ten witnesses were called and questioned by Iowa County district attorney James O'Neil, who would try the case. Billy Weston and Herbert Fritz gave statements to the court. Another witness, a Spring Green resident named Harper Harrison, somehow got access to Carlton in jail. He claimed under oath that the accused killer had confided to him that he had killed Emil Brodelle after the draftsman told him, "I'll get you yet!"

Harrison also recounted a far-fetched story from Carlton that he killed Mamah Borthwick because he thought she was a man who had come to

Brodelle's aid and that had he known who she was, he would not have attacked her.

Despite Carlton's weak appearance in the courtroom, Sheriff Williams said the man was still a threat to those around him. The sheriff testified that the murder suspect was granted the freedom to walk the corridor of the jail and that Carlton threw a pail filled with water at him in an attempt to injure him.

Prior to the hearing, the jail physician, Dr. W. S. Lincoln, checked Carlton's body for needle marks and deemed him to be free of "dope hunger."

Gertrude Carlton also told authorities that Carlton was not a drug user. She was later released without any charges filed against her. Sheriff's deputies put her on a train back to Chicago with only seven dollars in her pocket.

She told a reporter that her purpose for the trip was to retain a lawyer for her husband but offered nothing more. "Her only explanation was a cold shoulder to every question," the newsman wrote. "She was attired in black and presented a very neat appearance. Her countenance showed that she had been a victim of a great deal of worry and trouble."

Despite telling the reporter that she planned to stand by her husband during this ordeal, Gertrude Carlton would never be heard from again.

Searching for any possible motive, Chicago police detectives assisting with the case also wanted to determine whether the killer had abused drugs in the past. They interviewed a janitor who had worked for Carlton for a month at the Frances Willard School. "He was broke when he came down here," the custodian, John Keenan, told authorities. "I remember that well, for I loaned him a dollar to buy a pair of overalls the first day he worked for me. He seemed to be a good worker… But he appeared to me to be dopey all the time. He ate cigarettes. He must have smoked dozens of them in the few hours he was at school each day."

While at the county jail in Dodgeville, Carlton had become quite the attraction for local townspeople who gathered outside the jail, hoisted themselves up the wall, and peeked into the small window of his cell in an effort to catch a glimpse of him. Many had never seen a murder suspect or an African American man before.

Members of Chicago's Black community were under siege by reporters and lawmen alike looking for information about Carlton. The situation grew worse for South Side residents when a Black man was accused of killing a Chicago patrol officer just two days after the massacre at Taliesin. The deadly shooting occurred when the suspect, Simon Hogan, was confronted by a white police officer named George Trumbull, a four-year veteran of the Chicago Police Department, just after Hogan allegedly tried to rob a woman of one dollar. Trumbull was shot four times, including a bullet to his chest just below the heart. He collapsed on the street and died within seconds.

Hogan fled the scene on foot and was tracked down at a nearby rooming house at the corner of South State and Twenty-Sixth Streets. There, fifty-two armed officers surrounded the building with their guns drawn.

Cops demanded that Hogan surrender. When the suspect did not respond, officers fired a hail of bullets into the building through the walls and windows while innocent tenants were trapped inside. "Sleepy residents of the black belt for many blocks around, aroused by the fusillade, hurried into the streets and stood cowering at a safe distance as they watched the progress of the battle," a *Tribune* reporter wrote.

Hogan fired back with a revolver but was taken into custody after a police marksman shot the weapon out of his hand. The drama was captured in a front-page story under the screaming headline "Police Slain by Negro—Take Slayer in Pitched Battle—Police Capture Patrolman's Murderer after Storming Negro Stronghold."

The words *Negro Stronghold* falsely suggested that the building's Black residents had supported Hogan and taken up arms to defend him, when in reality, they were victims themselves and were afraid for their lives.

Hogan was later tried, convicted, and sentenced to life in the Illinois State Penitentiary at Joliet. Would a similar fate await Julian Carlton?

27

Edwin Cheney had the remains of his children, John and Martha, cremated after he returned to Chicago and laid to rest at a local cemetery. Like Frank had done with Mamah, Cheney did not hold a funeral service for his young son and daughter. Instead, he mourned the heart-wrenching loss in private.

Meanwhile, the death toll from the horrific event at Taliesin was rising. Both Thomas Brunker and David Lindblom succumbed to their injuries. Brunker's leg was burned so badly that doctors had planned for amputation in an effort to keep the man alive. The sixty-year-old Brunker had not been able to speak since the attack and was bedridden in a state of full paralysis. One of Brunker's ten children traveled to Spring Green to keep vigil by his bedside. She was told that her father was sleeping and would live through the night. She checked into the local hotel with hopes of seeing him in the morning. He died in his makeshift hospital bed before she could say goodbye. Brunker's funeral took place at St. Regis Church in nearby Ridgeway, Wisconsin, where he had attended as a boy.

Brunker's children would later file a lawsuit against Frank under the state's Workingmen's Compensation Act. The family demanded $3,000, asserting that "Brunker's death was in the service of his employer [Wright], and that he was killed while trying to stop the onslaught of the negro."

More hope was given for Lindblom's recovery since he had taken part in rescue and relief efforts at Taliesin. But after the adrenaline from that day wore off, his health declined rapidly, and the burns and hatchet wounds to his neck and shoulder were even worse than doctors had imagined. Frank attended the gardener's funeral, which was suspended after torrents of rain halted the funeral cortege on its way to the cemetery.

Now, Julian Carlton would have to answer for seven murders instead of five. The murder suspect had refused to eat since his arrest, and the district attorney was deeply concerned about the possibility that Carlton would escape a life sentence in prison, or more likely a hangman's noose, if he died quietly in his jail cell, thus robbing the survivors and the Spring Green community of justice. On September 30, 1914, more than a month after the murders, Carlton was taken by stretcher from the jail to the courthouse in Dodgeville for his formal arraignment. Carlton could not afford his own attorney, so a local lawyer named E. C. Fielder was appointed by the court to defend him. The murder suspect was guarded by two sheriff's deputies but appeared too sick to move, barely lifting his head from the stretcher. Fielder entered a plea of not guilty on Carlton's behalf, and the hearing ended quickly. In a surprise move, the judge announced that he would postpone the murder trial indefinitely until Carlton was physically fit to stand trial.

As the suspect was being carried out of the courthouse on a stretcher, Fielder was asked by a reporter whether he would mount an insanity defense for his client, now formally charged with the seven murders at Taliesin, in hopes that he would be sent to the state asylum. But the attorney played coy with the press and offered them no insight as to what his defense would be.

But there would be no defense and no trial. Nine days after his court appearance, Julian Carlton died in his jail cell in Dodgeville.

While incarcerated, Carlton starved himself and lost sixty pounds. He weighed only ninety pounds when he died. He had said very few words while in jail, but on the day of his arrest, Carlton had cryptically hinted that there was more to the story behind the murders than anyone knew.

"If I die, you'll never hear the real story," he reportedly whispered. "They'd better let me live if they expect to find out something."

What Carlton was alluding to, no one will ever know, but his words fed speculation that the killer may have had willing accomplices who helped him plan the murders. More likely, however, it was Carlton's final insult to the memories of the dead.

John Wright believed that Carlton may have been indirectly influenced in his killing spree.

"There were those of the clergy, too, who later from their pulpits used this tragedy as a moral lesson, calling forth endless expositions and quotations," he later wrote. "I wonder if their previous criticisms and prophesy of evil could have influenced [Carlton], who may have seen the possibilities for future glory for himself as the crime took shape in his warped mind."

In the October 11, 1914, edition of *The Butte Miner*, a Montana newspaper, editors dedicated a full page to the tragedy, using the deaths as a warning to those who defied moral law.

"'The wages of sin is death,' says the bible. Once more the truth of this maxim has been demonstrated in American life," the newspaper's pious editors gleefully wrote. "Death, disaster, misery in many forms still overtake those who transgress against the elementary laws of God… American millionaires, strong in power and wealth; beautiful women strong in the power of their charms, imagine for a moment that they can disregard all ties and live for pleasure alone, but they find that Nemesis still awaits them. Mrs. Mamah Borthwick Cheney is the latest conspicuous sufferer in a long list of tragedies of this kind."

There would be no funeral or even a burial plot in a potter's field for Julian Carlton. His remains were sent to the medical department at the University of Wisconsin, where his brain was removed and later studied by noted anatomy professor W. S. Miller in an effort to determine if Carlton had suffered some kind of brain injury that could have triggered his murdering spree.

The results of Miller's examination were never published. Carlton's body was cremated and his ashes dumped somewhere behind the medical school.

During this time, Frank received a mailbag full of letters from people from across the country. There were sympathy cards mixed in with letters of hate and condemnation for Frank and the late Mamah Borthwick. The architect did not read them. Instead, he tied them together in a large bundle and burned them.

The tragedy had also transformed Frank's son John. When he began working with his father, he vowed that he would play no role in Frank's life at Taliesin with Mamah. But his view toward her had softened as he witnessed Frank's intense pain.

"Something in him died with her, a something lovable and gentle that I knew and loved in my father," John Wright later explained. "I am convinced that the love that united them was deep, sincere and holy in spite of its illegality. I am convinced that the woman for whom he left home was of noble character."

John's mother, Kitty, was also deeply impacted by the killings. When a reporter visited her home at Oak Park a month after the murders, he found that the grass was tall and unkempt and that the flowering bushes were "ragged and sprawly." Ivy vines that had once looked splendid on the exterior of the house were now torn from the walls in some places. The reporter approached the front door and knocked. Kitty opened the door moments later, wearing a pastel-yellow morning gown with lace around the collar. She greeted the reporter with a puzzled look on her face. No journalist had called on her for several months, and she was a bit out of practice with her communications skills. They shared pleasantries, but this was no social call. The newsman quickly got to the business at hand. "What of this rumor that you are expecting Mr. Wright back at this home?" he asked.

The slight smile disappeared from her face. "You know I cannot reply to that. It would be most unwise and unnecessary."

"But they say—"

Kitty cut him off and shrugged. "They say many, many things."

She took a moment to arrange the lace at her neckline and smoothed her morning gown with her porcelain-white hands.

"I do not reply because I cannot," she continued. "If I could reply, but public curiosity is never satisfied, they would want to know more and more and more and I could never rest."

The reporter scrambled with his pencil to jot her quotes down on his notepad. He did not want to interrupt Kitty's train of thought. He had gone to the Oak Park house on a lark and without an invitation, hoping to find a story there. Based on past experience, he knew that if he got Kitty alone, she would not be able to resist his inquiries about her life.

"I am living the life of a recluse," she said. "I see no one, not even my friends. As to the rumors, I do not hear them. I will not hear them. I will not read a newspaper for fear that I may chance upon some article that will hurt me. Why should I be a victim of these rumors?"

Once again, Kitty worked to position herself for martyrdom in the press. She still had her children, and since she steadfastly refused to grant Frank a divorce, she still technically had her husband. But this interview opportunity had allowed her to slip back into the comfortable role of victim.

"That is why I will make no statement to the public," she announced. "I am here. You can see that. I am living my own life. He [Frank] is living his. What will happen? Heaven only knows I am in no way changed. I am the same woman I was then—well, years ago. I want to do the right thing and I feel that I am serving his best interests as well as mine by keeping silent. You understand don't you?"

The reporter nodded in agreement as he wrote.

"What is the public curiosity to me now?" she asked. "Nothing! So little

I do not even read the papers. Gossip is a thing apart. I know that people here are conjecturing wildly, but what these conjectures are I have no idea. It is best to wait and say nothing. You will [have to] pardon me. I have no statement to make."

Kitty smiled as she closed the heavy oak door. The reporter smiled too, knowing that her nonstatement had provided him with several juicy quotes for the next day's newspaper.

28

In December 1914, Frank decided to write to Mamah's Swedish mentor and collaborator Ellen Key after receiving her warm letter of condolences following the tragedy. He also wanted to notify Key that she would receive a portrait of Mamah taken by a professional photographer in June of that year. It was a stunning photo of Mamah seated sideways on a chair with her dark hair brushed back as she looked pensively and even seductively directly into the camera.

Dear Ellen Key.

Your kind words of Mamah are like balm to my heart. You will receive her picture under a separate cover. I am sending it today. It was made as a surprise for my birthday last June. There is nothing to say. The lightning struck—why, no one can say. All that remains to be done is to keep it from sinking in so deep that my usefulness will be gone. Or rather to take it as the heart of her would have me and put the soul of her into the forms that take shape under my hands. We lived—richly. She was taken—suddenly—without warning or pain to her I am sure. Just as we were beginning to feel that the bitter struggle was giving place to the quiet assurance of peace and the place we coveted together. I hope I can see you some time and we can talk of her. You have been a strength and comfort to us both and we have blessed you often.

With love and regard, Faithfully yours
Frank Lloyd Wright.

He would never get the chance to meet Ellen Key, as the war raging in Europe made transatlantic ocean travel unsafe for her.

Still in a depressed fog, Frank returned to Chicago to complete the work on Midway Gardens. There were many unfinished touches on the venue that he planned to make, but he felt uninspired. To make matters worse, the company safe was robbed, and developer Edward Waller was thrown into financial despair. Waller still owed creditors and unloaded the property by selling it for a loss to Schoenhofen Brewing Company, known for its Edelweiss beer. The beer company brought in a team of designers to finish the job by throwing buckets of paint around and adding what Frank called "obnoxious features out of balance and nasty."

The architect was outraged. "Where there had been form integral with materials and purpose, here was raw red, dead white, and bad blue paint. Another 'World's Fair' effect," he complained in his memoir. What was once an elegant entertainment complex for dance and orchestra music catering to the city's elite had turned into a vulgar beer hall for Chicago's working class.

Dissatisfied with the new ownership's direction, Frank returned to Wisconsin and threw himself into the reconstruction of Taliesin. He did this while owing back taxes on the family home in Oak Park and the bank threatening him with foreclosure. The house was broken into that April. Frank's daughter arrived home one night to find the living room "topsy turvy," but she told police that nothing appeared to have been stolen.

As was his habit, Frank paid little attention to his creditors while leaning on friends to lend him money to build a bigger and better retreat on what was now hallowed ground in Spring Green.

"More stone, more wood, more work—a more harmonious use for them all," Frank wrote later. "More work men, more money—sacrifices, not only creative work on my part but desperate attempts to find and eventually earn the money."

Frank hired a team of architects and artisans to work on the project, including an eighty-year-old Czech stonemason and Antonin Raymond, an artist from Prague who lived on the property with his French wife. As he had promised, Frank designed his massive new compound to dwarf the original Taliesin. His new studio was cavernous and large enough to hold almost a dozen working draftsmen. Frank and his men built new living quarters for the young architects in his employ as well as new servants' quarters and stables for his horses.

Frank's home within the compound was designed around enormous fireplaces and filled with expensive furniture, ornate rugs, and pieces from Frank's extensive collection of Japanese art: exotic prints and screens as well as sculptures that had somehow survived the fire. He also added a stone-floored room from which he could gaze out at the family chapel and Mamah's unmarked grave.

Frank thought of the property as a living thing and marveled at its resiliency. "Something was becoming clear, now, through all the brutalizing Taliesin had received," he wrote. "Something—no, not rebellion. Conviction. Purpose now lifted the crown of the head higher. Made the eye see clearer. The tread that had faltered for a moment in weakness and confusion became elastic and more as Work came alive again."

Frank spent long hours toiling in the soil outside the home to cultivate and rejuvenate Mamah's garden, watching the colorful dahlias return that spring as if they were unaware of the tragedy that had struck there.

Frank's home was too big for just one person. He dreaded the idea of rattling around in the large space accompanied only by the ghost of his beloved or perhaps the specter of her killer. In mid-December 1914, more than four months after the slayings, the grief-stricken architect received another letter from a stranger. Instead of burning it, as he had done with dozens of others, Frank unsealed the envelope that held three handwritten pages. Before even reading a word, he recognized that it had been written by a woman by the way that the writer's pen glided effortlessly across the pages.

My dear Sir,

Because I stand aghast at the immensity of your sorrow,
Because my own soul has been chastened by grief,
And I know how desolate are anniversaries and fete days,
I send to you my good wishes.
Rejoice that you are worthy to bear so great affliction,
That your strength is greater than human tragedy.

Sincerely, Madam Noel

Frank did not discard the letter. He kept it and likely read it over and over again. Although he still maintained a commitment in his heart for the woman who was sacrificed for their love, Frank was crippled by loneliness and intrigued by this caring stranger.

Maude Miriam Noel was not a young ingenue and adoring fan who was swept up in the romanticism of Frank's tragic, Romeo and Juliet–style love affair with Mamah Borthwick. Noel was forty-five years old and a mother of three from a prominent Southern family. She had been living in Paris for a decade while mourning the death of her husband, Emil Noel, three years prior. Like Frank, the expatriate American, who was called by her middle name, Miriam, was also an artist.

She had recently tied for first place in a prestigious sculpture competition in Paris.

After receiving Miriam's letter, Frank sat down three days before Christmas and wrote her a reply describing his isolation at Taliesin.

"I hunger for the living touch of someone—something immediately peculiar to myself," he wrote. "Inviolably 'mine.' Yes—at times almost anything or anything."

Miriam could feel the desperation in the architect's words. He was vulnerable now, and she seized on his weakness with a bold, smoldering response that outlined her true intentions.

"Let me crown your head with a wreath of violets and bind your hair with fillets of gold… I kiss your feet with my trembling lips," she wrote back. "I will come into your life for a little while. And then I will lose you because you will never understand, and then like Hagar, I will go forth to hunger and thirst in the wilderness, alone with my Ishmael, the poor frail child the world calls love."

Miriam had expressed her sexual desire for him as well as her own need to be cared for and sheltered by someone she could trust. At that point, Frank yearned to be wanted for his body and soul. He wanted to be made whole again. It would be an impossible task for any woman to achieve. Reading her seductive letter, Frank believed that she was up to the challenge. But Miriam's letter also came with a warning, one that he failed to recognize until it was too late.

29

As the horrors of 1914 gave way to the promise of the new year, Frank and Miriam continued their transatlantic correspondence. Her letters were increasingly sensual, and Frank likely blushed upon reading them. But they excited him just the same. He urged her to return to the United States and share his bed and his life with him. Once again, Frank had fallen in love.

When Miriam arrived in Chicago, Frank found her to be even more beautiful than the photograph she had sent to him.

Miriam was tall and thin with brown hair and green eyes. Her appearance was a departure for him, as Frank had previously preferred a more full-bodied woman like Mamah Borthwick.

Miriam also dressed differently from his late soulmate. While Mamah fancied flowing peasant dresses to hide her curves, Miriam dressed as if she were taking the Broadway stage. She wore expensive French-made dresses with soft brown velvet outlining her neck and arms. Miriam also enjoyed wearing exotic turbans and a large scarab, which she falsely claimed had been worn by Cleopatra. She was a sculptor and a self-proclaimed clairvoyant. She was eccentric and influenced by European styles and ideals.

Frank did not and could not replace Mamah in his life. Miriam Noel offered him something new and exhilarating.

She wore a sealskin cape and cap, and her fingers were adorned with several rings when she strolled into Frank's office for the first time in early 1915. Miriam placed her cigarette case on Frank's desk, fished out a smoke, and placed it between her delicate fingers and lips. Frank reached for a book of matches. He was not a smoker himself and fumbled a bit to ignite her cigarette. She took a long pull from the cigarette and blew out a plume of smoke toward the ceiling of Frank's office.

Miriam also had with her a worn copy of Mary Baker Eddy's book *Science and Health with Key to the Scriptures*, and she placed it on his desk.

"How do you like me?" she asked.

"I've never seen anyone quite like you," he stammered in response.

"She is beautiful," thought Frank. "A Parisien by adoption and preference. She appears brilliant, distinguished and sophisticated with a violet pallor and a mass of red-brown hair."

Frank had not confided his deepest thoughts with anyone since the tragedy. He had had a few discussions with his mother, Anna, but that was it.

"Drowning men—they say so—clutch at straws," he later wrote. "Here was no straw but enlightened comradeship, help, more light than I had to see by. Salvation maybe from blackness—blindness. I did not know. And here began the leading of the blind by the blind."

When Miriam moved into Frank's rented redbrick town house at 25 East Cedar Street, his son John took an immediate dislike to her and the influence she had on his father. John had read some of her steamy letters to Frank and referred to Miriam as *The Poetess-of-the-note from "Paree."*

"[She] wooed, grabbed and bagged him—then dragged, gagged and shagged him," he later wrote. "Dad was so dominated, seduced, coerced, chastised, conscripted, overridden, and beshawed, at times he wasn't even any man… Maybe Miriam was the victim of a satanic influence that incited and directed her course."

Miriam had no affinity for the devil or satanic worship. But there was darkness within her.

Unbeknownst to Frank, the new woman in his life was also a morphine addict who had a propensity for terrorizing her past lovers. While living in France, Miriam was arrested after setting out to "wreak vengeance" on a man who had wronged her.

While Frank and Mamah had been ideally suited for each other, the love affair between the architect and the Parisien widow was tumultuous at best. Frank detested Miriam's habit of smoking cigarettes, as only men were encouraged to use tobacco in the United States at the time. He also disliked the fact that she drank wine with almost every meal. He asked her to put away her exotic wardrobe and dress more modestly to fit in better with members of Chicago's café society. To her credit, Miriam did as Frank asked.

Originally, he had plans to bring her to Taliesin, but he thought better of it. He did not want what he believed was Miriam's wild eroticism to erode the purity of his monument to Mamah. Miriam took great offense to Frank's insistence of traveling to Spring Green without her as well as his unwavering and tireless dedication to keeping the memories of Mamah alive. "You worship the ghost of a dead woman," Miriam accused him in a letter. "A dead woman whom you tortured as you have tortured me and to whose memory you have given no real loyalty."

She was likely referring to the architect's quick leap into her arms less than five months after Mamah's death.

The arguments continued, and Frank moved his clothing and other belongings out of their Chicago apartment. Miriam vacated the apartment also, leaving a brief note behind. "I am going—the 'menace' to your safety no longer exists."

Miriam traveled to New Mexico to spend time with friends while Frank retreated to the comfort and warmth of Taliesin, where his children visited him often. For a brief moment, he seemed happy to be rid of her. She wrote to him in the early spring, describing how lonely she felt without him. Exasperated by their brief and volatile affair, he fired off a response notifying her that he was breaking off the relationship. "It cannot continue Miriam," he wrote to her wearily. "The disparaging discrepancy is too great, it counts too heavily against me as always—and I cannot be or do the things you need to give you happiness—Your demands are beyond me—Your expectations sinister in my sight… Reason is gone! Charity is gone—Now comes Fear—Hate—Revenge—Punishment—Then Regret—Shame, Humiliation—Ashes. It is the accepted Road—All ambitious Souls hear me! Sex is the Curse of Life!"

Frank had penned a stunning rebuke to Miriam, but his words lacked conviction. He eventually invited her back to Chicago and gave his word that she would become the new lady of the manor at Taliesin.

Her arrival at Spring Green set off a round of angry gossip from townspeople whose opinion of Mamah Borthwick had improved only after her murder. They were outraged that the famed architect had moved another single woman into his home, and there were renewed threats of tar-and-feathering parties for the couple.

The person most offended by the mere presence of Miriam at Taliesin was Nellie Breen, Frank's elderly housekeeper.

She chastised Miriam when Frank's children visited, sending her crying to her bedroom where she locked the door. Breen also stood guard at night to thwart any attempts from Miriam to enter Frank's bedroom. He could not put up with Breen's puritanical antics any longer and fired her in early October. But the housekeeper refused to go quietly. Upon her dismissal, Breen raided Frank's unlocked desk and stole a collection of letters sent to him by Miriam. She then got on a train to Chicago and marched into the *Chicago Tribune* newsroom, offering to sell the letters for a price.

Editors could hardly wait for another opportunity to smear the celebrity architect over another affair of the heart. They handed Breen a stack of cash and began reviewing the letters, which appeared to have been written by Miriam before and after Frank had briefly broken off their relationship. The letters revealed her deep concern about Frank's struggle to move beyond his love for Mamah and provided a glimpse of Miriam's manic personality and her penchant for lashing out at those she loved.

Beloved: If I could take you into the mysteries of this glorious day you would lose all your sorrow—It would fall from you like an unworthy garment. Twice, three days I have spoken to no one, yet I have danced and quivered and vibrated like a ray of light.

Oh dear Frank, I would take your burden if I could—would dissolve it in this love that is more than peace… It is love that makes me so happy. How I revel in it! When I think of how I overflow with love for you and how grudgingly you give it to me, and how carefully you pick and choose, lest some word or feeling rise within you which might seem disloyal to the past—that worthless old past which has left you nothing but an empty broken soul.

Miriam's letters got more mean-spirited from there.

You want to be freed beyond the law and are not wise enough to know that disaster always follows lawlessness. You have not learned—You have not learned—and I don't think you want to learn it. You are still too much in love with the Christmas Tree effect of life.

Do not come, I cannot see you again. It will precipitate another outburst. Your carnivals at Taliesin are not for me… My suffering is too intense to be described, but that doesn't matter either—only one thing matters—THAT YOU BE ENTERTAINED, AMUSED. No, no. I cannot—just cannot.

You are blind to God. Blind as I think no mortal ever was, seeking new distraction in a worldly folly—A PATHETIC, BITTER, AGING MAN!

Breen also presented a written record detailing each time Frank had traveled with Miriam from Chicago to Spring Green. The editor cleverly suggested that the housekeeper take her notes about the couple's interstate travel to federal authorities to "make a case."

The editor was referring to the Mann Act, also known as the White-Slave Traffic Act of 1910, which made transporting women across state lines for immoral purposes a federal crime. The law was put into place in an effort to curb prostitution, but the editor likely told Breen that the same law applied to her former employer when he escorted Miriam from Chicago, Illinois, to Spring Green, Wisconsin. The editor envisioned a series of scandalous stories to come, all filled with torrid details about Frank and Miriam's sex life. The architect's so-called Love Cottage at Taliesin was back in the headlines once again.

30

Nellie Breen left the *Tribune* newsroom and marched over to the federal building in Chicago where she demanded that Frank be investigated for violating the Mann Act. Superintendent Hinton C. Clabaugh of the Bureau of Investigation of the U.S. Justice Department, the precursor to the FBI, asked Breen to give a statement before they continued with any probe into the matter.

"I went to work at Spring Green with Mr. Wright with the express understanding that there would be no repetition of the Mamah Borthwick Cheney affair," Breen told authorities. "Everything went along alright until Mr. Wright sent to Paris and asked the sculptress [Miriam Noel] to come to his home in Spring Green and cheer him in his sorrow. His mother and the Wright children were at his home when she came and they immediately resented the visit and they left. Several times I stopped the sculptress from going into Mr. Wright's room and when it was announced she would be the Mistress of the Home, I left."

Breen then showed more letters sent between the romantic pair while Miriam was out of state in New Mexico. Federal agents planned to also investigate whether the couple had violated any postal laws.

Frank could hardly believe that his elderly former housekeeper could hatch a revenge plan so elaborate and surmised that Breen was being guided by someone, perhaps a journalist, to seek the attention of federal law enforcement. He was right. The architect asked friends in Chicago to point him to the best lawyer available to defend him against such allegations. They all recommended that he hire fifty-eight-year-old attorney Clarence Darrow for the job. Darrow had served briefly in the Illinois House of Representatives and had spent several years as a private attorney defending labor union members on bombing and even murder charges. In one case in southern California, Darrow was accused and later charged with bribing a prospective juror with an envelope stuffed with $4,000 in cash. His own trial ended in a hung jury, and the prosecutor never ordered him back to court after Darrow pledged to never practice law in the state again.

Surprisingly, he returned to Chicago with his reputation still intact.

Frank met with Darrow, and both deemed Breen's claims to be frivolous. The lawyer presented copies of Breen's letters to Superintendent Clabaugh and asked the federal agent to pursue extortion charges against the housekeeper. Learning of this, Breen marched back to the *Tribune* newsroom in a fury.

"So, they say I have been blackmailing Mr. Wright, do they?" she asked an editor. "Darrow has taken my letters to the federal building has he? Well, here is a copy of my only letter to Mr. Wright. You may judge for yourself as to what sort of 'demands' I made of him."

Breen handed the editor the letter, in which she demanded a meeting with her former employer.

> *Dear Mr. Wright… You and Miriam Noble are liable for arrest under the Mann Act upon evidence as yet solely in my possession. This evidence is so strong that if arrested, you may not be admitted for bail. Nothing about this will be done however, if you agree to separate [from Miriam] at once. That is, you can not keep her at Taliesin or*

Cedar Street, nor have her to visit you nor live with her. I think you know the folly of offering me money. The newspapers are muzzled and will stay muzzled unless you are arrested.

"N.B."

Breen then informed the editor that she had a postscript to the letter but did not keep a copy of it.

"It was lengthy and consisted almost entirely of friendly ridicule," she said. "And I will be glad to have it published if Mr. Wright will give it out."

Breen's explanation for her outrageous behavior and threats against Frank and Miriam was that it was all in an effort to shield the Wright children from the sins of their father.

Frank scoffed at the notion that Breen was trying to protect his children, as most of them were now adults themselves and living their own lives. He also had little interest in publishing Breen's postscript and waging war with her in the press. Frank would allow law enforcement officials to chart the next course of action. At a hearing on the matter, Clarence Darrow argued that the housekeeper was envious of Miriam Noel.

"In my opinion, what she [Breen] wanted was to run the house," Darrow told the district attorney. "I think there is some jealousy in the matter."

Frank also spoke at the hearing. "Mrs. Breen was a domestic in my employ and was disgruntled because of her discharge," he explained.

Federal immigration officials also expressed interest in the case after Breen falsely claimed that Miriam was Russian and not American. Immigration officials demanded that Miriam present them with evidence that she was in fact a U.S. citizen.

A short time later, Clabaugh dismissed the Mann Act investigation against Frank.

"We have sifted thoroughly the charges made by Nellie Breen," an unidentified federal agent told a reporter. "The main evidence so far is that she prevented the sculptress mentioned from going into Wright's room. The government cannot say who shall or who shall not go to the home of [Mr. Wright] for a visit unless it can be proved that the person went there in violation of the Mann Act. Unless something of a more definite nature is supplied, the government has no case in the Wright-Breen affair."

Breen refused to give up. She asked investigators to look closely at a trip to California taken by Frank and Miriam together and determine if they had broken any laws.

"It would be useless to attempt to prove a violation of the Mann Act just because Mr. Wright and Mrs. Noel went to California together," Superintendent Clabaugh stated. "It will be necessary to prove that the trip was made for purposes other than to visit [a] fair. Mrs. Noel has a perfect right to visit at Spring Green. The government has no right to tell anyone whom they shall or shall not visit, unless the visits are for unlawful purposes."

Federal investigators may have closed their book, but Frank was hardly done with the matter. He invited a reporter to Taliesin, where they sat for an interview in the spacious living room. After exchanging some pleasantries, Frank launched into a full-blown attack on the character of his former housekeeper.

"If the federal authorities have dropped the case, I'm afraid Mrs. Breen has not," he told a reporter. "I don't know what her next move will be, but I am sure there will be a next move. She may try to have me indicted by the Wisconsin authorities. What I fear most is that she may attempt to kill Madame Noel."

The horrible memory of Mamah's murder just a year before suddenly flashed through his mind. Why had he welcomed such chaos and danger into his life? It was a character flaw for sure, one of many. But again, Frank refused to take any responsibility or blame himself. He told the reporter that Breen's actions were part of a disturbing pattern.

"We learned that a Lake Forest woman went abroad, where she died, to escape stories Mrs. Breen set about her… Mrs. Breen has been a trouble maker since she came into my home. I thought when I employed her that any suspicion of sex interest would be eliminated from my household. If anyone imagines that I ever cared for her in that way, the answer is in Mrs. Breen's dried figure and shriveled, unpleasant face… I do not believe for a moment that Mrs. Breen ever had a sentimental thought regarding myself. But she was a masterful little creature and wished to dominate her environment."

At that moment, Miriam appeared in the living room wearing what the reporter later described as "a clinging gown of shimmering white." She handed the reporter her written statement, which read in part, "Because I love Frank Lloyd Wright and admire him more than all men and honor the life he has lived, I am at Taliesin, his beautiful country home. I understand and deeply sympathize with the struggles and terrible trials of his life… Now because of my deep love for him, he is being persecuted again. My real faith for him has never wavered and we have passed through deep waters together… If there is any justification of my position here, it is that the work we hope to do together and the strength we can give each other is more important than a form in which Mr. Wright has become obsolete."

After reading the letter, the reporter asked her, "In view of the fact that your letters have been made public, won't you give a few of Mr. Wright's letters to you [so] that the world may not be robbed of a complete literary symposium?"

"Never," she responded angrily. "His letters to me are sacred to me. The world has no business with them."

Miriam stormed out of the room.

Frank watched while she made her exit. He was beaming, drawn to her inner fire, which had brought him back to her time and again. "Madam Noel is one of the most brilliantly intellectual women I ever knew," Frank told his guest. "She is wonderful, not only as a literary woman but as an artist."

With the federal investigation now dropped and Miriam's letters returned to her, Frank, as he had done with Mamah before, planned to take Miriam with him on a trip to the Far East for what he called his "refuge and rescue" and back to the land and culture that had influenced him like no other: the empire of Japan.

31

In early 1916, Frank received a visit at Taliesin from an envoy of the Japanese government to formalize a long-held gentlemen's agreement to hire the architect to build a grand new hotel in the heart of Tokyo. Frank told reporters in 1913 that he had won the job, but three years went by without any indication from the Japanese whether the project was moving forward. The trauma of his personal life, the deadly massacre at Taliesin and the loss of Mamah, and the scandal over stolen love letters had dominated Frank's mind during this time. And after the great promise and financial debacle of the Midway Gardens project, Frank was looking for a bold new challenge, one that could prove to be the capstone of his illustrious career to that point.

The cost for the new hotel was set at $2,000,000, which would translate to roughly $60 million today. Frank and his team worked for nearly a year on the design plans in the workroom at Taliesin before sailing to Japan.

During this time, the architect looked for inspiration in the pages of *The Book of Tea* by Japanese art critic Okakura Kakuzo. Frank wanted to ensure that his architectural plans adhered to Okakura's idea of teaism, which according to the author, "inculcates purity and harmony, the mystery of mutual charity, [and] the romanticism of the social order."

"It is essentially a worship of the Imperfect," Okakura wrote. "As it is a tender attempt to accomplish something in this impossible thing we know as life."

Frank also learned that Chinese philosopher Lao Tzu believed in the sixth century BCE that the reality of a building was not found in its walls and roof but in the empty space they contained.

Frank felt illuminated by the ancient philosopher's ideas and would ultimately incorporate them into the design of the Imperial Hotel.

In late December 1916, after attending a farewell dinner in his honor at the Union League Club in Chicago, Frank, Miriam, and an entourage of architects headed for Japan on board the luxury liner *Empress of Russia.* The master architect cut a striking figure on the ship, wearing a black-belted cape and matching beret while walking the leisure deck with a rattan cane. Before Frank left Chicago, he told friends that he would build a big, modern hotel to serve as "the social clearing house for the official life of Japan. At the present time, there is absolutely no place in which foreigners can be entertained in Tokyo, and this…hotel is to be erected partly to enable those prominent in Japanese social life to entertain foreign guests. The building will be three stories high and named the Imperial Hotel… Although it will be open to the public, it will have a royal atmosphere about it."

Frank would not build a hotel. He pledged to build a palace.

The ship entered Yokohama Bay on a clear January morning under pure golden skies. Frank stood on the deck and stared out at the white sails of sampans billowing in the deep blue water and to the hills where straw-thatched houses appeared like natural extensions of the rock and earth.

"I was to have earlier feelings deepened, intensified," Frank wrote in his memoir. "Imagine if you have not seen it, a mountainous, abrupt land, the sea everywhere apparently risen too high upon it, so that all gentle slopes to the water's edge are lost."

For land travel, Frank had shipped his Overland Country Club automobile, which was too big for Japanese roads. "[The] ride from Yokohama to

Tokyo soon taught us that the narrow, crowded streets plotted for rickshaws did not lend themselves to comfort travel in an automobile," wrote John Wright, who was hired to serve as his father's primary assistant on the project.

Although the worldly Miriam had lived in Paris for ten years, for her, entering Japan was like setting foot on Mars. Frank did his best to keep her spirits up by remarking on the country's cleanliness and the style and dress of the Japanese women. While Miriam may have had some reservations about their new adopted homeland, Frank was overjoyed by his return to Japan.

"At last I had found one country on earth where simplicity, as natural, is supreme," he wrote in his memoir. "The floors of these Japanese homes are made to live on—to sleep on—to kneel on and eat from, to kneel upon soft silken mats and meditate upon. On which to play the flute, or to make love."

Frank immersed himself in Japanese culture and even tried his hand at making an "idealized" cup of tea, but he eventually grew bored by the repetition of the traditional ceremony. But he was there to work and immediately began construction on a temporary annex to house himself and other members of his team. His small apartment looked out on a beautiful garden and had a small dining room and living room with a fireplace and a tiny piano. Frank and Miriam slept upstairs, where he had a drawing board next to their bed.

"No foreigner yet invited to Japan had taken off his hat to Japanese traditions," he later wrote. "When foreigners came, what they had back home came too… And yet Japanese fine art traditions are among the noblest and purest in this world… It was my instinct not to insult them. The West had much to learn from the East."

Frank wanted to honor the architectural beauty of Japan while also creating something modern and new. The biggest challenge was not designing and building the spacious lobby and two hundred rooms for guests of the hotel; it was ensuring that the massive structure could withstand an earthquake. It was a conundrum that kept the architect up at night. He still bore the deep emotional scars connected to the original Taliesin, a compound he had designed and built for the purpose of recreation and freedom of love. That building became a trap for his workmen when Julian Carlton set it ablaze with the butchered bodies of Mamah Borthwick and John Cheney still inside. Death had cursed that place. Now he was building something on a grand scale where hundreds of lives would be dependent on the safety protocols that he had put into place.

There was no information at the time in standard engineering books to guide them, so with his son John by his side, Frank set up a crude testing apparatus on the ground behind their office. They drilled post holes and filled them with concrete. On top of the concrete pins, they built multiple platforms with weighted sandbags piled high atop them. They then strung a wire about six inches from the top of the pins and took readings to determine how the concrete pins were settling into the soil. Tokyo experienced small tremors frequently, and testing was done to see how the platforms holding sandbags of various weights responded to the rattling of the ground. Frank and John used all the data they had gathered to lay out the construction requirements for the hotel.

One day, they felt something much larger than a tremor. A small earthquake shook the city and knocked the brick chimneys off the old Imperial Hotel, which stood nearby. Terrified residents scurried for safety, but Frank did not move. He braced himself at his design table and kept working. He was desperate to discover a way to master nature's volatility.

The ongoing construction of the Imperial Hotel was big news throughout Japan, and Frank became the go-to architect for Japan's wealthiest men, foreign business leaders, and diplomats. The infusion of cash allowed Frank to quench his thirst for expensive Japanese prints and other pieces of Asian art that filled his small apartment. But while Frank was enjoying the luxury lifestyle, many of his workers, including his son John, were not. When John paid himself money that he believed he was owed from one of their commissions, his father became enraged.

Frank immediately sent John a cable dismissing him from the project. "You're fired! Take the next ship home," the cable read.

"You selfish, ruthless tyrant," John thought to himself. "To ask you for pay is alright if I don't get it, but sacrilege if I do. And I got it!"

John booked passage back to America on the Dutch ship *Rembrandt.* When he returned to Chicago, his mother, Kitty, informed him that Frank had written a viciously worded letter to her, accusing her of raising a thief. John would remain estranged from his father for several more years.

Now Frank was virtually alone and haunted by his own demons and petty jealousies. Construction of the Imperial Hotel dragged on and on. He wondered if he would ever complete the project of his dreams and return to Taliesin.

32

Frank was in the midst of a deep sleep when he felt himself beginning to sway. At first, he thought it was a dream, that he was somehow back onboard the *Empress of Russia*, facing turbulent waves in the center of the Pacific Ocean. But then he opened his eyes and saw the entire bedroom shaking around him. He was knocked off the bed and sensed shock after shock running through his body and felt the floor unsteady under his bare feet. It was another earthquake, minor in scale but still utterly terrifying for all those who were experiencing it.

"There may be [a] more awful threat to human happiness than [an] earthquake," he wrote. "I do not know what it can be."

Frank watched as plaster cracked on the walls and heard timbers groaning around him as if the building was going to come crashing down with him and Miriam stuck inside. He called this tremor and others like it a "terrible natural enemy to all building[s]."

On another occasion, a violent tremor lifted the entire construction site. Immediately following the gigantic jolt, a group of workers scattered for safety, knocking Frank to the floor as they ran, and he feared that he might get trampled to death while lying helplessly near the promenade entrance of the old hotel. "A moment's panic and hell broke loose as the wave motions began," he remembered. "As I lay there, I could clearly see the ground swell pass through the construction above as it heaved and groaned to hideous crushing and grinding noises. Several thunderous crashes sickened me."

He was constantly studying the small quakes and likened them to the movement of waves, not of sea but of earth. Frank decided that he would float his hotel on the soil as a battleship floats on salt water, by building the hotel with lighter and more flexible materials that could bend in any direction. "Why fight a quake?" he asked the members of his design team. "Why not sympathize with it and out-wit it?"

Frank divided the hotel into two parts, each sixty feet long, and connected them through a series of wall and floor joints. All supports were centered under the floor slabs instead of the edges of the walls. The architect compared the building technique to that of a restaurant waiter who carried a tray on an upraised arm with his fingers at the center.

"[I would] erect a building made of two hands thrust together, palms inward and fingers interlocking to yield movement," he later wrote. "But resilient to return to its original position when distortion ceased."

Frank and his Japanese construction team then built concrete cantilever slabs and inserted them continuously across the building to create the structure for the hotel.

"The great building thus became a jointed monolith with a mosaic surface of lava and brick," he wrote in his memoir.

As many as six hundred men would work on the project over the next four years. The Imperial Hotel was designed for flexibility and stability, while Frank's relationship with Miriam Noel was not. She showed signs of manic-depressive illness, or what we would today call bipolar disorder.

"Miriam, herself—as I had soon discovered—had for many years been the victim of strange disturbances." Frank recalled. "Sometimes unnatural exaggerations, mental and emotional. They would spoil life entirely for both of us for days at a time."

Frank complained that Miriam had a morbid nature and that she was prone to violence. In truth, Miriam likely had great difficulty becoming accustomed to Japanese culture and was initially unaware that the Imperial Hotel project would consume Frank's life for several years. But instead of recognizing this great rift between them and going their separate ways, Frank asked Miriam to marry him. She said yes. Miriam had long been referred to as *Mrs. Wright* on invitations to lavish social events while living in Japan, and Frank introduced her as such, just as he had done with Mamah Borthwick when the two journeyed to Europe together many years before. But there was still only one Mrs. Wright in the eyes of the law, and Kitty had held on to that title with an iron grip for so long. Why would she grant him a divorce now?

But time had beaten her down, and Kitty was hanging on to the memory of a man that she had fallen in love with when she was just seventeen years old, one who never truly loved her back. Frank learned through his eldest daughter, Catherine, that Kitty was finally willing to grant him a divorce. This time, she did not run off to the press. Instead, she opted for a more private parting of the ways. Kitty wanted a cash settlement of $10,000, alimony of $150 per month, and all the furniture in their Oak Park house. The divorce decree was signed by Judge E. Ray Stevens of Sauk County, Wisconsin, after both Frank and Kitty presented evidence that they had been separated for five years.

Still, celebrity journalists of the day somehow got word of the divorce and smeared Frank's name on the front pages of newspapers across the country. *The Buffalo News* ran the headline "Marriage Assailant Divorced."

"Branded an assailant of the institution of marriage and left a social outcast because of his unconventional association with an affinity when marriage to her was impossible…the Chicago builder now is free to marry again if he wishes," the reporter wrote. "Though his career has been marked by various and sundry love affairs, earning him the sobriquet of 'wooer of many women,' it was his strange romance with Mamah Borthwick Cheney, the wife of a neighbor, that inspired his long struggle for marital freedom and turned world-wide attention to his spectacular assault on American decorum."

Although it was now widely known that Frank was living with Miriam Noel in Japan, there was not one mention of the potential new Mrs. Wright in the article. Instead, it was an exhaustive rehash of his love affair with Mamah and its tragic, bloody ending.

It appears that, like Frank, journalists were also tortured by the memory of a dead woman.

Miriam maintained an intense jealousy of Frank's enduring loyalty to Mamah and shot daggers at any woman who looked Frank's way. During one fit of rage over Frank's perceived flirtation with one of Miriam's friends, she rushed at him and attempted to stab him with a knife.

Frank had reached his breaking point with her. "I loved her enough to kill her and myself," he wrote to a friend. Miriam left Frank and moved temporarily to a summer resort outside Tokyo called Ikao. He was free of her but could not function in her absence. Frank wrote Miriam a letter and, in a rare moment of candor and self-reflection, took blame for their relationship woes.

> *To the woman by my side—I feel that no words of mine can show my regret for what I am and shame for what I do… I guess my talent has screened me from myself all along—It is well that I have to come face to face with myself unequivocally at last. And when my need is greatest I am alone.*

Miriam eventually returned to their Tokyo apartment and into Frank's arms. Upon their reconciliation, he felt whole again, romantically speaking, but grew more and more concerned about money trouble. His divorce from Kitty had nearly broken him financially. Frank complained about the settlement to his son John. "She bargained to sell back to me, at a price I could not afford to pay, the 'name' I gave her, to help her on her way," the architect groused.

Still, the lack of money did not stop him from continuing to amass a large collection of expensive Japanese prints. As he had done throughout his life, if Frank wanted something, he bought it and worried about paying for it later. He filled his apartment with Asian treasures, "Chinese paintings and embroideries…old lacquer boxes, carved ivories, brocades, jade and all sorts of beautiful things," wrote Miriam.

Much of the collection of art and artifacts was nearly destroyed when flames broke out at the old Imperial Hotel. Earlier that evening, Miriam had refused to accompany Frank to a garden party at the American embassy in Tokyo. At first, Frank chalked it up to another of Miriam's erratic mood swings, but she insisted that something was about to go wrong that night. Frank left her at the apartment only to rush back a few hours later when he saw plumes of smoke coming from the building. When he arrived, he saw Miriam throwing all their belongings, including Frank's $40,000 collection of Japanese prints, out a window, attempting to save them. Had she attended the party at the embassy, all Frank's treasures would have been ruined. At that moment, Frank began to share Miriam's belief that she was clairvoyant. The cause of the fire was never determined.

Meanwhile, construction of the new Imperial Hotel was plagued by delays. Although Frank was quick to cast the blame elsewhere, pointing fingers at his Japanese laborers and even monsoon seasons, his senior draftsman, Antonin Raymond, claimed that construction was slowed by the master architect's constant tinkering with the hotel's design. Rumors spread among Tokyo's expatriate community that Frank had gone mad. His benefactors inside the imperial royal household were also deeply concerned about delays and cost overruns. Frank was brought into several meetings with hotel board members where he was accused of wasting time and money.

His only ally was board chairman Baron Okura Kihachiro, a wealthy eighty-year-old entrepreneur. During one tense meeting with Frank seated by his side, Okura stood and addressed his fellow board members. Normally quiet and composed, he pounded the table with both fists as he spoke. Frank watched the display and leaned on his interpreter to fill him in on what was happening.

"The Baron says that if the young man [Frank] will remain in Japan until the building is finished, he, the Baron will himself find the necessary money," the interpreter told Frank.

Okura ended his statement by telling his fellow board members that if they did not accept his proposal, they could all go to hell.

Frank stayed in Tokyo until the hotel project was nearly complete. One wing remained to be built, but it was a carbon copy of another wing that was finished and furnished. Frank was confident that his Japanese construction team would cap the project in time for its scheduled opening. "I could go home with a good conscience," he later wrote. "My clients, headed by the Baron, were generous, added substantial proof of appreciation to my fee."

After a champagne luncheon hosted by board members and a traditional tea ceremony attended by his fellow builders to bid him farewell, Frank and Miriam stepped aboard the *Empress of Asia* in late July 1922. Although she was not married to Frank, Miriam signed her name as *Miriam L. Wright* on the ship's passenger manifest. The fifty-year-old woman also shaved a year off her birthdate while Frank gave his true age, fifty-two.

Before his departure, Frank visited his creation one last time. "Here was the real thing," he wrote about the Imperial Hotel. "This could have happened nowhere but in Japan. Here was the spirit I had tried to compliment and respect in my work."

A group of thankful workers and draftsmen followed Frank's car to the pier at Yokohama Harbor, hooting and hollering out the window of their automobile. "Banzai. Wrieto-San, banzai!"

Frank and Miriam were both overwhelmed by the adulation they had received. As the passenger ship sailed out of the harbor, the couple congratulated themselves on a job well done. The lengthy project had taxed them both mentally and physically. Frank believed that all rough waters were now behind him, foaming in the wake of the ship that was bringing him back to America. He was dead wrong.

33

When Frank returned to the United States, he told friends and journalists alike that he planned to replicate the success of the Imperial Hotel project by building similar grand structures in great cities around the world. Before traveling back to Taliesin, Frank and Miriam stayed at Chicago's Congress Hotel, where he gathered a group of reporters and offered his perspective of the Japanese mindset. "They are very much afraid of us," Frank said. "They look upon us as a great giant which can crush them if it wants to… The Japanese have taken the steps they have because they feel they must do so to protect themselves if possible. They know the white man has swept over races from its path at will—and that they may be the next to become extinct."

He was talking about the steady rise of Japanese militarism, and his words served as a prescient warning of what was to come two decades later when Japanese war planes attacked the American military installation at Pearl Harbor.

Then Frank shifted gears and filled journalists in about his future plans.

"I shall rest a while," he told them. "And then I shall determine whether I am to make my headquarters in Chicago, or in Los Angeles where I have an office."

The architect had established a presence on the West Coast during the construction of Hollyhock House, a lavish home and theater arts complex that he had designed with his eldest son, Lloyd Wright, while he was in Japan.

The longer Frank had stayed and worked in Japan, the less he thought of Chicago. The city had given him both tremendous opportunity and great grief. He tripped over his tongue once again by calling the city a crude and vulgar place. When he was asked to describe a suitable coat of arms for the city, Frank suggested that an onion be emblazoned on its shield with a pig on the right and a poet on the left.

"Chicago is Indian for onion, in name as in reputation, unesthetic," he said. "Because culture has been stuck on its surface as a businessman's expedient or bought by the rich as luxury. Commonplace elegance is everywhere; harmonious elegance is desperately rare."

Newspaper readers in Chicago were stung by Frank's words, and once again he retreated to the relative safety of Taliesin.

Meanwhile, some six thousand miles away in Tokyo, a group of renowned architects from around the world got their first glimpse of the nearly finished Imperial Hotel and were less than impressed. The master builders thought that Frank's marvel was an architectural mess. Their spokesperson, Louis Christian Mullgardt, whose designs had been celebrated at the Panama-Pacific International Exposition in San Francisco, was particularly cruel in his critique, calling the construction of the Imperial Hotel "fantastic and prehistoric" and referring to Frank's decorative work as "Yucatanese, Aztec, and Navajo piffle." Mullgardt and his colleagues examined the hotel's stonework and were bowled over with laughter. "It's suggestive of a well-known cheese," he told a reporter, alluding to Swiss cheese. "And this is *earthquake country*. The swimming pool is also a mosquito farm. The errors are so numerous and flagrant that it may be said this structure should have never been built."

When word of Mullgardt's stinging criticism reached Frank, he fired back at the architect, accusing him of trade assassination. Later, another critic charged Frank with exploiting the Japanese people by foisting "a pet child of his imagination on an unsuspecting community."

Frank would not engage any further, as he was faced with another calamity, the death of his mother, Anna Lloyd Wright. Frank had been estranged from her for several months after banning her from Taliesin because of her constant fighting with Miriam. At one point, Anna gave her son an ultimatum. She demanded that he choose between her and his longtime lover. Frank chose to remain with Miriam. He felt as if he had spent most of his adult years in the eye of a hurricane with dark, ominous clouds circling around him. It was time for him to step out of the storm and away from all the things that brought unnecessary drama to his life.

"I have waded through rivers of tears and blood to find it with a ruthlessness seldom if ever heard of," he told his mother. "But always with a fool's sincerity and hope at least and a man's courage."

Due to her declining health, Anna needed around-the-clock medical care. Frank wanted to send her to a nursing home, but his sister Jane Porter insisted that he would have a battle on his hands. "A sanitarium is out of the question for Mother unless you want to take her there chloroformed. She won't go."

Jane told her brother that their mother had an uncanny ability to rally if anyone thought she was nearing her deathbed. "She comes through wherever she is."

Against their mother's wishes, Frank and Jane eventually sent Anna to the Waldheim Park sanatorium in Oconomowoc, Wisconsin, where she lived for three months before her death at age eighty-four. Her funeral was held at the Unity Chapel on the Lloyd Jones family property, and she was buried under a row of tall pine trees. Her nephews served as pallbearers.

There is no record to determine whether Frank and Miriam attended the funeral. Still, the woman who birthed him and had set him on a path toward greatness was now gone. He felt another great void, not as heart-wrenching as the loss of Mamah, but it was a loss of a strong female force in his life. Her death would pull him deeper into Miriam's orbit. Frank would marry her in a secret midnight ceremony overlooking the Wisconsin River. He handed her a wedding ring with a simple inscription, *From Frank to Miriam*. He had struggled to achieve simplicity in his life and his designs. Further romantic complications would continue to keep his personal life on shaky ground, but his adherence to the Japanese concept of *shibui*, the delicate balance of simplicity and complexity, would lead to arguably his greatest achievement as an architect and one that would save countless lives.

34

On September 1, 1923, the day of the Imperial Hotel's grand opening, arriving VIP guests felt a small tremor in the lobby. It was approximately 11:58 a.m. A few miles away at the docks of Yokohama Harbor, all the smiles disappeared from the faces of well-wishers saying their farewells to loved ones aboard the *Empress of Australia* as it was about to set sail for America. A young U.S. naval officer named Ellis M. Zacharias was standing on the dock at the time. "For an appreciable instant, everyone stood transfixed," he said, "by the sound of unearthly thunder."

Moments later, all felt a second and more severe jolt that lasted fourteen agonizing seconds as Japan was rocked by a 7.9-magnitude earthquake after a sixty-mile line of the Philippine oceanic plate cracked and collided with the Eurasian continental plate. Zacharias and everyone gathered on the dock were lifted off their feet as the pier collapsed under them before they all plunged into the water. Most would soon be washed away by a forty-foot tsunami that was triggered by the massive earthquake. Oil tanks on the hillside ruptured, spilling millions of gallons of oil into the harbor and setting the ocean ablaze. "Yokohama dropped like a pancake," said another witness, a Mrs. Wright (no relation) of London. "I was in my house on the bluff and was buried by the falling masonry and beams… The screams of people buried in the wreckage I will never forget. With the dead and dying lying everywhere, it was a charnel house."

In Kamakura, three hundred residents were killed instantly when a twenty-foot-high wall of water crashed over the small town. "A tidal wave swept out a great section of the village near the beach," said another survivor, Henry W. Kinney, the Tokyo-based editor of *Trans-Pacific* magazine. "I saw a thirty-foot sampan that had been lifted neatly atop the roof of [a house]. Vast portions of the hills facing the ocean had slid into the sea."

Katherine Elder of Iowa was riding in a streetcar in Yokohama when the earthquake lifted the train off the rails. She managed to climb out of the car, holding her sister's baby in her arms. Showers of cinders and ashes from burning buildings nearby set her clothes on fire, and she had to jump into a canal with the child to avoid being consumed by flames. Fires broke out in every direction, and the smoke and flames could be seen for miles. Seven hundred people living in a twelve-story tower overlooking Tokyo's Asukayama Park were crushed to death when the building collapsed. The cities of Tokyo and Yokohama were virtually destroyed within minutes.

A Japanese radio operator named Taki Yonemura managed to send word of the disaster to the Radio Corporation of America's outpost in San Francisco, California. "Conflagration subsequent to severe earthquake at Yokohama today," the wireless cable read. "Practically, the whole city is ablaze… The flames are spreading to the surrounding towns. It's a scene like hell."

All tunnels and bridges were destroyed, killing those who were attempting to flee, and Mount Fuji had virtually disappeared behind a cloak of heavy black smoke. By late afternoon, a three-hundred-foot tornado of fire had formed and spun its deadly flames across Tokyo, destroying everything in its path. Over 140,000 people would die in just forty-eight hours.

"[There are] dead and dying on every hand," one journalist wrote from the scene of the devastation. "Survivors who can grope their way through fire, smoke and rubbish are leaving." Those lucky few who managed to survive the earthquake and fires sought refuge at whatever shelter was available to them, but nearly all the buildings in Japan's capital city had been destroyed. The Imperial Theatre had crumbled to the ground. There was nothing left of the Mitsukoshi department store but a mountain of rubble.

But there in the middle of all that devastation, Frank Lloyd Wright's Imperial Hotel was still standing.

An American named S. F. Murphy had registered at the hotel while coincidently on a business trip to sell seismic records to Tokyo University. "I was in the grill room," he told a reporter. "After the quake hit us, the grill [room] shook like a leaf. We plunged through the broken windows of the building, which remained standing."

The Imperial Hotel floated like a battleship on the soil, just as Frank had planned. The excruciating detail that he had put into his sketches and the seemingly never-ending study and tests of the topography, the building platforms, and much smaller earthquake waves had been successful. Everyone who was inside the hotel when the earthquake struck lived. Frank's insistence that his plans for a large reflecting pool not get scrapped due to cost overruns was also critical to the hotel's survival, as hotel workers formed a bucket brigade to take water from the pool and pour it on window sashes and frames to prevent the building from burning when flames jumped onto the property from across the street.

After building the first version of Taliesin, which had ultimately become a fortress of death, the architect found redemption with his design of the Imperial Hotel, a fortress of life.

But this news was slow to reach Frank, who was living at his studio on Vermont Avenue in Hollywood, California, at the time. He had read that Yokohama and Tokyo had been obliterated. He could not sleep for several days over grave concern about the fates of his many Japanese friends and colleagues, including Baron Okura Kihachiro.

Tokyo's Imperial Hotel, incorporating Frank Lloyd Wright's innovative and life-saving earthquake-proof design. (Getty Images)

"Finally, on the third night at about two in the morning, the telephone rang," he wrote in his memoir. "The [San Francisco] *Examiner* wished to inform me that the Imperial Hotel was completely destroyed. My heart sank."

The newspaper editor had mistaken the Imperial Hotel for the now gutted Imperial Theatre. Frank held a great lump in his throat until he received a telegram from Baron Okura. "Hotel stands undamaged as a monument to your genius," Okura wrote. "Hundreds of homeless provided by perfectly maintained service. Congratulations."

In the days to follow, the Imperial Hotel was transformed into a center for emergency relief, housing hundreds of refugees and providing thousands of meals to those left homeless.

When Baron Okura's cable was shared with news editors around the world, Frank was given high praise for his efforts. "The Imperial Hotel remains today a monument to the skill and ingenuity of an American architect," wrote a reporter for the *Los Angeles Times*. "Its immunity from the awful wreckage that laid waste to the greater part of Tokyo is a splendid tribute to the invincibility of science under the attacks of nature in her fiercest manifestations… Frank Lloyd Wright…has demonstrated that man can safeguard himself against the earthquake as certainly as the cyclone cellar can defeat the whirlwind or the lightning rod can circumvent the thunderbolt."

Soon, architects around the world began to incorporate Frank's design methods into their own construction plans to erect buildings that could withstand earthquakes and other calamities. The number of lives saved by the sheer genius of Frank's flexible architectural design style remains immeasurable today.

35

A year after the deadly earthquake, Baron Okura, as the formal representative of the Japanese imperial household, asked Frank to lead efforts to rebuild Tokyo, which included the construction of new living quarters for Emperor Yoshihito and other members of the royal family. The architect was honored by the request but knew that such a project would take as long as a decade to complete. He politely declined the offer to return to Japan "even to assume deification."

Frank did send Baron Okura several design plans and drawings to aid with the massive reconstruction effort. Then he turned inward and back to his mission of redesigning America.

His personal life remained in turmoil for a period of time. His marriage to Miriam would only last a few short years and ended as explosively as it had begun. The second Mrs. Frank Lloyd Wright moved out of Taliesin after just six months. She had felt like a prisoner living remotely in the Wisconsin countryside. Unlike wealthy members of the expatriate community back in Tokyo, farmers and their wives shunned her in Spring Green. Miriam's feeling of isolation encouraged her growing morphine addiction. Frank tried to get treatment for his wife, but she refused. Miriam later told reporters that she left Frank after she had suffered a nervous breakdown because he had "struck her, deserted her, tormented her and worst of all admitted that he was bored with her."

About a year into his separation from Miriam, Frank was staying at Taliesin when fire broke out once again inside his rebuilt home. He had just come from his bedroom and was sitting outside in a small gazebo-like dining area, eating his dinner. He heard a clap of thunder and saw a flash of lightning illuminate the property. From his vantage point inside the tiny structure atop a hill, Frank could see down to his bedroom, where smoke began pouring out the windows.

"Again, there it was. Fire!" he recalled in his memoir. "I called for water… I thought I had to put the fire out when an ominous crackling above the bedroom ceiling indicated [that] fire had gotten into the dead spaces beneath the roof."

Flames quickly tore through the home, and two of Frank's employees, his driver and a Japanese apprentice, recommended to him that they try to save what they could inside the home.

"No, fight the fire," Frank ordered. "Fight, fight, fight I tell you. Save Taliesin or let [it] all go!"

He had not been there when Julian Carlton burned the original Taliesin to the ground and murdered Mamah and most everyone else inside. He could not have prevented that tragedy. But Frank vowed that he would do everything in his power to save the home that he had rebuilt in their memory.

He stood on the roof with his feet burning and lungs seared by smoke while pouring buckets of water on the flames, which had now reached the workrooms. There was no way to save Taliesin now. In twenty minutes, half of the structure had burned to the ground. Ironically, the fire was not caused by lightning but by faulty wires inside Frank's home telephone. He was fortunate that no one was burned badly or killed in the blaze. This time, there was no ghoulish hatchet man waiting outside Taliesin to bring more hell to those who managed to get themselves out of the burning home alive. Still, he was devastated. There was an estimated $150,000 in damage to the property. Taliesin was gone.

As Frank inspected the damage wearing singed socks and trousers, a voice of hope came to him. "But, Frank, Taliesin stands where you stand."

The words did not come from some apparition. Instead, they were spoken softly by the new love in Frank's life, twenty-seven-year-old Olgivanna Milanoff. They had met while both attended a performance of the Russian Ballet in Chicago. She was described as a "Byzantine Madonna" with narrow eyes, slender hips, and the grace of a dancer. Olgivanna was the granddaughter of a Montenegrin duke and war hero named Marko Miljanov. Her father, Jovan Lazović, had served as Montenegro's chief justice for three decades. Olgivanna, who referred to herself as a rhythm instructor, had been raised in Russia and fled to America after the October Revolution of 1917.

Like Mamah Borthwick had been, Olgivanna was married at the time she met Frank. She would also remain by his side during the painstaking reconstruction of Taliesin.

Frank went through forty design sheets before he came up with the proper layout for his new home. The second Taliesin disaster had humbled him and taught him patience.

"Taliesin's radiant brow was marked now by pain and sorrow," he wrote. "But it should come forth and live again with a serenity unknown before."

He would build something even larger than its predecessors. He added a second level to the home with a Juliet-style overlook into the living room below, a cantilevered balcony that he affectionately called the "Bird Walk," as well as two new bedrooms that would soon be filled.

After nearly two years of estrangement, Frank asked Miriam for a divorce, but she refused and took him to court instead, accusing him of adultery.

During the initial court hearing, Frank's attorney called her "a gold digger, not a wife."

He then picked up a stack of sealed envelopes and waved them around the courtroom. "I have 100 filthy letters of hers, sent to bankers and contractors in which she blackened Mr. Wright's character," attorney Levi Bancroft told the judge. "And if I turned them over to federal officials, she'd go to the penitentiary for writing obscene matter."

Miriam told the judge that she was open to the idea of returning to her husband, but Frank scoffed at the notion. "The attempt at reconciliation was a farce," Frank told reporters who were covering the court proceedings. "I am unwilling to permit the name of the other woman [Olgivanna] to be dragged into the dirt if I can save her [Miriam] from herself."

Minneapolis Daily Star HOME

U. S. SIFTS WRIGHT SCANDAL

SHEPARD INDICTMENT UPHELD

ARCHITECT AN
DANCER FOUN
IN LOVE NES
AT WILDHURS

JUDGE DENIES DEFENSE PLEA DEATH CHARGE BE THROWN OUT

Lake Minnetonka 'Love Nest' Principals in New Tangle With Law

WILL FIGHT EXTRADITION

WRIGHT LEAPS AT LAWYER FOR DANCER'S MATE

'I Love Olga,' Says Wright, Held in Minneapolis Cell; Admits Parentage of Child

MAID SAYS PAIR LIVED QUIETLY IN TONKA COTTAGE

Frank Lloyd Wright found himself back in the headlines with another sex scandal in 1926 involving his second wife, Miriam Noel Wright, and his future wife, Olgivanna Milanoff. (MINNEAPOLIS STAR)

Weeks after the hearing, Miriam showed up at Taliesin and attempted to storm the gates, but she was refused entry to the property. She then threw rocks at the house and broke a few windows. Exhausted after her spectacle, Miriam booked a room at a Spring Green hotel and offered a statement to reporters. "I am without money," she said. "I need a home and as long as I remain Mr. Wright's legal wife, I intend he shall take me in."

Miriam later returned to Taliesin with local police officers and a search warrant to scour the property for Frank's new mistress, but Olgivanna was visiting Chicago at the time. Undaunted, Miriam attempted to get her deported as an "undesirable alien."

When that effort failed, Miriam offered Olgivanna a warning about the famous architect. "He will eventually cast off everyone who loves him, taking a new love as fast as he wears out the old," she told a reporter while sobbing. "Yet, I would do it all over again. That is my cross. For mine is a greater tragedy than Mamah Borthwick's. She is dead. And I live on. Oh, how I loved him."

In the fall of 1926, Miriam joined forces with Vladimir Hinzenberg, Olgivanna's ex-husband and father to her young daughter, Svetlana, in a campaign to have Frank and Olgivanna arrested by U.S. marshals on charges of violating the Mann Act. Hinzenberg also feared that the couple planned to take his daughter out of the country and wanted to file kidnapping charges against them. Hinzenberg's attorney, Harold Jackson, joined a federal raid at a home on the shores of Lake Minnetonka in Minnesota, where Frank was living with Olgivanna at the time under fake names. Authorities investigating whether the unmarried couple had violated the Mann Act, crossing state lines for sexual activity, had been tipped off to the location by a neighbor who recognized the famous architect. When the neighbor and his wife visited the home, they heard the cries of a baby in a bedroom. "It is mine," Olgivanna said of the infant. Frank admitted to them that he was the infant girl's father and then came clean about his real name. "I am through with my wife [Miriam] forever," Frank told the couple. "And I am going to see this thing through."

The neighbor called the police, and officers rushed to the home with Hinzenberg's lawyer, who said that he could positively identify the couple. "You dog!" the lawyer snarled at Frank while officers were placing the architect under arrest. Hearing this, Frank lunged at Jackson, but he was tackled by detectives before he could reach him. Jackson was ordered to wait outside the house while officers handcuffed Frank and Olgivanna, who were then placed in separate police cars and driven to the Hennepin County jail. Frank handed money he had in his pockets to the warden, who wrote his name down in the jail record.

"A warden took me down a long corridor along brutal, heavy animal cages built tier on tier," he recalled. "The clang of the gates he opened and shut as he went echoed and reverberated behind us… He clanged our way to the far end where the 'better element' of jaildom, the high-swindlers and bootleggers were kept… Scarcely able to breathe, I sat down on the mattress. Saw it stained. Was it blood?"

Olgivanna was also booked on charges of allegedly violating the Mann Act and placed in a jail cell. The next morning, the warden asked if she would be willing to give a statement to reporters. She had not slept and was exhausted and dirty from having spent the night in a dank cell. She also missed her child, who had been taken away from her upon their arrest. But instead of telling newsmen to go away, Olgivanna decided to express her humiliation and weariness during a lengthy jailhouse interview. "I have been driven from place to place like a wild beast," she told the newsmen. "But I will stick to Frank Lloyd Wright. He is my man. My little baby brought me through this year. The happiness it gave me to watch her grow kept me alive. Now the crash has come. It is awful but I suppose we still have something to be thankful for—this terrible year. It is over at last."

Olgivanna told reporters that she had read a letter to Frank from Miriam where she vowed that she would never return to him. "I suppose it was foolish of me, but I believed her and so did Frank… She [Miriam] found out about me and kept writing to Frank and threatening us. Then my baby was coming. I wasn't sorry, I was happy. I wanted the baby, but Miriam kept making trouble… I used to say, 'when she knows that I am a mother, she will be merciful. She is a mother too, she will understand.'"

Olgivanna claimed that Miriam had learned she was pregnant and tried to raid the hospital three days after their daughter, Iovanna, was born, and Olgivanna was forced to flee the hospital on a stretcher.

"Miriam would give us no peace."

When reporters caught up with Frank in his jail cell, he stated, "I regard [Olgivanna] as my wife. I love her and intend to marry her as soon as legal obstacles can be removed. I have nothing to conceal. The facts will show that I am morally justified in everything I have done."

Miriam promised never to give Frank such satisfaction. "I will never divorce Frank Wright as long as I live," she told a journalist.

Then, in an attempt to stick the knife in even deeper, Miriam announced that she would demand an investigation into the 1914 murders of Mamah Borthwick, her children, and the workmen at Taliesin, falsely implying that Frank had played a role in the massacre.

Kitty Wright, who had been out of the public eye for several years, emerged back into the spotlight to defend her former husband. Kitty and son John Wright both traveled to Minnesota to show their support for the couple.

A group of Frank's friends and business associates in Chicago also wrote a letter to the Minneapolis federal district attorney, Lafayette French, who was overseeing the case, and asked him to withdraw criminal charges against Frank and Olgivanna. "He has our sympathy in his present difficulties," the letter stated. "And we implore you not to permit your high office to be used as an instrument of persecution and revenge."

Feeling a tremendous heartache over her separation from their baby, Olgivanna was taken from the county jail and placed in a sanatorium until her arraignment in federal court. While there, she penned a letter of her own to be printed in the *Wisconsin State Journal* where she described the late stages of her pregnancy and the torment she experienced at the hands of Miriam. "The little life by my heart was beating strongly, ready to come and see the world," Olgivanna wrote. "I went to Chicago to prepare for that coming and met the catastrophe—the persecution of Miriam Wright, who called newspaper men, photographers and detectives to make sensational attacks upon me and the life I was guarding, a terrible scene and shock, just one week before my baby was born. Only mothers can understand the agony and suffering I had to go through."

Frank and Miriam engaged in their own battle of words in a newspaper, with each writing their own stories to be printed in full. Frank said that the loss of Mamah Borthwick had left him "so sick of heart that he would have welcomed death" and that his grief and vulnerability was exploited by Miriam. "My mental condition being what it was—distressed, and asking nothing better in life than to quit it, I acceded [to her]… I lived with Miriam Wright literally [as a] pawn to her ungovernable behavior, which was aroused whenever she was crossed in the most trivial things. In all this, there was something sinister and elusive that baffled me."

The news editor allowed Miriam to read Frank's story before she penned her response. Detailing her own version of their relationship, she claimed that Frank made love to her the very first night they met. "[He] said that he had at last found a woman who understood him and who was beautiful and charming enough to be his real companion." Miriam then accused Frank of having numerous affairs while they were together. "I know that he is a selfish man who loves nobody," she continued. "He never had a real love in his life… Is the public so stupid as to believe for a moment that a man would live 12 years with [a] woman with no ties but love and then abandon her for another woman unless there was something abnormal, something wrong in the makeup of this man who now repudiates what he held dearer than anything else except himself?… When a man's cup of sin runs over, nobody can help him. He must pay for the suffering he has caused."

Miriam then filed a $50,000 lawsuit against Frank, claiming that she had loaned him money that he never paid back. A sheriff's deputy in Iowa County seized several rare Japanese prints from Taliesin and had them sold to pay Miriam $15,000 of the amount she claimed to have given her husband when they lived together. As this happened, a judge in Minnesota granted Frank and Olgivanna the freedom to leave the state with their newborn daughter and live temporarily in California.

The case dragged on for several more months until Frank and Miriam reached a divorce settlement in late July 1927 as he agreed to pay her a lump sum of $36,000 for alimony.

Miriam took her financial windfall and traveled to Los Angeles.

"And now I'm going to live," she told a reporter while wearing her customary cape and fur-lined turban. "I've had several offers from Hollywood and I'm going to drop in tomorrow and have some screen tests taken. I might stay and work in a [motion] picture and then I'm going to Chicago to settle my affairs and go on to Paris."

When asked if she would avoid any romantic entanglements in the future, Miriam smiled and shook her head. "No, I'm not through with men. Men are wonderful."

Weeks later, Miriam would be arrested for sending a nasty note about Frank through the mail. Miriam sent the letter to a friend, who turned it over to Frank, who then sent it to federal authorities in Washington, DC, alleging that Miriam had broken federal obscenity laws. Since Miriam had written the note and then mailed it, she could be charged with transportation of obscene materials. According to the complaint, the letter was "too lewd to be placed upon the records of the court." Federal agents quietly approached her inside a hotel dining room in Chicago. They suggested that Miriam leave her table and follow them to her suite where they would read the arrest warrant in private to avoid her any embarrassment. But she would not budge.

"Read it here," she told them. "Shout it from the rooftops!"

After her arrest, Miriam sought revenge by attempting to get federal agents to reinvestigate Frank's cohabitation with Olgivanna at Taliesin. She wrote letters to every sitting U.S. senator. Three responded—George Norris of Nebraska, Lynn Frazier of North Dakota, and James Reed of Missouri—and another probe into the alleged Mann Act violation was launched.

Criminal charges against Miriam for the lewd note were eventually dropped when Frank refused to testify against her.

When Frank's divorce from Miriam was announced, one local newspaper reporter reflected on what he called "one of Wisconsin's most [incredible] records of unconventional homelife."

The newsman referred to Frank as a genius beyond all question. "Nobody can estimate the immense value of his contribution to his art," the journalist wrote. "But he has ignored the rules of life that bind the rest of us, and has borne a supreme burden of unhappiness. Perhaps it is the price of genius."

The federal charges against the architect and the mother of his new child were also dropped, paving the way for Frank's third marriage. But would Olgivanna create the same drama for him that his other wives had caused?

36

Miriam Wright's plot to destroy her ex-husband crumbled altogether in the spring of 1928.

The federal Mann Act investigation against Frank and Olgivanna was closed, and Miriam's attempt to deport Olgivanna to Montenegro or Russia also collapsed. "I am beaten by matrimony, by wealth, by lawyers and senators and congressmen," Miriam told a reporter.

Deflated but not yet defeated, Miriam took out her anger by breaking into one of Frank's suburban homes in La Jolla, California, and smashing everything in sight. She threw expensive china against the walls, destroyed floor lamps, and tore apart manuscripts that Frank had left in his office.

Neither Frank nor Olgivanna were inside the residence at the time, but their maid saw the giant mess and immediately called police. Miriam was quickly arrested nearby and did not deny the crime; instead, she was proud of the destruction.

"It was not an act of vengeance," she told the arresting officers. "It was a case of their having ruined my home and I decided to wreck theirs. If [the] police had given me ten more minutes, I would have made a complete job of it."

Miriam was charged with a count of malicious mischief. Olgivanna arrived on the scene while Miriam was in handcuffs. The angry ex-wife offered Olgivanna sixty-nine dollars to pay for the damage. Miriam had seventy dollars in her purse but needed a buck to get a bus back to San Diego. Police estimated the damage to Frank's home at over $1,000. Olgivanna took Miriam's settlement offer of cash in the hope that she would never see her again.

While still looking over his shoulder for any sign of his volatile ex-wife, Frank also faced another crisis as the Bank of Wisconsin seized Taliesin and all the assets inside the home to satisfy $40,000 of unpaid loans. Inside the inner garden at Taliesin, fifty local farmers and businessmen gathered as the bank auctioned off Frank's farm equipment, oriental rugs, Asian sculptures, wood carvings, paintings, and Japanese prints. The bank purchased the property back for $700,000. Frank had lost Taliesin and all the treasures he had collected around the world, but he still had Olgivanna and their baby Iovanna by his side. He also adopted Olgivanna's older daughter, Svetlana Hinzenberg.

On August 25, 1928, exactly one year after his divorce from Miriam was finalized, Frank married Olgivanna at an estate at Rancho Santa Fe, a suburb of San Diego.

"We are together, well and happy," Frank said in a statement. "We're going to put new life into new buildings in the great Arizona desert spaces during the next year or two."

The couple needed a fresh start and a reprieve from the madness and pain inflicted on them by Miriam. Although Frank would later buy Taliesin back from the bank, his focus was already shifting from the rolling fields of the Midwest to the sunbaked desert region of the American Southwest. He purchased several hundred acres of land just northeast of Scottsdale, Arizona, and over the course of the next decade, he would build Taliesin West.

Originally, Frank desired to build a simple camp in the desert with fifteen cabins, but like all his projects, his ideas expanded, and the camp eventually grew into a sprawling complex. "The terrain changed absolutely," he said regarding the difference between Wisconsin and Arizona. "Here we came to the desert where there are astonishing and exciting new forms. In Wisconsin, by way of age, erosion has softened everything. Out there [in Arizona], everything was sharp, savage. Everything was armed and it was an entirely new experience." He used the natural materials around him, stone from local quarries, Arizona cotton to build canvas panels, and rough-sawed pine from trees grown tall in the northern part of the state to create not only a home but an architectural community that would last for generations.

Taliesin West, he said, "is a look over the rim of the world."

There were few distractions in his personal life. Miriam died in 1930, alone in a Milwaukee, Wisconsin, hospital while she was recovering from a surgery. She had been working on a manuscript detailing her life as Mrs. Frank Lloyd Wright. Miriam had come up with the perfect subtitle for her book: *The Biography of an Undisciplined Soul.*

Olgivanna Lloyd Wright, Frank's third wife, stayed by his side for the rest of his life and helped him create Taliesin West in Arizona. (Taliesin West Preservation)

"What was left of a remarkably vital high-spirited woman, who for fifteen years [was] psychopathic, had been going up in flame, seldom knowing real rest unless by some artificial means, had found it," Frank later wrote about his second wife. "At last, she was beyond [the] reach of exploitation."

Without the constant threat of Miriam hanging over him, his new wife, and their young children, Frank was able to focus solely on his work, and he flourished. As Mamah Borthwick had done during her relationship with the architect, Olgivanna championed her husband's genius and even collaborated with his work. Together, they established the Taliesin Fellowship, which allowed aspiring builders and designers from around the country to travel to Chandler, Arizona, and Spring Green, Wisconsin, to learn from the master architect. Frank's students also assisted with some of his greatest creations. In 1934, Frank was hired by a department store president from Pittsburgh, Pennsylvania, named Edgar Kaufmann Sr. to build him and his wife Liliane a summer retreat in the Appalachian mountains. Frank visited the location they had in mind in Connellsville, Pennsylvania. The Kaufmanns had fallen in love with a place called Bear Run and envisioned a cottage where they could look out at a nearby ravine and waterfall. During Frank's inspection of the property, he noticed a rock ledge rising high above the waterfall on the other side of the ravine. Suddenly, he came up with an idea. "The natural thing would be to cantilever the house from that rock bank over the falling water," he thought to himself.

He raced back to Taliesin in Wisconsin and began discussing the project with his apprentices. But how would he recreate the vision he had swirling in his head on paper? Frank procrastinated a bit while thinking the project through. Meanwhile, the client was getting anxious and slightly frustrated by his so-called lack of progress. Finally, Frank grabbed a pencil and three pieces of colored tracing paper, one to design the basement, the next to design the first floor, and the last to sketch out what he wanted the second floor to look like. His apprentices all stood around wondering if this was how it felt to watch Mozart or Beethoven compose one of their classical masterpieces. The master architect worked feverishly, designing each section of the home along with the elevations. He wore down a full set of pencils until he finally threw his writing utensils down on the drafting table in a dramatic indication that he was finished. In just two hours, Frank Lloyd Wright had designed what would become the most famous modern home in the world, Fallingwater.

Seven years later, in 1943, while another war raged across the globe, Frank was commissioned to build a museum in New York City to house works of art that had been collected over several decades by millionaire businessman Solomon R. Guggenheim. Now seventy-eight years old, Frank shifted his design focus away from earthly things like Fallingwater and Taliesin West. Instead, he looked toward the sky. While every construction and reconstruction of Taliesin in both Wisconsin and Arizona had been grounded by nature, Frank referred to his new design as "Archeseum, a building in which to see the highest" amid a city filled with "soulless skyscrapers." Some New Yorkers were less than flattering when describing the building, which to them looked at best like "an upside down cake" and at worst, a "great stone toilet bowl."

The new museum would take Frank more than a decade to build, and the final result was awe-inspiring. The exterior was designed to resemble a seashell with logarithmic spirals, while the interior turned the conventional museum setting on its head by guiding visitors from the top of the building downward on a continuous ramp overlooking an open rotunda.

There was no building like it anywhere else in the world. As the project neared completion, Frank described the uniqueness of the museum to reporters. "For the first time, a building has been designed that destroys everything square, rectilinear," he boasted. "You see paintings under the same conditions in which the artist did them, as they would rest on an easel, illuminated by a mixture of light and artificial light… [It is] a building that creates [an] atmosphere instead of a frame in which to show a painting."

A newspaper correspondent working for the *Evening Standard* of London was given a private tour of the museum in July 1958 when Frank had just turned ninety-one years old. The newsman described the aged architect as "an alert, sharp eyed figure…a tall lean white-maned patriarch, cheerful, testy and garrulous by turns," who poked his walking stick into every corner of the Guggenheim building site while he inspected the progress. He also referred to the museum itself as "a spaceship mysteriously grounded among the staid apartment houses facing Central Park."

Later that month, Frank took out a clean sheet of drafting paper and designed his own tomb.

Frank's first wife, Kitty, died in March 1959 in Santa Monica, California, just one day shy of her eighty-eighth birthday. Her remains were cremated. Frank was not immediately informed about her passing. When he asked one of his children why he had not been told, David, his fourth child with Kitty, reportedly shrugged his shoulders and replied, "You never showed any interest."

Although Kitty may have been far from Frank's mind in his later years, he did reflect on a chance meeting that he had with her years after their divorce in his memoir. They had bumped into each other while attending an art exhibition in Chicago. "I remember an echo of my earlier youth," he wrote. "A tall, graying, but still handsome woman came toward me smiling. A moment's hesitation. And then I recognized Catherine [Kitty]. I had not seen her in fifteen years. These years seemed to have dealt gently and she looked—frankly—young and happy."

The following Easter, Frank and Olgivanna, both dressed in white, spent the day at Taliesin West, enjoying a holiday celebration at their home complete with balloons and tables lined with multicolored eggs. After lunch, they watched a movie in Taliesin's theater and then listened to a classical music performance by celebrated pianist Carol Robinson. It was an exhausting day, and Frank grew agitated, as he had been kept up past his 7:30 bedtime.

Over the next six days, he looked worn down. Frank was not the alert, sharp-eyed figure he had been while giving a tour of the Guggenheim just months before. The next Saturday, he attempted to drag himself back to the theater to watch a dance recital given by his wife and their daughter, Iovanna, who was now thirty-three years old, and several other performers. Frank complained to his wife that he was experiencing severe discomfort in his stomach and bowels. "The pain. Can't bear it," he told Olgivanna. "Mother, chop the old tree down."

He was rushed to St. Joseph's Hospital in Phoenix where doctors discovered an intestinal blockage. They performed surgery to remove the blockage two days later. Frank woke up after the operation and requested a glass of milk and some fresh air. Instead, he was placed in an oxygen tent. Olgivanna slept over at the hospital and remained by her husband's side. His condition was "satisfactory," so there was hope that he would eventually be released from the hospital and allowed to return home.

THE CAPITAL TIMES

FRANK LLOYD WRIGHT DIES

Pass Withholding, Nelson Pleads

Succumbs to 5-Day Illness

Call One-Day Hearing Halt

Appears Before Solons

One Witness Still to Be Quizzed By Prosecution

World Loses Greatest Architect

Services to Be Held At Taliesin East Next Week

Frank Lloyd Wright died in 1959 at age ninety-one. He is widely considered to be America's greatest architect. (Capital Times)

During the early morning hours of April 9, 1959, Frank's gallbladder burst while he was in his hospital bed. Seconds later, his heart stopped. Doctors could not resuscitate him. Frank Lloyd Wright was dead.

At some point during his thirty-year, peaceful marriage to Olgivanna, he told her that he wished to be buried in the small cemetery by the Unity Chapel in Spring Green next to his slain soulmate, Mamah Borthwick. Olgivanna, who had always been comfortable in her relationship with Frank and never felt that she had to compete with the ghost of a dead woman, honored his request. The casket carrying the master architect's body was pulled by horses to the same plot of thick blue grass where he had buried Mamah forty-five years before. The box was lowered into a hole a few feet away from her gravesite.

"A dream? In realization ended," Frank once wrote about his love for Mamah. "No. Woven, a golden thread in the human pattern of the precious fabric that is life: her life built into the house of houses. So far as it may be known—forever!"

AUTHOR'S NOTE AND ACKNOWLEDGMENTS

The Solomon R. Guggenheim Museum was designated an official New York City landmark in 1990. It was the youngest building ever to receive this distinction. The Guggenheim is one of eight buildings designed by Frank Lloyd Wright on the list of UNESCO's World Heritage Sites.

Although Frank was buried near Mamah Borthwick in Spring Green, Wisconsin, their eternal rest together was disturbed upon the death of Olgivanna in 1985. In her own will, Olgivanna wished to have Frank's remains exhumed from the Lloyd family cemetery in Wisconsin, cremated, and taken to Scottsdale, Arizona, where they were mixed with her ashes and interred at an undisclosed location somewhere on the grounds of Taliesin West.

I first learned about Frank Lloyd Wright's fascinating story over a cup of coffee while meeting with Hollywood producer Taylor DiGilio in Los Angeles. I was pitching Taylor and his company, Appian Way (owned by Oscar-winning actor Leonardo DiCaprio), the book I had been writing at the time, which would be called *Blood in the Water: The Untold Story of a Family Tragedy*. After talking about how best to adapt that project into a feature film, I asked Taylor what he and his team were working on.

"Do you know the architect Frank Lloyd Wright?" he asked me.

"Of course."

"Do you know what happened to him back in 1914?"

"No, tell me."

Taylor gave me a synopsis of the story, and I was hooked. Originally I had planned to focus solely on the murders at Taliesin, but Frank and Mamah would not let me. As I plunged myself into my research, I discovered a true love story involving two people who had the courage to fight for their love against all comers: scorned spouses, tabloid journalists, the clergy, and pious members of Edwardian society.

As Frank had once written in a letter about Mamah to Ellen Key, "We lived—richly."

During the research for this book, I leaned on the Frank Lloyd Wright Foundation for information about the master architect as well as dozens of newspaper articles from the time. I also incorporated details from these tremendous books: *Frank Lloyd Wright: An Autobiography*; Mark Borthwick's endearing family memoir, *A Brave and Lovely Woman: Mamah Borthwick and Frank Lloyd Wright*; Meryle Secrest's *Frank Lloyd Wright: A Biography*; John Lloyd Wright's insightful memoir, *My Father Who Is on Earth*; *The Fellowship: The Untold Story of Frank Lloyd Wright & The Taliesin Fellowship* by Roger Friedland and Harold Zellman; Paul Hendrickson's richly reported book, *Plagued by Fire: The Dreams and Furies of Frank Lloyd Wright*; and William R. Drennan's blistering account, *Death in a Prairie House: Frank Lloyd Wright and the Taliesin Murders*. For anyone looking for more information about Frank and Mamah, add these books to your personal library.

I would also like to thank my wife, Kristin, for your continued love and support while I was juggling this project and a complicated theatrical production at the same time. I promise that I won't do that again! You make me a better person and a better writer. I love you! I would also like to thank my amazing and accomplished daughters, Bella and Mia Sherman. I hope you'll find Mamah Borthwick as inspiring as I did. I'd like to thank my uncle Jim Sherman for your continued toughness and humor in spite of difficult circumstances. I would like to thank my incredible in-laws, Steve and Martha Goldsmith, and also Nate, Jenny, Jack, and Lyla York as well as Garrett, Rosemary, and Millie Goldsmith. Of course, I cannot forget my rock star literary agent, Peter Steinberg, and the team at UTA, including Olivia Fanaro and Keya Khayatian, Ike Zhang, Andrew Lear, and Matthew Baskharoon. Thank you again! And a huge thanks to my editor, Anna Michels, and the marketing and publicity team at Sourcebooks. You all do such a great job, and writing and publishing is a team effort. I've got the very best team members on the planet.

I'd like to also thank Dave Wedge, Corly Cunningham, Toby Duane, Bobby and Ellen Bandera, Marc Lidsky, Mark Pine, Derek Capolino, Andy Little, Huffa Eaton, Tom and Kristy Cunningham, Lisa Doucet, Paul Ciolino, cousins Chris and Matthew Neal, Mark Sullivan, Joe, Suzy and Paul Rapoza, devoted fan Karen Teece, and the wonderful readers at Club RED for their friendship and support. A big thanks also to my incredible assistant, Nick Franco.

It's now time to step back from the keyboard, pour a glass of pinot noir, and figure out where the next writing journey will take me. When I find out, so will you.

Casey Sherman

DON'T MISS *HELLTOWN*, ANOTHER THRILLING TRUE CRIME NARRATIVE FROM CASEY SHERMAN!

CHAPTER ONE

West Barnstable, Massachusetts
1968

Edie Vonnegut was nervous about bringing the boy home to meet her father, who was holed up in his writer's shed off the back of their Cape Cod farmhouse on Scudder Lane. Seventeen-year-old Edie had learned to traipse lightly around her father, Kurt, especially when he was working.

"Wait here," Edie told her date, a handsome, young ice hockey player from nearby Hyannis. "He said that he wants to meet you. I'll be back in a sec."

Edie left the boy standing at the edge of Coggins' Pond at the back of the property as she tiptoed toward the wooden door and knocked.

"What?" an exasperated Vonnegut asked. "What now?"

Edie pushed open the door, paused for a moment to calm her nerves, and stepped inside. Standing at the threshold atop a wooden plank that held Thoreau's quote, *Beware of All Enterprises That Require New Clothes*, the daughter saw her father's lanky frame hunched over his Smith Corona typewriter with its space bar indented by his thumb from years of use and self-abuse. His head wore a halo of gray cigarette smoke, and underneath, Edie could see the grimace on his worn and wrinkled face. It was a look that terrified her siblings and on numerous occasions had sent their mother, Jane, to the laundry room, where she would lock herself inside to cry alone for hours.

The boy heard a rumble of chatter coming from the studio, followed by the slamming of the door as Edie marched out with her arms flailing and her long, brown hair blowing in the Cape Cod breeze. She turned once to flip her father the middle finger and then stomped toward the main house, leaving the boy to fend for himself at the edge of Coggins' Pond.

The boy jogged up the hill just as Vonnegut exploded out of his study and intercepted him on the beaten path back to the house.

"I'm going to say one thing, so let me be perfectly clear," the writer barked. "Don't you fuck my daughter. Don't you dare fuck her!"

Vonnegut's words startled the boy. He had only come over to take Edie for ice cream and a movie, and now he was being subjected to a bizarre, sexual interrogation from the girl's domineering dad.

Scared and confused, the boy simply nodded and picked up his pace toward the main house.

Vonnegut watched him go and hoped that his words would sink in. The writer then retreated back to his studio and continued the daunting work of editing his latest novel, a book that he intended to call *Slaughterhouse-Five*.

Locked away in his study, Vonnegut reached for another Pall Mall and struck a match. After taking the smoke into his lungs, his mind returned to his daughter. She had been a real sweet kid, but now that she was older, she'd become a bitchy little flibbertigibbet.

He felt that he had a right to be overly protective of the teenager. She was beautiful after all. Edie was gifted with a svelte, athletic figure that had turned every boy's head at Barnstable High School. She wore her skirts short and her hair long, parted in the middle with brown curls cascading over her shoulders. Vonnegut knew he did not need to worry much about the boy he had just encountered in the backyard. The kid seemed polite enough.

Instead, he fretted over a new crowd that Edie was hanging out with down the road in Provincetown. That group seemed aimless, uninspired, and hungry for only drugs and sex. Hippies were taking over the tip of Cape Cod, and Kurt Vonnegut Jr. feared that his precocious daughter could get washed away with the tide.

Like Edie Vonnegut, Sydney Monzon was fascinated by Ptown, which was only a thirty-minute drive from the place where she grew up but a world away from her parents' stuffy home in the village of Eastham, which ran up the Cape's long, giraffe-like neck. Commercial Street, with its eclectic vibe, was the closest that Sydney could get to the counterculture eruption that was happening in places like Haight-Ashbury in San Francisco and Greenwich Village in New York, at least for now. She had recently told her sister Linda and her closest friends that she wanted a new life, one filled with adventure and exploration. Sydney was a year out of Nauset High School, where she had graduated in 1967. Blessed with a radiant smile and delicate features, Sydney made friends easily, but she was desperate to break away from the ordinary.

In her high school yearbook, she wrote that she was leaving with the belief that "the future holds more valuable hours than has the past." While her classmates waxed their surfboards to tackle the waves at nearby Coast Guard Beach, Sydney, or "Snyd" as she was called, could often be found curled up under a tree with her nose in a book. She loved to read the work of philosophers like Bertrand Russell and quoted them often. Sydney paraphrased Russell in her senior quote: "Some men would rather die than think; in fact, they do," she wrote. Sydney was drawn to intellectuals, which was why no one raised any concern about the friendship she had struck with Tony Costa, a handsome young man in Provincetown whom she called Sire. The pair was often seen riding their bicycles together down the narrow streets and alleyways in the center of town. Sydney had told her sister Linda that their relationship was casual and platonic. She was living with another man, a local fisherman named Roland Salvador, at the time. Still, Linda had her suspicions that her sister had fallen hard for her new friend and that Sydney's relationship with Roland had hit a dead end. On Friday, May 24, 1968, Linda Monzon left her two-room cottage at 25 Watson Court, in Provincetown's historic district, and began walking up the hill toward Commercial Street. At the top of the hill, she noticed a small figure standing next to a car. Linda recognized her sister immediately and smiled. Sydney was tiny: about four feet, eleven inches tall, she weighed less than one hundred pounds. Friends had playfully teased her that she had been the model for the Baby First Step doll, which was hugely popular among little girls at the time.

"Hey, Linda, can you come here?" Sydney shouted. "I need to talk to you."

"I can't, Sis," Linda said, looking at her watch. "I'm already late. I'll just see ya later."

Sydney gave her sister a troubled look. Linda waved it off as some minor boy trouble and made herself a mental note to dig in further when the sisters were alone. Linda kept walking while Sydney got into the passenger seat of Costa's car, a 1963 Oldsmobile, and drove away.

He took his eyes off the road briefly and let them rest on Sydney's body. She wore a pair of white Levi's bell bottoms with cuts above the knees and a sleeveless, pastel-orange blouse that was tucked into her small waistline. Her silky brown hair was parted in the middle and flowed over her shoulders. Sydney caught his gaze and then looked into the back seat where she spotted a pair of gloves, a laundry bag, and a small screwdriver.

"Where are we going, Sire?" she asked nervously.

Costa smiled. His eyelids were heavy.

"We need to get some pills," he told her. "And then I'll take you to a place where a thousand tiny Tinkerbells will descend upon you and carry you to fantasy's domain."

Sydney realized where they were headed: an ancient cemetery near Corn Hill Beach in North Truro. They had gone there several times before to get stoned. But Costa was now out of drugs and low on cash. They would need to replenish the stash Bonnie-and-Clyde style. He rolled down his window to let in a gust of damp salt air. The breeze seemed to revive him. They drove past the doctor's office on Route 6A and saw that all the lights were out. The doctor had closed his shop early to enjoy the long Memorial Day weekend, the unofficial start to the busy summer tourist season on Cape Cod.

They waited for nightfall and switched seats. Sydney was now behind the steering wheel. She adjusted the cushion so that her bare feet could reach the pedal.

"All right, love. You can drop me off at the telephone booth over there by the hamburger stand," Costa told her. "When I'm done pillaging the doctor's office, I'll wait for you in the phone booth. I'll just pretend that I'm making a call if anyone shows up."

Sydney nodded. She could hardly imagine what her father, Bertram, a drywall contractor and U.S. Navy veteran, would think about the idea that his daughter was about to pull off a drug store robbery.

"I'll hide the dope over there," Costa said, pointing to a row of bushes. "We can pick the stuff up after we see that everything is all right. Then we'll head home, okay?"

"Yeah, I'll drive down the road a ways and will come back in about an hour. Is that cool with you, Sire?"

"That sounds groovy."

Sydney let the young man out and sped off. She drove back to Eastham, back toward her mundane past, where she had once fretted over simple things like decorating for the prom with its "Over the Rainbow" theme and working on the yearbook committee. Sydney had even supplied a baby picture for the Nauset Tides yearbook of her in a dress, balanced against the grill of her father's car. She had been the epitome of the all-American girl until the move up to Ptown. Sydney pulled the car over near the Eastham Windmill and waited. The giant gristmill, with its large wooden sails, had towered over the town green since 1793. It was the oldest structure of its kind on Cape Cod and a source of great pride for local residents, but for Sydney, it was a symbol of a small town that was stuck too far in the past. She fiddled with the radio and landed on Hugo Montenegro's orchestral from the Clint Eastwood film *The Good, the Bad, and the Ugly*, which was nearing the top of the Billboard charts. She now felt a bit like a desperado herself as she sat in wait for her companion to make his score.

Tony Costa made his way ninja-like to the medical office just as a Truro police officer drove past on his nightly patrol. Stealthily, he crept toward the back of the building and tested a window to see if it was unlocked, but the office was totally secure. He then wedged a screwdriver into the muntins that separated the glass panes and tripped the lock.

Costa climbed into the office, drew the shades, and slid the gloves on both of his hands. He had put together his cat burglar kit in a hurry and realized now that he was wearing two left-handed gloves. The pill closet was located at the front of the building, so he navigated his way slowly through several small offices with locked doors. Costa had carpentry experience, so he easily managed to remove the doors by pulling out their hinges. He did not want to trash the office. His sole mission was to obtain the pills he needed and nothing more, at least not yet. He found the pill closet and examined it with a small penlight.

"Gold mine," he whispered to himself.

Suddenly, the penlight shut off. The battery was dead. He did not panic; instead, he pulled out a book of matches and a tiny glass of denatured alcohol from his laundry bag. Using a piece of clothesline rope for a wick, he lit the end to create a makeshift lantern. He had used the kit to cook up dope and had now transformed it into an alcohol lamp. He trembled with excitement as he gazed into the pill closet. He had never seen such an abundance of drugs before. Reading each label carefully, he stuffed sealed bottles of Nembutal, Seconal, Dexedrine, and so-called black beauties into his laundry bag, filling it to the brim.

Costa found his way back to the open window and slipped out as silently as he came.

He hid the drugs in the woods and strolled over to the phone booth to wait for Sydney. Two cars passed by before she pulled into the parking lot, hugging the steering wheel with her diminutive frame. He opened the passenger door and climbed in next to her.

"What happened, Sire? Where's the stuff?" she asked. "Did you get anything?"

"Did I get anything, love? There's more dope in there than a pharmaceutical warehouse," he replied. "The bag's over there in the pine grove. Let's go get it and get out of here."

Sydney drove over to the wooded area and watched as her companion retrieved the laundry bag.

"Are we headed back to Ptown?" she asked.

"I've got a stash in the woods," he told her. "You know the place. We can sort the stuff out there and put it all into the ammo cans. It'll be safer than riding all the way into town with it."

Costa had purchased several army surplus tank ammunition canisters that were airtight and water resistant. The cans were now buried in a thicket near Cemetery Road. Sydney stepped on the gas pedal, and soon the pair wound their way down the twisting country lane. She gripped the steering wheel tightly around each hairpin turn while her companion increased the volume of the car radio. The local station was now playing "Blue Turns to Grey" by the Rolling Stones, his favorite band.

He sang along with the tune, imitating Mick Jagger.

Sydney kept her focus on the road. The difficult drive was made worse by a heavy rain that began to pelt the windshield. She flipped on the wipers as he guided her off the main road to a dirt track, an old carriage trail, barely wide enough to fit his car. They could hear the bushes and long vines scraping against the sides of the Oldsmobile as they bounced over tiny moguls and deep puddles before coming to a small clearing about a mile into the woods.

"We're here," he told her, smiling.

Costa reached over and wrapped his long arms around her small shoulders. They kissed as droplets of rain rolled down the windshield like tears on a baby's cheek. Sydney moved closer, finally straddling him. He held her tightly, breathing heavy with excitement now, as he ran his hands over her compact body. Sydney met his soft touch with her own delicate caress.

This is perfect, he thought to himself. They were alone in the Oldsmobile, but they were not alone. The young man's split personality, an alter ego he had named Cory, had come along for the ride.

Don't do it, Cory, he urged the alter ego. *She doesn't deserve to die.*

Costa suddenly broke the embrace.

"Love, why don't we sort and stash this stuff now, before we get too involved in each other's bodies and minds and forget what we came here for."

Sydney nodded and adjusted her blouse. They got out of the car, and he grabbed the heavy laundry bag from the back seat. He reached for her hand as they ran through the rain toward a large pine tree at the edge of the clearing. Sydney giggled as the mud squished through her bare toes. She said something to her companion, but he didn't hear it. The young man's inner voice was now raging loudly in his skull.

He set the bag down at the base of the tree and dug through wet leaves until his fingers found one of the canisters. Sydney began rifling through the bag, handing him bottle after bottle. The drugs filled three full ammo cans.

"Are we done yet, Sire?" she asked him. "We're getting soaked to the bone out here."

"We are just about done, love," he responded. "Why don't you head back to the car?"

Tony Costa reached his hand inside a fourth ammo can and felt the thick wooden handle of a large knife.

"You fucked my head up bad tonight, Cory," he muttered to himself as he pulled out the weapon. "Let's leave her alone."

Suddenly, he felt the sharp edge of the blade against his neck.

You'll die too, motherfucker, Cory threatened. *Just like the rest of them.*

Costa looked over at Sydney, who was walking with her back turned toward the Oldsmobile. He jumped to his feet and gave chase, running toward her with the knife held high in his right hand. Sydney heard the rustling of leaves under his feet and then the splash of a puddle as he drew closer. She spun around quickly and could see her companion's crazed eyes, nearly illuminated in the darkness. Her own eyes followed his raised arm as it swung down upon her.

"Sire!" she screamed.

The blade cut into Sydney's shoulder, triggering a fountain of blood that sprayed across the young man's shirt. He lifted the knife and struck her again and again.

READING GROUP GUIDE

1. What do you think of the idea of a "true calling"? Was Frank always going to be an architect because of his mother and his own personality, or did he have a choice in the matter?

2. Are you inspired by nature? Do you have a favorite piece of art that was inspired by nature?

3. Frank realizes that architects are both praised for everything that goes right and blamed for everything that goes wrong. What other professions act in this manner? Is it right to put all the responsibility—good or bad—on one person in any situation?

4. How does Frank seem to you? How does he write about himself and his accomplishments (or otherwise)? Do you think you would have liked to know him personally?

5. Consider Frank's relationship with his mother. Is it a healthy relationship? How does she treat him versus his sister?

6. How did societal norms and laws of the time hold Frank and Mamah back in their relationship? Do you think they would have less trouble attempting to be a couple nowadays?

7. Consider how Mamah and Kitty were portrayed in the media at the height of the scandal. How did the differences convey what society wanted from a woman at the time?

8. Frank found that the bad publicity around his personal life was making his working life more difficult as well, as architecture is a client-based business. How much do you care about the personal life of someone you're working with? Would Frank's behavior concern you enough not to hire him?

9. Do you believe Frank truly loved Mamah? How does his behavior after her death lead you to believe one way or the other?

10. Were the difficulties Frank faced throughout his life his own doing? Do you believe he could've done something about the way he acted to alleviate or avoid altogether these burdens?

11. What do you make of Frank Lloyd Wright's legacy? Are you a fan of his architecture? What do you think makes someone a genius, and do you believe he was one?

NOTES

PROLOGUE

"men in sooty, bloody clothes": *The Rose Jar: The Autobiography of Edna Meudt* (North Country Press, 1990), 176.

CHAPTER ONE

"I happened to be": Frank Lloyd Wright, interview by Hugh Downs, *Wisdom*, NBC, May 8, 1953.

A graduate of Amherst College: *Frank Lloyd Wright: An Autobiography* (Duell, Sloan and Pearce, 1943), 10.

"children should be seen": "The Architect's Father: A Reconsideration of William Carey Wright, the Father of Frank Lloyd Wright," This American House, July 16, 2023, https://thisamericanhouse.com/the-architects-father-a-reconsideration-of-william-cary-wright-the-father-of-frank-lloyd-wright/.

"There were berries": *Frank Lloyd Wright: An Autobiography*, 10.

"She was very sweet": "Architect's Father."

"When she told me": "Architect's Father."

"She seemed so full": "Architect's Father."

"Yours was a prophetic": Meryle Secrest, *Frank Lloyd Wright: A Biography* (Alfred A. Knopf, 1992), 53.

"It was always": *Frank Lloyd Wright: An Autobiography*, 12.

"Well, let's see if": *Frank Lloyd Wright: An Autobiography*, 15.

"a pittance in keeping": *Frank Lloyd Wright: An Autobiography*, 10.

"frail little thing": *Frank Lloyd Wright: An Autobiography*, 17.

"Ready now, Frank?": *Frank Lloyd Wright: An Autobiography*, 18.

"Four o'clock": *Frank Lloyd Wright: An Autobiography*, 18.

"Ringing accuracy": *Frank Lloyd Wright: An Autobiography*, 20.

"So he limped along": *Frank Lloyd Wright: An Autobiography*, 20.

"Yes, yes. I know": *Frank Lloyd Wright: An Autobiography*, 21.

"Your muscles will be": *Frank Lloyd Wright: An Autobiography*, 22.

"simple, shingle wooden": *Frank Lloyd Wright: An Autobiography*, 29.

"These sons and daughters": *Frank Lloyd Wright: An Autobiography*, 30.

"The spot of red": *Frank Lloyd Wright: An Autobiography*, 26.

"Study nature, love nature": "Frank Lloyd Wright and Nature," Guggenheim New York, accessed August 5, 2025, https://www.guggenheim.org/teaching-materials/the-architecture-of-the-solomon-r-guggenheim-museum/frank-lloyd-wright-and-nature.

CHAPTER TWO

She beat the girl: "Architect's Father."

"She lived much in": *Frank Lloyd Wright: An Autobiography*, 49.

"Father ought to realize it": *Frank Lloyd Wright: An Autobiography*, 49.

"Perhaps the father": *Frank Lloyd Wright: An Autobiography*, 49.

"Well, Mr. Wright": *Frank Lloyd Wright: An Autobiography*, 50.

"All real crises in": *Frank Lloyd Wright: An Autobiography*, 51.

Despite a poor academic record: Roger Friedland and Harold Zellman, *The Fellowship: The Untold Story of Frank Lloyd Wright & the Taliesin Fellowship* (Harper Collins, 2006), 13.

"dull pain": *Frank Lloyd Wright: An Autobiography*, 52.

"opened for his pupil": *Frank Lloyd Wright: An Autobiography*, 53.

"Standing out from the crowd": *Frank Lloyd Wright: An Autobiography*, 54.

"Some fell dead on": *Frank Lloyd Wright: An Autobiography*, 55.

Several workers were killed: Mark Gajewski, "Capitol Collapse," Historic Madison, accessed August 11, 2025, https://www.historicmadison.org/capitolcollapse.

"a vivid tragedy": *Frank Lloyd Wright: An Autobiography*, 55.

"good and conscientious": *Frank Lloyd Wright: An Autobiography*, 55.

"unsatisfied longings, humiliations": *Frank Lloyd Wright: An Autobiography*, 52.

CHAPTER THREE

The inferno had swept: "The Great Chicago Fire of 1871," Chicago Architecture Center, accessed August 11, 2025, https://www.architecture.org/online-resources/architecture-encyclopedia/the-great-chicago-fire-of-1871.

"There are great architects": *Frank Lloyd Wright: An Autobiography*, 59.

"Here at the university": *Frank Lloyd Wright: An Autobiography*, 59.

"On no account let": *Frank Lloyd Wright: An Autobiography*, 60.

He had stubbornly resigned: *Frank Lloyd Wright: An Autobiography*, 63.

"too sentimental": *Frank Lloyd Wright: An Autobiography*, 64.

"A human item": *Frank Lloyd Wright: An Autobiography*, 65.

"industriously varied without variety": *Frank Lloyd Wright: An Autobiography*, 66.

"Were all American cities": *Frank Lloyd Wright: An Autobiography*, 66.

Frank believed that the city's: *Frank Lloyd Wright: An Autobiography*, 66.

"fine-looking, cultured fellow": *Frank Lloyd Wright: An Autobiography*, 67.

"Let me see your drawings": *Frank Lloyd Wright: An Autobiography*, 68.

"All right, take him on": *Frank Lloyd Wright: An Autobiography*, 68.

"I've been expecting you": *Frank Lloyd Wright: An Autobiography*, 69.

"cozy restaurants": *Frank Lloyd Wright: An Autobiography*, 75.

"You've quit already": *Frank Lloyd Wright: An Autobiography*, 74.

"I have been very sad": Friedland and Zellman, *Fellowship: The Untold Story*, 15.

He also believed that Silsbee: Friedland and Zellman, *Fellowship: The Untold Story*, 16.

"I believed the *Raisonné*": *Frank Lloyd Wright: An Autobiography*, 75.

"Adler and Sullivan, architects": "Chicago Construction: A Backward Glance Reveals Many

Miles of Rising City Roofs and Its Panorama Is Worthy of Its Creators, the Architects," *Inter Ocean* (Chicago), January 7, 1888.

"He's looking for someone": *Frank Lloyd Wright: An Autobiography*, 90.

"a small man immaculately": *Frank Lloyd Wright: An Autobiography*, 90.

"You've got the right kind": *Frank Lloyd Wright: An Autobiography*, 92.

"Oh, my boy": Friedland and Zellman, *Fellowship: The Untold Story*, 17.

CHAPTER FOUR

"pretty much had her": *Frank Lloyd Wright: An Autobiography*, 78.

"I was grown up pretty well": *Frank Lloyd Wright: An Autobiography*, 78.

"Why all this fuss": *Frank Lloyd Wright: An Autobiography*, 87.

"I've had pretty nearly everything": *Frank Lloyd Wright: An Autobiography*, 88.

"The heavens weeping out of doors": *Frank Lloyd Wright: An Autobiography*, 105–6.

"Now look out, Wright": *Frank Lloyd Wright: An Autobiography*, 106.

"superior taste in matters": *Frank Lloyd Wright: An Autobiography*, 109.

"center of the united fundamentalist": *Frank Lloyd Wright: An Autobiography*, 108.

"I became a good pencil": *Frank Lloyd Wright: An Autobiography*, 104.

The club's notebook contained: Friedland and Zellman, *Fellowship: The Untold Story*, 18.

"The Auditorium progresses steadily": "Architectural Alphabet: Con It Over and Imperial Chicago Will Rise Before You," *Inter Ocean* (Chicago), January 27, 1889.

"a magnificent example": "Auditorium Supplement," *Inter Ocean* (Chicago), December 11, 1889.

"a gorgeous civic and social": *Frank Lloyd Wright: An Autobiography*, 109.

"The young husband found": *Frank Lloyd Wright: An Autobiography*, 110.

"Your sole interest is here": *Frank Lloyd Wright: An Autobiography*, 110.

CHAPTER FIVE

"The Winslow House had burst": *Frank Lloyd Wright: An Autobiography*, 128.

"I don't want to go": *Frank Lloyd Wright: An Autobiography*, 128.

"The children were their mother's": *Frank Lloyd Wright: An Autobiography*, 111.

"The architect absorbed": *Frank Lloyd Wright: An Autobiography*, 113.

"He bought my clothes": John Lloyd Wright, *My Father Who Is on Earth* (Southern Illinois University Press, 1994), 26.

"Papa's parties were the best": Wright, *My Father*, 43.

"It was my misfortune too": *Frank Lloyd Wright: An Autobiography*, 118.

"Papa told him he could": Wright, *My Father*, 36.

"Never mind, Mr. Wright": *Frank Lloyd Wright: An Autobiography*, 119.

"I can't run away": *Frank Lloyd Wright: An Autobiography*, 127.

"I'd rather be free": *Frank Lloyd Wright: An Autobiography*, 127.

"well equipped arsenal": "Spare that Tree… Architect Wright Will Defend his Shade with Guns," *Inter Ocean* (Chicago), August 26, 1900.

"one of the most remarkable men": Secrest, *Frank Lloyd Wright: A Biography*, 146.

"The innovation…makes it": "Art by Architects, Exhibition of Chicago Club Contains Many Fine Pictures," *Inter Ocean* (Chicago), March 25, 1900.

"The machine is intellect": Frank Lloyd Wright, "The Art and Craft of the Machine," address to Chicago Arts and Crafts Society, Hull House, March 6, 1901, https://projects.mcah.columbia.edu/courses/arch20/pdf/art_hum_reading_50.pdf.

Frank took with him: "An Architect's Journey: Frank Lloyd Wright's Photographs of Japan, 1905," Frank Lloyd Wright Trust, accessed August 11, 2025, https://www.wrightsjapan1905.org/learn/an-architects-journey/.

"Men and women so care": *Frank Lloyd Wright: An Autobiography*, 195.

"I saw the native home": *Frank Lloyd Wright: An Autobiography*, 196.

"By heaven, here was a house": *Frank Lloyd Wright: An Autobiography*, 197.

CHAPTER SIX

Her father, Marcus: Mark Borthwick, *A Brave and Lovely Woman: Mamah Borthwick and Frank Lloyd Wright* (University of Wisconsin Press, 2023), 18.

"loaded with beautiful specimens": Borthwick, *Brave and Lovely Woman*, 32.

"Miss Mamah Borthwick's rendition": Borthwick, *Brave and Lovely Woman*, 32.

"[Martha] was uniformly counted": Borthwick, *Brave and Lovely Woman*, 36.

"the largest class": "Literary Class-Day at Ann Arbor," *Chicago Tribune*, June 19, 1892.

"The favorite scriptural verse": Borthwick, *Brave and Lovely Woman*, 41.

"Ed Cheney sings in Allen's": Borthwick, *Brave and Lovely Woman*, 42.

"And now my sovereign master": Borthwick, *Brave and Lovely Woman*, 43.

"She will help in sending": Borthwick, *Brave and Lovely Woman*, 48.

He was even prosperous: Albert Nelson Marquis, ed., *Who's Who in Chicago: The Book of Chicagoans, A Biographical Dictionary of Leading Men and Women in the City of Chicago and Environs* (A. N. Marquis, 1905).

Mamah invited more than a dozen: *Michigan Alumnus* 6 (1900): 39.

The bride wore a wedding dress: Borthwick, *Brave and Lovely Woman*, 61.

CHAPTER SEVEN

"one of the oldest": "Marcus S. Borthwick," obituary, *Inter Ocean* (Chicago), April 23, 1900.

Blurring the interior: "Arthur and Grace Heurtley House," Frank Lloyd Wright Trust, accessed August 11, 2025, https://flwright.org/explore/arthur-heurtley-house.

Cheney purchased a lot: Paul Hendrickson, *Plagued by Fire: The Dreams and Furies of Frank Lloyd Wright* (Vintage Books, 2019).

The house was also designed: "Mamah Borthwick and Edwin Cheney House," Frank Lloyd Wright Trust, accessed August 11, 2025, https://flwright.org/explore/cheney-house.

"Romeo and Juliet shall live": *Frank Lloyd Wright: An Autobiography*, 138.

"Everything personal or otherwise": *Frank Lloyd Wright: An Autobiography*, 163.

Those who cosigned: Secrest, *Frank Lloyd Wright: A Biography*, 198.

"I had added tired": *Frank Lloyd Wright: An Autobiography*, 162.

"When the top was down": Wright, *My Father*, 50.

Frank cut a dashing figure: Wright, *My Father*, 52.

CHAPTER EIGHT

"Every tone in her voice": Secrest, *Frank Lloyd Wright: A Biography*, 193.

"tragic lines": Friedland and Zellman, *Fellowship: The Untold Story*, 29.

"endearingly tender and light": Secrest, *Frank Lloyd Wright: A Biography*, 161.

"The motor car brought": *Frank Lloyd Wright: An Autobiography*, 163.

"He [Cheney] was a prince": Secrest, *Frank Lloyd Wright: A Biography*, 192.

"Marriage not mutual": *Frank Lloyd Wright: An Autobiography*, 163.

"I am going to leave": Borthwick, *Brave and Lovely Woman*, 112.

"I would in any case": Borthwick, *Brave and Lovely Woman*, 120.

"a monster of awkwardness": "Larkin Company Administration Building," Frank Lloyd Wright Foundation, accessed August 11, 2025, https://franklloydwright.org/site/larkin-company-administration-building/.

CHAPTER NINE

One of the great: Frank Lloyd Wright Trust, accessed August 11, 2025, https://flwright.org/explore/frederick-c-robie-house.

There, she studied writing: Borthwick, *Brave and Lovely Woman*, 123.

Robie told Frank: "A Brief History of the Robie House by Frank Lloyd Wright," Rost Architects, January 23, 2023, https://www.rostarchitects.com/articles/2023/1/23/the-robie-house-by-frank-lloyd-wright.

Frank oversaw every phase: Eleanor Gibson, "Frank Lloyd Wright's Robie House Was His Most 'Consummate Expression' of Prairie Style," Dezeen, June 5, 2017, https://www.dezeen.com/2017/06/05/robie-house-frank-lloyd-wright-150-anniversary-prairie-style-20th-century-architecture-usa/.

So strongly did he believe: Friedland and Zellman, *Fellowship: The Untold Story*, 30.

"I am leaving the office": Borthwick, *Brave and Lovely Woman*, 133.

"He left…quick": Wright, *My Father*, 54.

They found their way: Borthwick, *Brave and Lovely Woman*, 136.

CHAPTER TEN

"Frank Lloyd Wright left Thursday": Hendrickson, *Plagued by Fire*, 180.

"Frank Lloyd Wright of 500": News of the Society World, *Chicago Sunday Tribune*, October 3, 1909.

"unity, truth, beauty": "Unity Temple," Frank Lloyd Wright Trust, accessed August 12, 2025, https://flwright.org/explore/unity-temple.

"Simplicity and Repose": Frank Lloyd Wright, "In the Cause of Architecture," *Architectural Record* 23, no. 3 (March 1908): 155–65, https://www.architecturalrecord.com/ext/resources/news/2016/01-Jan/InTheCause/Frank-Lloyd-Wright-In-the-Cause-of-Architecture-March-1908.pdf.

"to get a sense": "Unity Temple."

"We extend to the architect": "Unity Temple."

When Frank and Mamah arrived: "Elope to Europe—Architect Frank Lloyd Wright and Mrs. Edwin Cheney of Oak Park Startle Friends," *Chicago Sunday Tribune*, November 7, 1909.

CHAPTER ELEVEN

Their work resulted: "Elope to Europe."

"A wife pledging faith": "Elope to Europe."

"Investigation of the circumstances": "Elope to Europe."

"Will you seek a divorce": "Elope to Europe."

"sought by any means": "Elope to Europe."

"This all is scarcely": "Elope to Europe."

"We have six children": "Elope to Europe."

"Oak Park, Oct. 20": "Elope to Europe."

"This is simply": "Elope to Europe."

"Her sex will stigmatize": "A Line-O'-Type or Two," *Chicago Daily Tribune*, November 8, 1909.

"Mr. Cheney is not in": "Frank Lloyd Wright's Wife Says She Is Confident He Will Return to Her," *Chicago Daily Tribune*, November 8, 1909.

"I think you will believe": Friedland and Zellman, *Fellowship: The Untold Story*, 30.

"Ellen Key greeted me": Borthwick, *Brave and Lovely Woman*, 136.

"How many souls seeking": *Frank Lloyd Wright: An Autobiography*, 164.

"I, too, now sought": *Frank Lloyd Wright: An Autobiography*, 165.

"Walking hand in hand": *Frank Lloyd Wright: An Autobiography*, 163.

"The year dad left": Wright, *My Father*, 58–59.

CHAPTER TWELVE

"heart disease with involvement": Borthwick, *Brave and Lovely Woman*, 149.

"Reconciliation between Frank Lloyd Wright": "Frank Lloyd Wright's Son May Repair Family Break," *Chicago Daily Tribune*, January 18, 1910.

Kitty did share: "Wright Is Repentant," *Grand Forks Herald*, January 20, 1910.

"attacked and severely beaten": "Wright Is Repentant."

"You have a wife and children": Hendrickson, *Plagued by Fire*, 228.

"It is a constant increasing": Frank Lloyd Wright to Anna Lloyd Wright, July 4, 1910, Frank Lloyd Wright Foundation, #1502.281.002.

"I had one time thought": Frank Lloyd Wright to Anna Lloyd Wright.

"I dread the aspect": Frank Lloyd Wright to Anna Lloyd Wright.

"It is the character given": Frank Lloyd Wright to Anna Lloyd Wright.

"You knew and Catherine knew": Frank Lloyd Wright to Anna Lloyd Wright.

"Trying to live, at a frightful cost": Hendrickson, *Plagued by Fire*, 226.

"The fight has been fought": Hendrickson, *Plagued by Fire*, 229.

CHAPTER THIRTEEN

While Frank was making: Borthwick, *Brave and Lovely Woman*, 182.

When the application called: Borthwick, *Brave and Lovely Woman*, 182.

"I feel that I cannot discuss": "Oak Park Soul Mates Part," *Chicago Daily Tribune*, August 3, 1910.

"It is a tribute to": "Oak Park Soul Mates Part."

"Mrs. Wright, with the same zeal": "Oak Park Soul Mates Part."

"from the gaze": "Found at Fox River Camp," *Crystal Lake Herald*, August 11, 1910.

"secluded by a group of trees": "Found at Fox River Camp."

"Cheney, when discovered": "Found at Fox River Camp."

"This is the question": "Mrs Cheney Back? 'No,' Says Husband," *Inter Ocean* (Chicago), October 11, 1910.

"is coming home to square": "Oak Park Awaits Wright," *Chicago Daily Tribune*, September 24, 1910.

"I must beg not to be": "Oak Park Awaits Wright."

"Mr. Wright says that": "Wright Returns to Oak Park Wife," *Chicago Sunday Tribune*, October 9, 1910.

"Doesn't Mr. Wright think": "Wright Returns."

"No, he says he has": "Wright Returns."

"At night, the house": "Wright Returns."

"I am accustomed to being": Secrest, *Frank Lloyd Wright: A Biography*, 206.

"Each morning I wake up": Friedland and Zellman, *Fellowship: The Untold Story*, 31.

CHAPTER FOURTEEN

"The passions have all": *Frank Lloyd Wright: An Autobiography*, 166.

"Those who regard monogamy": Ellen Key, *Love and Marriage*, trans. Arthur G. Chater (G. P. Putnam and Sons, 1911), 1, 5–6.

If I sink: Borthwick, *Brave and Lovely Woman*, 189.

"What you term": Secrest, *Frank Lloyd Wright: A Biography*, 206.

It was a book that Frank: Borthwick, *Brave and Lovely Woman*, 192.

CHAPTER FIFTEEN

Frank brought her manuscripts: Borthwick, *Brave and Lovely Woman*, 200.

Like the Villa Medici: Secrest, *Frank Lloyd Wright: A Biography*, 209.

"I scanned the hills": *Frank Lloyd Wright: An Autobiography*, 168.

"Was there no natural": *Frank Lloyd Wright: An Autobiography*, 168.

"I saw the hill-crown": *Frank Lloyd Wright: An Autobiography*, 169.

"crown the exuberance": *Frank Lloyd Wright: An Autobiography*, 170.

"bespeaking strength and comfort": *Frank Lloyd Wright: An Autobiography*, 171.

"About June 28, 1909": "Cheney Divorces Wife Who Eloped," *Chicago Sunday Tribune*, August 6, 1911.

"While we lived together": "Cheney Divorces Wife."

"had left him without": "Cheney Divorces Wife."

"a Griselda waiting patiently": "Cheney Divorces Wife."

"distasteful": "Architect Wright in New Romance with 'Mrs. Cheney,'" *Chicago Sunday Tribune*, December 24, 1911.

"Whether it was for": "Partition in Wright Home Is Torn Down," *Omaha Evening World Herald*, November 16, 1911.

"All I can say is": "Partition in Wright Home."

Dear Papa: Borthwick, *Brave and Lovely Woman*, 211.

I have as you hope: Borthwick, *Brave and Lovely Woman*, 213.

On Christmas Eve, 1910: "Architect Wright in New Romance."

"The spot [in Spring Green, Wisconsin]": "Architect Wright in New Romance."

"Mrs. Cheney's" divorce: "Architect Wright in New Romance."

"When they found it": "Architect Wright in New Romance."

"a score of curious villagers": "Architect Wright in New Romance."

"I'm Wright": "Architect Wright in New Romance."

"Mr. Wright went north": "Architect Wright in New Romance."

"We have nothing to say": "Architect Wright in New Romance."

"beautifully ornamented Christmas": "Mrs. Wright to Tell of 'Hegiras,'" *Chicago Daily Tribune*, December 25, 1911.

CHAPTER SIXTEEN

"I see this as an opportunity": "Spend Christmas Making 'Defense' of 'Spirit Hegira,'" *Chicago Daily Tribune*, December 26, 1911.

"In the first place": "Spend Christmas."

"She was always Mamah": "Spend Christmas."

"The children, my children": "Spend Christmas."

"Mrs. Wright wanted children": "Spend Christmas."

"Mrs. Wright had little time": "Spend Christmas."

"I believe we can": "Spend Christmas."

"I felt that I would": "Spend Christmas."

"I believe in them": "Spend Christmas."

"You mean that the material": "Spend Christmas."

"There will be people": "Spend Christmas."

"I want to say this": "Spend Christmas."

"My home stretches": "Spend Christmas."

"set about the rooms": *Frank Lloyd Wright: An Autobiography*, 169.

"All the cream the boy": *Frank Lloyd Wright: An Autobiography*, 170.

"a complete living unit": *Frank Lloyd Wright: An Autobiography*, 171.

"was to be an abstract": *Frank Lloyd Wright: An Autobiography*, 171.

CHAPTER SEVENTEEN

"There will be no": "Ask Sheriff's Aid to Oust Wright," *Chicago Daily Tribune*, December 27, 1911.

"I was asked to open": "Ask Sheriff's Aid."

"They want him to leave": "Ask Sheriff's Aid."

"I don't know yet": "Architect Buys Arms to Defend His Soul Mate," *St. Louis Post-Dispatch*, December 27, 1911.

"This love affair of his": "Ask Sheriff's Aid."

"A man in any other": "Couple Part, Children Merry. Both Sides Reticent," *Baraboo Weekly News*, December 28, 1911.

"People of wealth": "Couple Part, Children Merry."

"blinded egoist": Friedland and Zellman, *Fellowship: The Untold Story*, 49.

"scandal, distortions of truth": Wright, *My Father*, 64.

"a fine bunch of dubs": "Fine Bunch of Dubs Were There, Frank Lloyd Wright Delivers Tirade against the Newspaper Men," *Daily Gate City* (Keokuk, IA), December 29, 1911.

"I still love": "Forms Profane; Spirit Sacred," *Los Angeles Times*, January 7, 1912.

"Of the dark, somewhat": "Mamah Borthwick Defends Acts," *Chicago Examiner*, January 1, 1912.

"Yes, I am Mamah": "Mamah Borthwick Defends Acts."

"But for the life of me": "Mamah Borthwick Defends Acts."

"I just wanted to show": "Mamah Borthwick Defends Acts."

"We both live in monogamy": "Forms Profane; Spirit Sacred."

CHAPTER EIGHTEEN

His mother's name: Hendrickson, *Plagued by Fire*, 195–96.

"The law we repeat": "The Huntsville Lynching," *Decatur Weekly News*, July 27, 1900.

"His captors gave him": "Prayer Was Spoken for Doomed Man," *Elba Clipper*, April 23, 1907.

There were sixty-one men: "Lynchings: By Year and Race," University of Missouri-Kansas City Law School, accessed August 12, 2025, https://law2.umkc.edu/faculty/projects/ftrials/shipp/lynchingyear.html.

"a druid-bard who sang": *Frank Lloyd Wright: An Autobiography*, 167.

"I turned to this hill": *Frank Lloyd Wright: An Autobiography*, 168.

CHAPTER NINETEEN

"Many of them were": *Frank Lloyd Wright: An Autobiography*, 172.

After their wedding: "Cheney Rewedded after His Wife's Hegira," *Rock Island Argus*, August 15, 1912.

"By the remarriage": "Cheney Rewedded."

"into her own soul mate": "Ellen Key May Be Put In False Light," *Inter Ocean* (Chicago), March 28, 1912.

"You will be interested": Borthwick, *Brave and Lovely Woman*, 231.

"I would be delighted": Borthwick, *Brave and Lovely Woman*, 233.

Friends of Mrs. Coon: "True Love Put above Man Law," *Virginian Pilot*, September 9, 1912.

"I wanted a home": *Frank Lloyd Wright: An Autobiography*, 173.

But journalists had long: "Cheney-Wright Soulmates Leave for Japan," *Chicago Examiner*, January 12, 1913.

CHAPTER TWENTY

Citizens who were angry: "Rioting in Jap[an] City Spreads," *Tampa Times*, February 11, 1913.

The new hotel had: Secrest, *Frank Lloyd Wright: A Biography*, 214.

"the largest [hotel]": "Hotel News," *San Francisco Call and Post*, June 8, 1913.

"We will take up": "Suffrage Notes," *Inter Ocean* (Chicago), September 30, 1913.

The project was announced: "Proposed Midway Gardens at Sans Souci," *Chicago Tribune*, February 22, 1914.

"Frank, in all this": *Frank Lloyd Wright: An Autobiography*, 176.

"Frank, I know you": *Frank Lloyd Wright: An Autobiography*, 177.

"I knew it": *Frank Lloyd Wright: An Autobiography*, 177.

"It was a rush job": Wright, *My Father*, 71–72.

"Mrs. Ellen Deeley": "Chafee Grant in Hero Role—Routs Assailant of Girl," *Chicago Tribune*, October 9, 1913.

African American men like: Hendrickson, *Plagued by Fire*, 216.

"He [Carlton] was a good": Hendrickson, *Plagued by Fire*, 295.

"quick service and hot": *Frank Lloyd Wright: An Autobiography*, 178.

CHAPTER TWENTY-ONE

Another neighbor claimed: Hendrickson, *Plagued by Fire*, 296.

"the goings on": *Rose Jar*, 174.

"They're simply too": "Mrs. Cheney and Five Others Slain," *Chicago Tribune*, August 16, 1914.

"fast growing up": *Frank Lloyd Wright: An Autobiography*, 180.

"Most places of the": *Frank Lloyd Wright: An Autobiography*, 181.

"Don't need cards": *Frank Lloyd Wright: An Autobiography*, 183.

"Money troubles now": *Frank Lloyd Wright: An Autobiography*, 184.

"This will be a wonderful": Midway Gardens advertisement, *Chicago Tribune*, June 27, 1914.

"Too many persons": R. F. Webster, "Crowd at Opening," *Chicago Tribune*, June 29, 1914.

Dear Ellen Key: Borthwick, *Brave and Lovely Woman*, 254.

"Mamah…was a cultured": Wright, *My Father*, 80.

CHAPTER TWENTY-TWO

"They're trying to": Hendrickson, *Plagued by Fire*, 296.

"I'll knock your": Hendrickson, *Plagued by Fire*, 296.

"I need this for": Borthwick, *Brave and Lovely Woman*, 258.

"We were treated": Hendrickson, *Plagued by Fire*, 296.

"A rug has become": William R. Drennan, *Death in a Prairie House: Frank Lloyd Wright and the Taliesin Murders* (Terrace Books, 2007), 90.

"Oh, Mama, look": "A Terrible Tragedy," *Iowa County Democrat*, August 20, 1914.

"The liquid ran under": "Awful Crime in Wisconsin," *Chicago Tribune*, August 16, 1914.

"I plunged through": "Awful Crime in Wisconsin."

"The door was a wall": "Madman at Rope's End," *Cincinnati Enquirer*, August 16, 1914.

"The ax struck me": "Trapped Victims in Fire, Slew as They Escaped," *Sunday Review* (Decatur, IL), August 16, 1914.

"I cannot give a": "Madman at Rope's End."

CHAPTER TWENTY-THREE

"Hail Mary, full": Meudt, *Rose Jar*, 175.

"It is bad to be nearly": Meudt, *Rose Jar*, 175–76.

"That is not Martha": Meudt, *Rose Jar*, 176.

Dear Mother: "Negro Murders Six in Wright's Bungalow," *Chicago Sunday Tribune*, August 16, 1914.

"What's happened, Dad": Wright, *My Father*, 81.

At around 2:00 p.m.: Borthwick, *Brave and Lovely Woman*, 264.

"I have often tried": Wright, *My Father*, 82.

"Thirty-six hours earlier": *Frank Lloyd Wright: An Autobiography*, 185.

"The Carlton's, Julian": "Negro Murders Six."

CHAPTER TWENTY-FOUR

Some men surmised that Carlton: "Trapped Victims in Fire."

When asked what: "Negro Murders Six."

"Shadows of men": Wright, *My Father*, 82.

"[pushing] madly to see": Wright, *My Father*, 83.

"She for whom Taliesin": *Frank Lloyd Wright: An Autobiography*, 185.

"Dawn across the valley": "Wright Buries Mamah of Hills in Night Grave," *Chicago Daily Tribune*, August 17, 1914.

The young boy could: Secrest, *Frank Lloyd Wright: A Biography*, 222.

"Satsuma. $250 in": "Wright Buries Mamah."

"I will rebuild it all": "Wright Buries Mamah."

"Once, years ago": "Wright Buries Mamah."

"We will bury her": "Wright Buries Mamah."

CHAPTER TWENTY-FIVE

"I am sure that he": "Wright Buries Mamah."

He called it a: *Frank Lloyd Wright: An Autobiography*, 185.

"We made the whole": *Frank Lloyd Wright: An Autobiography*, 186.

"I watched his great": Wright, *My Father*, 84.

"His face bore the expression": Wright, *My Father*, 84.

"The August sun": *Frank Lloyd Wright: An Autobiography*, 186.

"All I had left to show": *Frank Lloyd Wright: An Autobiography*, 186.

"Memories rushed": Wright, *My Father*, 85.

"But I would come back": *Frank Lloyd Wright: An Autobiography*, 186.

"Days strangely without": *Frank Lloyd Wright: An Autobiography*, 187.

"My mother was": *Frank Lloyd Wright: An Autobiography*, 188.

To you who have: "Frank Lloyd Wright to His Neighbors," *Weekly Home News* (Spring Green, WI), August 20, 1914.

CHAPTER TWENTY-SIX

"They jumped on me": "Wright Buries Mamah."

"He admits he went": "Wright Buries Mamah."

"Mr. Wright has many": "Enemies of Wright Are Blamed," *Cincinnati Enquirer*, August 18, 1914.

"My husband had": "Wright Buries Mamah."

"He would not tell": "Wright Buries Mamah."

"William Weston and David": "Wright Rebuilds His Bungalow as Memory Temple," *Chicago Daily Tribune*, August 18, 1914.

"I didn't like Carlton": "Wright Buries Mamah."

"he was morose and sullen": "Wright Buries Mamah."

"He seemed to be nervous": "Wright Buries Mamah."

The day before: "Wright Rebuilds His Bungalow."

He toyed with a glass: Hendrickson, *Plagued by Fire*, 299.

Harrison also recounted: "Carleton Is Held on Murder Charge," *Fennimore Times*, September 2, 1914.

Gertrude Carlton also told: Hendrickson, *Plagued by Fire*, 294.

"Her only explanation": "Wife of Love Castle Murderer in Town," *Freeport Journal Standard*, August 31, 1914.

"He was broke": "Wright Rebuilds His Bungalow."

"Sleepy residents of the": "Police Slain by Negro," *Chicago Daily Tribune*, August 18, 1914.

CHAPTER TWENTY-SEVEN

Brunker's funeral took place: "The Bungalow Dead Grows to Seven," *Chicago Daily Tribune*, August 19, 1914.

"Brunker's death was": "Heirs of Murdered Man Sue Wright for $3,000," *Mattoon Commercial-Star*, September 13, 1914.

More hope was given: "Seventh Victim Is Dead in 'Love Castle' Tragedy," *Freeport Journal-Standard*, August 19, 1914.

As the suspect: "Love Bungalow Slayer in Court on Stretcher," *Chicago Daily Tribune*, September 30, 1914.

"If I die": "Murders at Taliesin," *Dodgeville Chronicle*, August 21, 1914.

"There were those": Wright, *My Father*, 83.

"The wages of sin": "The Fate of the House Built on Sin," editorial, *Butte Miner*, October 11, 1914.

There would be: "Slayer's Brain Is Examined," *Urbana Courier-Herald*, October 16, 1914.

During this time: *Frank Lloyd Wright: An Autobiography*, 190.

"Something in him": Wright, *My Father*, 86.

When a reporter visited: "Mrs. Wright Has Turned Hermit in City Home," *Mattoon Commercial-Star*, September 17, 1914.

"What is the public curiosity": "Mrs. Wright Has Turned Hermit."

CHAPTER TWENTY-EIGHT

Dear Ellen Key: Borthwick, *Brave and Lovely Woman*, 272–73.

"Where there had been": *Frank Lloyd Wright: An Autobiography*, 191.

Frank's daughter arrived: "Robbers Busy in Oak Park," *Chicago Daily Tribune*, April 12, 1915.

"More stone, more wood": *Frank Lloyd Wright: An Autobiography*, 190.

Frank thought of the property: *Frank Lloyd Wright: An Autobiography*, 190.

My dear Sir: Hendrickson, *Plagued by Fire*, 316.

"I hunger for the living": Friedland and Zellman, *Fellowship: The Untold Story*, 39.

"Let me crown": Friedland and Zellman, *Fellowship: The Untold Story*, 40.

CHAPTER TWENTY-NINE

She is beautiful: *Frank Lloyd Wright: An Autobiography*, 201.

"Drowning men": *Frank Lloyd Wright: An Autobiography*, 202.

"[She] wooed, grabbed": Wright, *My Father*, 111.

While living in France: Secrest, *Frank Lloyd Wright: A Biography*, 242.

"You worship the ghost": Secrest, *Frank Lloyd Wright: A Biography*, 243.

"I am going": Secrest, *Frank Lloyd Wright: A Biography*, 244.

"It cannot continue": Secrest, *Frank Lloyd Wright: A Biography*, 244.

Beloved: If I could: "The Love Letters of the New Companion," *Washington Herald*, November 28, 1915.

Oh dear Frank: "Love Letters."

You want to be: "Does It Pay After All?," *Cincinnati Post*, November 12, 1915.

Do not come: "Does it Pay After All?"

You are blind to God: "Does It Pay After All?"

The editor cleverly: "Stolen Letters Show No Case," *Chicago Daily Tribune*, November 6, 1915.

CHAPTER THIRTY

"I went to work": "Wright, Accused of Love Plot, Denies," *Baraboo Weekly News*, November 11, 1915.

"So, they say I": "Nellie Breen Shows Letter Sent to Wright," *Chicago Daily Tribune*, November 10, 1915.

Dear Mr. Wright: "Nellie Breen Shows Letter."

"In my opinion": "Wright, Accused."

"We have sifted": "Wright, Accused."

"It would be useless": "Stolen Letters Show No Case."

"If the federal authorities": "Architect Fears Jealousy of Woman," *Bismark Daily Tribune*, November 9, 1915.

"We learned that": "Architect Fears Jealousy of Woman."

"Because I love Frank": "I Love Him, Says Mrs. Noel," *Muskogee Daily Phoenix*, November 14, 1915.

After reading the letter: "Sculptress and Beauty Pens Letters of Love," *Washington Post*, November 14, 1915.

With the federal investigation: *Frank Lloyd Wright: An Autobiography*, 194.

CHAPTER THIRTY-ONE

Frank wanted to ensure: Okakura Kazuko, *The Book of Tea: A Japanese Harmony of Art, Culture and the Simple Life* (Duffield, 1906), 3.

"It is essentially a worship": Okakura, *Book of Tea*, 3.

Frank also learned: Friedland and Zellman, *Fellowship: The Untold Story*, 40.

"The social clearing": "Frank Lloyd Wright Given Farewell Dinner," *Chicago Daily Tribune*, December 23, 1916.

"I was to have earlier": *Frank Lloyd Wright: An Autobiography*, 194.

"[The] ride from Yokohama": Wright, *My Father*, 96.

"At last I had found": *Frank Lloyd Wright: An Autobiography*, 196.

"When foreigners came": *Frank Lloyd Wright: An Autobiography*, 214.

Frank immediately sent: Wright, *My Father*, 101.

CHAPTER THIRTY-TWO

"There may be": *Frank Lloyd Wright: An Autobiography*, 214.

He called this tremor: *Frank Lloyd Wright: An Autobiography*, 214.

"A moment's panic": *Frank Lloyd Wright: An Autobiography*, 220.

"Why fight a quake?": *Frank Lloyd Wright: An Autobiography*, 214.

"[I would] erect a building": "Frank Lloyd Wright Tells of Designing Famous Tokio [*sic*] Hotel," *Wisconsin State Journal*, November 28, 1927.

"Miriam, herself": *Frank Lloyd Wright: An Autobiography*, 204.

"Branded an assailant": "Marriage Assailant Divorced," *Buffalo News*, December 24, 1922.

"I loved her enough": Hendrickson, *Plagued by Fire*, 324.

To the woman: Hendrickson, *Plagued by Fire*, 325.

"She bargained to sell": Wright, *My Father*, 111.

"Chinese paintings": Secrest, *Frank Lloyd Wright: A Biography*, 259.

"The Baron says": *Frank Lloyd Wright: An Autobiography*, 219.

"I could go home": *Frank Lloyd Wright: An Autobiography*, 221.

"Here was the real thing": *Frank Lloyd Wright: An Autobiography*, 221.

A group of thankful workers: *Frank Lloyd Wright: An Autobiography*, 221.

CHAPTER THIRTY-THREE

"They are very much": "Japanese Fear US," *Chicago Sunday Tribune*, August 20, 1922.

"I shall rest a while": "Japanese Fear US."

When he was asked: "Onion, Pig and Poet, Symbols of Chicago," *Omaha Daily News*, February 20, 1918.

"Chicago is Indian": "Chicago Told It Is Onion City," *Salt Lake Telegram*, February 20, 1918.

Their spokesperson, Louis: "New Hotel in Japan Causes Architect War," *San Francisco Chronicle*, October 23, 1922.

"a pet child of his": "Architecture of Japan," *Construction Magazine*, September 19, 1923.

"I have waded through": Secrest, *Frank Lloyd Wright: A Biography*, 274.

"A sanitarium is out": Secrest, *Frank Lloyd Wright: A Biography*, 277.

"She comes through": Secrest, *Frank Lloyd Wright: A Biography*, 277.

Against their mother's: "Frank Lloyd Wright's Mother Dies at Oconomowoc," *Platteville Journal and Grant County News*, February 21, 1923.

CHAPTER THIRTY-FOUR

"For an appreciable instant": Joshua Hammer, "The Great Japan Earthquake of 1923," *Smithsonian Magazine*, May 2011, https://www.smithsonianmag.com/history/the-great-japan-earthquake-of-1923–1764539/.

"Yokohama dropped": "Japan's Horror," *Glasgow Herald*, September 10, 1923.

"A tidal wave swept": Hammer, "Great Japan Earthquake of 1923."

Katherine Elder of Iowa: "Falling Tower Kills 700," *Argus* (Melbourne, Australia), September 3, 1923.

"Conflagration subsequent to severe": "Whole City Ablaze, Scene Like Hell," *Argus* (Melbourne, Australia), September 3, 1923.

"[There are] dead": "Japan Earthquake Death List Grows," *Lincoln County News*, September 6, 1923.

An American named S. F. Murphy: "Japan's Horror."

"Finally, on the third": *Frank Lloyd Wright: An Autobiography*, 222.

"Hotel stands undamaged": "Wright Now Acclaimed as World Leader," *Capital Times* (Madison, WI), October 18, 1923.

"The Imperial Hotel remains": "A Building That Stood Firm," *Los Angeles Daily Times*, September 19, 1923.

CHAPTER THIRTY-FIVE

He politely declined: "Want American to Help Rebuild Japan," *South Bend Tribune*, October 30, 1924.

Miriam later told: "How Famous Architect's Love Life Crashed Again," *Fresno Bee*, July 11, 1926.

"Again, there it was": *Frank Lloyd Wright: An Autobiography*, 261.

She was described: Secrest, *Frank Lloyd Wright: A Biography*, 428.

"Taliesin's radiant brow": *Frank Lloyd Wright: An Autobiography*, 273.

"I have 100 filthy": "Wife Says That Frank Lloyd Wright Is Now with Olga," *Capital Times* (Madison, WI), February 26, 1926.

"The attempt at reconciliation": "Wright Case Reconciliation Fails Today," *Capital Times* (Madison, WI), May 20, 1926.

"I am without money": "Fists of Third Dead Love Beat in Vain at Love Cote," *New York Daily News*, June 6, 1926.

Undaunted, Miriam: "How Famous Architect's Love Life Crashed Again," *Fresno Bee*, July 11, 1926.

"He will eventually": "How Famous Architect's Love Life."

"It is mine": "Famous Builder of Men's Homes Can't Keep His Own Intact," *St. Louis Star and Times*, October 26, 1926.

"You dog!": "Wright Leaps at Lawyer for Dancer's Mate," *Minneapolis Star*, October 21, 1926.

"A warden took": *Frank Lloyd Wright: An Autobiography*, 283.

"I have been driven": "Olga Vows She Will Stick by Frank," *Capital Times* (Madison, WI), October 22, 1926.

"I suppose it was": "Olga Vows."

"Miriam would give": "Olga Vows."

When reporters caught: "Olga Vows."

"I will never divorce": "Miriam Will Press Mann Act Charges," *Capital Times* (Madison, WI), October 22, 1926.

"He has our": "Wright's Former Wife Offers Aid in Legal Battle," *Eau Claire Leader*, October 29, 1926.

"The little life": Olgivanna Milanoff, "Olgivanna Tells of Life with Wright," *Wisconsin State Journal*, November 4, 1926.

Frank said that the loss: Frank Lloyd Wright, "Women Have Crucified Me," *Greensboro Daily Record*, November 23, 1926.

"[He] said that he had": Miriam Noel Wright, "Frank Never Loved Any of Us Says Miriam," *Greensboro Daily Record*, November 23, 1926.

"And now I'm": "Mrs. Wright to Besiege Hollywood," *San Francisco Examiner*, September 21, 1927.

"No, I'm not through": "Mrs. Wright to Besiege Hollywood."

"Read it here": "Government Steps into Wright Case. Miriam Arrested for Lewd Note," *Sheboygan Press*, October 6, 1927.

"Nobody can estimate": "Around Wisconsin," *Burlington Free Press*, September 1, 1927.

CHAPTER THIRTY-SIX

"I am beaten": "Defeat Admitted by Mrs. Wright in Love Battle," *Oakland Post Enquirer*, April 20, 1928.

"It was not an act": "Wife of Noted Architect in Wrecker Role," *Long Beach Press Telegram*, July 14, 1928.

"We are together": "Frank Lloyd Wright Marries Same Day Divorce Is Granted," *Rochester Democrat and Chronicle*, August 27, 1928.

"The terrain changed": Wright, interview by Downs.

"is a look over": *Frank Lloyd Wright: An Autobiography*, 452.

Miriam had come up: "Miriam Wright Dies Suddenly in Milwaukee," *Arizona Republic*, January 4, 1930.

"What was left": *Frank Lloyd Wright: An Autobiography*, 298.

"The natural thing": Secrest, *Frank Lloyd Wright: A Biography*, 416.

While every construction: "Building Stirs Controversy After Death of Architect," *Fort Worth Star-Telegram*, April 12, 1959.

"For the first time": "F.L.W's Building, 'Atmospheric,'" *Kansas City Star*, July 27, 1958.

The newsman described: J. W. M. Thompson, "I Stroll in Mr. Wright's One Floor Wonder," *Evening Standard* (London), July 7, 1958.

When he asked one: Secrest, *Frank Lloyd Wright, A Biography*, 563.

"I remember an echo": *Frank Lloyd Wright: An Autobiography*, 365.

"The pain. Can't bear": Friedland and Zellman, *Fellowship: The Untold Story*, 525.

"A dream?": *Frank Lloyd Wright: An Autobiography*, 365.

ABOUT THE AUTHOR

Casey Sherman is a *New York Times*, *Los Angeles Times*, *Wall Street Journal*, *USA Today*, and *Boston Globe* bestselling author of nineteen books, including *The Finest Hours* (now a major Walt Disney Studios motion picture starring Chris Pine and Casey Affleck) and *Patriots Day* (now an acclaimed motion picture from CBS Films starring Mark Wahlberg and Kevin Bacon). Sherman's true crime bestseller *Helltown* is now in development as a limited television series for Amazon Studios. Sherman will serve as executive producer on the project, which is slated to star Oscar Isaac (*Dune*), with director Edward Berger (Netflix, *All Quiet on the Western Front*), and produced by Team Downey (Robert Downey Jr. and Susan Downey, HBO's *Perry Mason*). Sherman's other books include *A Murder in Hollywood*; James Patterson's *The Last Days of John Lennon*, which spent more than twenty-three weeks on the *New York Times* bestsellers list; *12: The Inside Story of Tom Brady's Fight for Redemption*; and *Hunting Whitey: The Inside Story of the Capture and Killing of America's Most Wanted Crime Boss*. Sherman has appeared on more than one hundred television and radio programs and is a contributing writer for *TIME* magazine, *Esquire*, the *Washington Post*, the *Daily Beast*, *Boston Magazine*, and the *Boston Herald*.